Landscape Reinvented

The Uffington Enclosure Award 1778

Anthony Parsons and Sandra Millikin

Published by The Uffington Museum Trust 2014
©Anthony Parsons and Sandra Millikin

ISBN 978-0-9930747-0-7

Dedicated to the memory of Angel Lockey of Moor Mill 1726–1789
"…for he was a Man in whom was no Guile"

Cartography by Giles Darkes
Artwork by Bronwen Thomas
Book design by Red Paper Design
Printed by Berforts Information Press

This project has been funded by the Heritage Lottery Fund All-Our-
Stories programme and by the Uffington White Horse Show Trust

Contents

I. Preface

The authors (who have lived in Uffington since 1983 and 1971 respectively) stumbled upon the Uffington Enclosure Award during a disagreement with a neighbour, over the right of vehicles to use a footpath. By chance we discovered a 1967 letter from the County Surveyor of Berkshire (Uffington was in Berkshire until county boundaries changed in 1974) which stated that the footpath in question was defined in *'an annex to the Enclosure Award'* and was only four feet wide suggesting that it was never intended for vehicles. We consulted the original Award at the Berkshire Record Office in an effort to see whether we could support our case and verify the County Surveyor's assertion.

Confronted with 33 sheets of closely written 18th century script (we have reproduced part of a page from the award in **figure 1**) we appreciated that we would first have to transcribe this mapless and indexless document before we could start to interpret or research its contents. Since the award contained a fascinating amount of detail relating to the landscape which forms the background to our daily lives, it seemed worth spending many hours transcribing the document into something which would form the basis not only for our research but hopefully for that of others.

Enclosure was a significant and even life changing event for landowners, tenants and parishioners of Uffington, Woolstone and Baulking, and today's landscape around these villages still reflects very closely the changes wrought by enclosure.

The story of Parliamentary Enclosure illustrates the power of large landowners and the efficiency of an administrative process carried out with revolutionary zeal and which evolved through the English Midland counties. The Act of Parliament setting up the Uffington Enclosure Commission was passed in early 1777, and the landowners finally approved the commissioners' report on 29th May 1778. Before the passing of the Act a lot of preliminary work would have been done. After the passing of the Act landowners and their agents and lessees would have searched their records or their memories to establish their land rights, be they ownership, occupation, the right to use common land or receive tithes. Commissioners analysed and argued about how to resolve fairly what must have often been conflicting claims. Surveyors and cartographers recorded 119 allotments, qualitymen assessed values, scribes recorded in detail the decisions made and bookkeepers assessed the expense to be attributed to each landowner. Roads were defined and exchanges of land agreed. Many quill pens would have been re-sharpened and boot-leather worn through in those 15 months.

We have tried to indicate the most important facts about enclosure as accurately as possible, relying on documents where possible, but also using our best judgment in the interpretation of the old records and sometimes relying simply on local knowledge. But it is beyond the scope of this book to provide a definitive history of this period. We hope our work will be a starting point, not an ending, and that others will find our transcription and interpretation into maps helpful for future research. Inevitably readers will notice errors and omissions and we welcome amplifications and corrections. Equally, we would welcome access to other relevant documents of the period which readers might own, or know about, and which might improve the accuracy and breadth of this study.

Eighteenth century spellings often differ from those we use today. For example Icknield way was Ickleton Way, Baulking was Balking, enclosure was spelled 'inclosure'. We have used modern spelling within the text but in the maps the older spellings may be used. In the interests of economy we have not always been historically precise in our use of certain terms. For example strictly 'open fields' describe the large fields used for growing crops before enclosure; we sometimes use the term to cover all open areas which were subsequently enclosed: fields, common land, meadows etc. Also we may describe Woolstone and Baulking as 'parishes' whereas at the time of enclosure they were 'hamlets' or 'chapelries' within the parish of Uffington.

We could not have published this book without generous financial support from the Heritage Lottery Fund and the White Horse Show Trust. We received steadfast support of colleagues associated with Tom Brown's School Museum in Uffington, advice and encouragement from Dr Peter Durrant and his colleagues at the Berkshire Record Office, and we are grateful to Muriel Lindo and Liz Robinson for photographic work and school packs respectively. Thanks also to Elizabeth Rosser for allowing us to reproduce images of her original of the Watts map. Sharon Smith kindly proofread our manuscript.

We thank Giles Darkes, Bronwen Thomas for professional cartography and artwork respectively and John Walker for book design. The Vale and Downland Museum in Wantage have allowed us to reproduce their early 19th century painting of the Wantage market place. We have also received advice from David Godfrey of the Oxfordshire Field Paths Society for which we are grateful. Assistance from the archivist at the library of The Queen's College Oxford, was also most helpful. We researched documents at the National Archive in Kew, and accessed online sites of the British Library, the Berkshire, Wiltshire and Oxfordshire County archives and many others. We acknowledge permissions to reproduce images from the National Library of Scotland and the Berkshire Record Office and finally we acknowledge the use of satellite views in two images obtained using Google software.

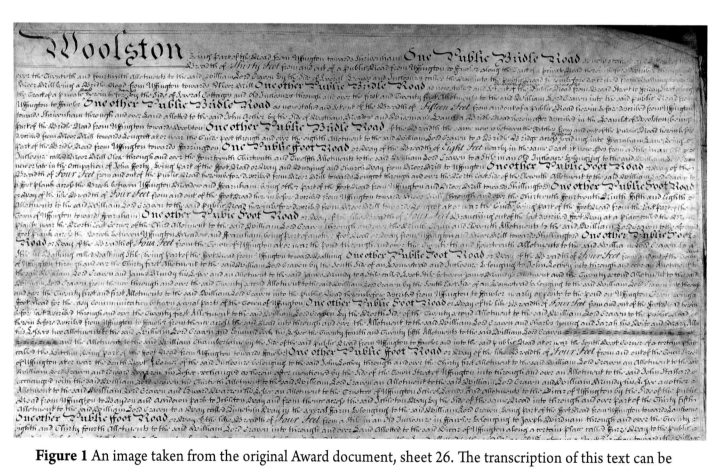

Figure 1 An image taken from the original Award document, sheet 26. The transcription of this text can be found in appendix 5.

Image reproduced courtesy of the Berkshire Record Office.

II. Enclosure in 18th century England

Enclosure was a process of tidying up land ownership and associated rights and allowing one person to cultivate or graze a distinct parcel of land, rather than using it communally.

There are many books about enclosure as it was an important part of English agrarian history (see for example refs 1 - 5), so we will outline only the main features before focussing on the Uffington enclosure which is the subject of this book.

Enclosure in some form (usually informal) had been taking place over many centuries before systematic large scale enclosure began to occur in about the mid-18th century. In earlier periods enclosed agricultural areas, or 'closes', were created around villages, either carved out of the ancient woodlands or from open and common fields; (the word 'field' was reserved historically for large open tracts of agricultural land.) Such old enclosures, usually irregular in shape, would have been clustered around many villages in central England; the village of Uffington and the hamlets of Woolstone and Baulking were no exception. Interestingly the oldest record of an enclosure in Berkshire is from the late 14th century and was a small pasture located in Woolstone (ref 1). The 'old enclosures' around our three villages are shown in figures C, D and Q.

Parliamentary enclosure was a large operation. Each parish or parishes to be 'enclosed' required a private Act of Parliament to give it legal force. Between 1760 and 1800 there were almost 1500 such Acts and the total area enclosed was 2.5 million acres (ref 2). The area enclosed in Uffington, Baulking and Woolstone was 3670 acres (figure J).

The primary purpose of enclosure was the transformation of agricultural land managed communally into parcels of land managed in 'severalty' or single ownership. This was often accompanied by creation of hedges and fences isolating the parcels from their neighbours; but this physical enclosure was not in fact the essence of the process, notwithstanding that the term enclosure somewhat misleadingly suggests it was. Enclosure also comprised variation of rights such as the definition of public and private roads running through and alongside the new allotments of land, the commutation of tithes and similar obligations, with land allotted in recompense so that annual liabilities were capitalised. Enclosure was a complex process.

Parliamentary enclosure affected a large swathe of land across central England running from Lincolnshire and South Yorkshire to Somerset and Dorset (ref 2).

The motives for Parliamentary enclosure are still debated by historians (refs 2–5). The 18th century saw many efforts to improve agriculture generally. Large landowners would see in a rising national population an opportunity to profit significantly from their land holdings if the land could become more productive. Pre-enclosure fields were divided into strips owned or tenanted by different individuals, although what was grown in a given field or collection of strips would usually be agreed collectively. In the 18th century this was seen as inflexible, fertility was declining, spaces between strips were wasteful and were a source of weeds. And it was certainly inconvenient for a given owner or tenant to move from one strip or set of strips to another to carry out day-to-day farming.

Common pasture land was often overgrazed, rights of common might be abused and the common itself encroached upon by adjacent landowners or their tenants. Yet also there would have been opposition from smaller farmers to enclosure since they often valued the flexibility of grazing on commons, and 'wastes' alongside roads. Villagers and especially the poor might lose sources of free firewood, grain from gleaning after the harvest and other lesser but valuable rights.

The Manor of Uffington: the Craven family

From the 10th century until the dissolution of the monasteries in the 16th century the manor of Uffington belonged to the Abbey of Abingdon. After the dissolution it passed to the Crown (1537-38). It passed through different hands (ref 21) but in 1620 it was conveyed by the then owners Francis and Elizabeth Jones and their son Abraham to Elizabeth Craven.

Elizabeth's son was created Viscount Craven of Uffington and until the 1950s the manor of Uffington remained part of the Craven estate.

The Cravens owned land in other parts of the country as well. The family did not live in Uffington but they maintained an agent in the village who looked after their properties, dealt with tenants, collected rents, and generally acted as the representative of Lord Craven in Uffington. He lived in the three gabled brick and chalk house now known as The Manor which is on the corner of the road to Fernham, opposite the old schoolhouse which now houses the museum.

The seat of the Cravens was at Hampstead Marshall near Newbury in Berkshire. The eldest son of Lord Craven was known as Viscount Uffington. In the 1950s the estate decided to sell its holdings in Uffington and their properties were offered to the then tenants, some of whom bought but some of whom did not. Those not sold to tenants were offered at public auction when cottages generally fetched prices in the hundreds. The Craven connection remains in for example 'Craven Cottage' in Broad Street, the former public house known as 'The Craven'

Fulwar Craven, 4th Baron Craven
by James Latham

Box 1

on the Fernham Road and the group of houses built in the 1970s known as 'Craven Common'.

At the time of enclosure the Lord of the Manor was the Sixth Baron Craven, William Craven (1738 to 1791). He was the son of a clergyman and succeeded his uncle William Craven the Fifth Baron, in 1769, as a young man. He would have been thrown into the business of enclosure very shortly thereafter.

The Fifth Baron only held the title for five years, having succeeded his cousin Fulwar Craven in 1764. Fulwar's name appears frequently in the Award as many of the leases referred to were granted by him. He died childless and hence was succeeded by his cousin.

William 6th Baron Craven 1768 by Francis Cotes

Also encouraging the fashion for Parliamentary Enclosure was the increasing availability of loans by way of mortgage to cover the expenses of Enclosure; but the interest on such loans required the greater productivity promised by Enclosure.

Finally for some landowners there may also have been an element of copying what others were doing without necessarily doing a careful analysis. Enclosure was fashionable.

There has been much debate over the social impact of Enclosure. Some say it made agriculture more efficient and enabled better land productivity and to support an increasing population. Others say that it rewarded the rich at the expense of the poor. Our examination of the Uffington Award is intended only to provide information about what happened on the ground, rather than judge the value of the changes wrought by Enclosure here.

III. The Uffington Enclosure Award

3.1 Scope of the Award

Parliamentary enclosure in Berkshire started in the north-west of the county, an area which included Uffington (ref 1). Ashbury was enclosed in 1772 and Childrey with Letcombe Bassett in 1774. The residents of Uffington and neighbouring parishes would have been aware of the process.

There was of course a clear hierarchy of landowners from the Lords of the Manor (William Lord Craven in Uffington) who owned large tracts of land, the Vicar who was entitled to land and tithes as a result of his office or 'living', progressing through yeoman farmers and down to cottagers who owned or occupied only very small parcels of land.

Although we refer to the Uffington Enclosure Award, the land it covered was not restricted to the 'township ' of Uffington, but it included the hamlets of Baulking (spelled Balking) and Woolstone (spelled either Woolston or Wolverston in the text) and part of Kingston Lisle and Fawler which were in the adjacent parish of Sparsholt. Although these places have been situated in Oxfordshire since the 1974 boundary changes, they were at the time of Enclosure in Berkshire. Figure B shows the area covered by the Act, the names of the Lords of the Manor around the time of enclosure and the vicars and impropriators (or lay rectors) of the two relevant parishes, Uffington and Sparsholt.

Much land was owned by the Lord of the Manor (or another landlord) but let to a different occupier or 'tenant' so more than one person would be affected by enclosure of a particular piece of land.

Land tenure

Ownership of land in England is a complex subject. There are now and were in the past different forms of ownership, or 'tenure' of land. The most familiar type of ownership nowadays is what we call 'freehold' where the owner of the land (who may be more than one person) is the absolute owner and no one else has any type of ownership.

There may be rights granted to others to use this freehold land in some manner, for example a right of way across a piece of land to get to another piece of land, or the right to have a drainage pipe under a piece of land, or even the right to hunt across the land. Land may be mortgaged, so that the lender has rights relating to the land. But the lender is not the owner.

At the time of the Enclosure Act and indeed until 1925 when legislation regularised and simplified land ownership, there were more types of ownership than this absolute or freehold ownership.

Leasehold land was land owned under a lease granted for a period of years or for a lifetime of an individual. This is the 'term' of the lease. Leases for a term of years remain common today but leases for life were abolished in 1925. Leases for life were by their nature for indefinite and unascertainable terms.

Leases are a type of property and can pass under a will or intestacy in most instances. However leases for life would end on the death of the lessee.

During the period of Enclosure we have, in Uffington, records of three kinds of tenancy under Lord Craven; these are recorded in a tabulation which cross references properties in the 1785 Craven map

Box 2 describes some aspects of the relationship between landowner and tenant at the time.

Early in 1777 the Act was passed ...'for Dividing, allotting, and enclosing certain Open and Common Fields, Common Meadows, Common Pastures, Downs, Commons, and other Commonable Lands, within the Township of Uffington, and the Hamlets of Balking and Woolston, otherwise Woolverston, and within the Hamlets of Kingston Lisle and Fawler, in the County of Berks.' Features of this Act are described in Box 3. The Act appointed Commissioners to realise the objectives of the Act and gave legal force to their decisions. It gave quite detailed directives in many areas to the Commissioners, for example that the chalk figure known as The White Horse was to belong to the Manor of William Lord Craven even though this would mean moving the boundary between Uffington and Woolstone. It is apparent that many matters had been negotiated before the Act was finalised. This, together with their experience derived from previous Parliamentary enclosures, helps to

explain how the Commissioners' work could be completed over a relative short period, 15 months.

Because not all pieces of land of the same size had the same value, some being more productive or more desirable than others, deciding how the land would be reallocated was a major potential area of dispute between those with interests in the land. Commissioners were required by the Act to take account of the area of a parcel of land and also its location and its quality. This would apply to the land owned before enclosure and to land allotted in the enclosure process.

We have not found any documentary evidence of how this process proceeded in Uffington, other than the Act and Award themselves. But there must have been a lot happening in the background, a lot of negotiation and disagreement and compromise. If one thinks of how easily neighbours can disagree about the location of a boundary, it is easy to envisage what sort of issues

Box 2

Tenants at Rack Rent This arrangement covered the majority of Craven premises whether small cottages and their gardens, or houses and homesteads together with small closes and much larger fields with areas up to 150 acres. In our records the total area under rack rent was 2116 acres with rent of £1746 collected. Rent was payable annually and presumably adjusted annually. Managing such rents would have been a major task of the Craven Steward.

Leaseholds These were long term tenancies based on leases often agreed several decades earlier with Lord Craven's forebears. Again they covered cottages, homesteads, closes but the total area covered by this arrangement was only 105 acres.

Copyholds Again these were long term arrangements with the privileges granted to each tenant, and the exact

services he was to render to the Lord of the Manor in return for them, described in the roll or book kept by the Steward who gave a copy of the relevant entry to the tenant. Copyholds were often on three lives so that when the first died the copyhold passed to the next, often a wife or son. There was a mechanism for adding a third person at this time (see example in Box 9) This was clearly an arrangement which gave priority to long term management of the land by a family.

These various and obsolete types of ownership or tenure generally created obligations which limited the right of the owner in some way. A copyholder owed allegiance to the Lord of the Manor. Other obligations might be by way of a rent payable in money or in some kind of produce, such as a tithe payable to the church.

The Act

The private Act of Parliament, passed in early 1777, provided the legal authority for the work of the enclosure commissioners. It defined the extent of their powers and the powers and limitations of the landowners, tenants and others affected by Enclosure. Its purpose is summarised: *'Lands or ground lie intermixed and dispersed in small parcels and are therefore incapable of any considerable improvement.......yet enclosure cannot be established without the aid and authority of Parliament.'*

The Act is 49 pages long. It enabled enclosure of both the parish of Uffington, which included the township of Uffington and the hamlets of Woolston and Baulking, and part of the parish of Sparsholt, that is the hamlets of Kingston Lisle and Fawler. See figure B.

A few landowners owned land in both parishes, and they no doubt wished the Commissioners to have the flexibility to deal with their land wherever situated. For example Abraham Atkins was Lord of the Manor of Kingston Lisle which included Fawler and Baulking. Lord Craven also had interests in Uffington, Baulking and Kingston Lisle. Both Hardwell Farm and *'the piece of common ground called Baulking Green'* were excluded from enclosure. The remaining area of Sparsholt parish (see figure B) was enclosed in 1800.

The Act appointed five commissioners to carry out the Uffington enclosure award and three of these individuals were also responsible for the Kingston Lisle and Fawler award. Arrangements were made for commissioners to be replaced if any one was unable to serve. Those with the authority to appoint replacements were as follows:

- James King:
  Lord Craven

- William Fillingham:
  John Archer (impropriator of Uffington)
  and George Watts (vicar of Uffington)

- Francis Burton:
  Queen's College Oxford (impropriators of Sparsholt) and Philip Brown (vicar of Sparsholt)

- John Brothers:
  the majority of proprietors present at the relevant meeting (but excluding those named above)

- John Watts:
  the majority of proprietors present at the relevant meeting (but excluding those named above)

In fact Francis Burton died before starting work as a commissioner so Queen's College and Philip Brown appointed a successor, John Mitchell.

Commissioners were required to prove their impartiality by swearing an oath to serve *'without favour or affection to any person whatsoever'.* Allotments were to be made *'in proportion to shares, rights and interest of common, tithes and other properties,'* and having regard to *'quality, situation and convenience'* of a piece of land as well as its area. Commissioners were to be paid £1-11s-6p per day.

There is considerable emphasis in the Act on the commutation of tithes, of which the two vicars, Watts and Brown, and the impropriators, Archer and Queen's College were the beneficiaries. The vicars were also entitled to continue to hold glebe land. Typically tithes were converted to allotments of land, but where tithe payers had insufficient landholdings or rights to cover their commitments, on-going annual payments were specified. Tithes were categorised: Small tithes, Great tithes and also St John's tithes (payable to 'Chapel Wardens' in Kingston Lisle.) In Kingston Lisle and Fawler there was some dispute regarding the payment of certain tithes and the impropriator and vicar were invited within the Act to proceed to the Assizes Court to resolve this matter

As well as tithes other arrangements were required to be terminated with compensation in lieu; these included:

The right of Queens College (or their tenant) to depasture or graze one ox at a piece of pasture land called Ox Lease between Whitsun and St Michael the Archangel (May and September)

Vicars Watts and Brown were exonerated in the future from the obligation to keep a bull and a boar for the use by the inhabitants of their respective parishes for serving their cows and sows

The Act sought to foresee and deal promptly with problems which might arise from its implementation. For example

- Commissioners had the right to settle disputes arising out of their work including the authority to hear witnesses testify under oath. This did not extend to disputes over title to land; but disputes of this nature were to be resolved in such a way as not to delay the work of the commissioners.

- Landowners were required to signify agreement within 12 months to the allotments to which they had been assigned. Provision was made for guardians, husbands, trustees etc to sign on behalf those who were lacking legal capacity; these persons included *'infants, ideots, lunatics, those 'across the sea', feme covert* [ie married women], *those with incapacity or disability'* [ie mentally or physically ill].

- Nothing in the Act could extend, revoke, make void, alter or annul any will or settlement or prejudice other claims regarding land.

- George Watts was authorised within the Act to borrow up to £210 to meet the cost of fencing

etc; there is no mention of similar arrangements for Philip Brown, vicar of Sparsholt.

The Act also sets out many practical steps the commissioners had to follow:

- Allotments may be anywhere within the parish.

- Owners may retrieve trees, underwood, thorns, bushes etc from their previous holdings within six months.

- Proprietors may start fencing and ditching before completion of the award.

- Swing gates may be installed to prevent sheep or cattle from destroying banks, drains, woods, young hedges and fences. There should be no lambs for four years because of the damage they might cause to young hedges.

- All former roads were deemed to be part of allotted land. The new roads and ways specified in the award were to be maintained at the expense of all inhabitants.

- A notice was to be placed on the church door announcing the termination of rights of common at the appropriate time. Violators' cattle would be impounded and released only on payment of 2/- per beast.

- Stone pits were to be assigned which could be used in common by landowners and their tenants for the repair of public and private roads.

Finally the commissioners were required to complete the two awards for Uffington and Kingston Lisle and file copies on parchment in both in the Court of Common Pleas in Westminster as well as in the Common Chest of the Church. A copy was to be accessible to interested parties on payment of a fee.

Some landowners

The names of major landowners appear frequently in the Enclosure Award. These were the people with the greatest interests in land in the area covered and presumably also the most influential since social and economic power was generally measured by land ownership. They tended not to live in the parish.

The largest and most important of these was the Lord of the Manor of Uffington, William Lord Craven, who is the subject of Box 1.

Here is some information about a few of the others:

The Wiseman family owned land in Woolstone from 1583 (ref 21) when Edmund Wiseman inherited land from William Weldon. This passed to William Wiseman and then down through the family to a date before 1712 when it was sold to **Bartholomew Tipping** who became Lord of the Manor of Woolstone. Wisemans Ham, an old enclosure near Lower Woolstone is one record of the Wiseman family in the Award.

Bartholomew Tipping lived at Woolley Park near Chaddleworth in Berkshire. He was the seventh person with that name. His dates were 1735 to 1798 and he was High Sheriff of Berkshire. Woolley Park had been the seat of the Tipping family since the middle of the sixteenth century. Bartholomew Tipping VII died unmarried so the estate passed out of the family with his death into the Wroughton family, being inherited by his niece Mary-Anne who married the Rev Philip Wroughton. In the early 19th century the estate became part of the Craven estate.

Lovelace Bigg owned at the time of Enclosure the manor of Hall Place Woolstone which had originally been owned by the Saunders family. He was an absentee landlord. Lovelace was born in 1741 and died in 1813. He lived at Manydown Park, Hampshire (and later at Chilton Foliat near Hungerford). This was sold to Thomas Bigg in 1754, who left it to his brother the Rev Walter Bigg. Walter's son was Lovelace Bigg who succeeded to the property and in 1789 took the name of Wither (Lovelace Bigg-Wither).

might have arisen when land previous occupied by one person was taken away and given to another.

Aside from the issues of fairness and equivalency, there was also the technical and onerous task of carrying out precise surveys of the land so that it could be properly delineated on the ground. So before re-distribution could start, all the

existing strips would have to be surveyed and their ownership and value assessed, rights of common would be have to be recorded.

One notable feature of the Uffington Enclosure Award is that most of the roads and paths defined in the Award almost 250 years ago still exist little altered, as do many of the hedges and boundaries.

3.2 The Commissioners and Landowners

The men to whom these tasks were entrusted were 'the Commissioners'. They were a group of professionals, usually land surveyors, who emerged in the 18th century and specialised in enclosure. It

was presumably a lucrative occupation and successful commissioners would have been much in demand.

The five Commissioners were:

It was allegedly said of Lovelace by an unrespectful tenant that his face 'could have been very fine if a horse had not sat on it.'

His son Harris Bigg-Wither sold Hall Place to Captain Butler in 1828. Harris was in 1802 engaged to the novelist Jane Austen but the engagement was broken off after only a day and she never married! Captain Butler sold part of the estate, Woolstone Farm, to Lord Craven, but retained the rest until well into the 20th century.

The **Fettiplace** family were a large and important old Berkshire family holding property in the Wantage area and in Oxfordshire. William Fettiplace (c1463 to 1528) left land in Uffington and Sparsholt and other parishes in Berkshire to the **Provost and Scholars of Queen's College Oxford**.

The last Fettiplace baronet Sir George Fettiplace had died in 1743 and land passed through the female line to Thomas (who took the name of Fettiplace). He died in 1767 and was succeeded by his son Robert

who died in 1799 leaving his brother Charles as the heir. At the time of the Childrey enclosure award in 1772, a few years before that of Uffington, the manor at Childrey was in possession of Robert's Trustees, presumably Trustees in Bankruptcy. These same trustees are named in the Uffington Award.

Another landowner whose name appears in the Award is **Lord Spencer**. The Earls of Spencer are one of the biggest landowners in England, with estates primarily in Warwickshire and a seat at Althorp. The family is best known today for Lady Diana Spencer who married Prince Charles and became Princess of Wales.

It was John Spencer, the first Earl Spencer (1734 to 1783) who held land at Uffington during the Enclosure period. He had inherited the estates of the Duchess of Marlborough. These included property at Baulking and Shellingford sold in 1796. The former was in the area covered by the Uffington Enclosure Award in which Earl Spencer was allotted 8 acres.

- James **King** of Daventry in the county of Northampton

- William **Fillingham** of Newark upon Trent in the county of Nottingham

- John **Brothers** of Hungerly in the parish of Wykin in the county of the city of Coventry

- John **Watts** of Sulgrave in the said county of Northampton and

- John **Mitchell** of South Weston in the County of Oxford (John Mitchell replaced Francis Burton who died very soon after the first meeting; see Box 3)

These men were not local. They came from the Midlands where a lot of enclosure was carried out and it seems likely that they had been involved in other enclosures. They must have been men of integrity with considerable diplomatic and commercial skills and experience. The profession of Commissioner was a prosperous one and William Fillingham for example became quite rich through the practice of acting as Commissioner.

The Commissioners appointed a surveyor, George King of Daventry, (who later prepared estate maps for Lord Craven and Reverend Watts, presumably on a private basis, see figures K and L). Three men were appointed to assess the quality and value of the units of agricultural land involved in the enclosure process. They were John Hughes of Odstone in the parish of Ashbury, John Pocock of Fawley and John Stephens of Farnborough. These were local men.

Also named at the beginning of the Award were the larger landowners plus four other individuals – three yeomen and a blacksmith - who became signatories to the Award document. Presumably the yeomen and the blacksmith were selected to represent the interests of the smaller landowners and tenants.

Those named were:

- Rt Honourable William Lord **Craven** Baron Craven of Hampstead Marshall in the county of Berks

- Abraham **Atkins** of Kingston Lisle in the said county of Berks Esquire

- John **Archer** of Welford in the said county of Berks Esquire impropriator of the parsonage of Uffington in the said county of Berks

---

Box 5

John Archer: Impropriator of Uffington parish

John Archer's name appears frequently in the Enclosure Award.

He was the impropriator or lay rector of Uffington. He held the 'advowson' of Uffington which meant he had the right to nominate an individual to become the vicar of Uffington. George Watts was the vicar at the time of Enclosure and there was a connection of friendship between the two (see below).

As impropriator John Archer received tithes from property owners in the parish together with the vicar. As part of the enclosure process these tithes were translated into allocations of land, with John Archer being allocated over 500 acres and the Vicar just 230 acres. But one obligation of the impropriator was to pay for repairs and maintenance of the chancel of the parish church.

John Archer did not live at Uffington however but at Welford near Newbury. Together with George Watts he had a close connection with the Shirley family of Peasemore which is not far from Welford. John Shirley (1714 to 1775) was vicar of Welford and held the Manor of Peasemore. His goddaughter was Henrietta Watts, one of George Watts' two daughters.

By his will John Shirley left the Manor of Peasemore to Joseph Allen, John and Mary Allen, and after their deaths to '*my worthy friend John Archer Esq*'.

Interestingly the link between Uffington, Welford and Peasemore between 1760 and 1810 is also shown through those holding the Peasemore advowson: John Archer (1761), Catherine Ready (1791), George Watts (1801) and Thomas Hughes (1807).

We have not researched Archer's history in any detail, in particular how he acquired the Uffington impropriatorship. However Welford Park was like Uffington before the Dissolution of the Monasteries in 1536 in the care of the monks of Abingdon Abbey.

John Archer was born in about 1729 and died in 1800. He was twice married, first to Lady Mary FitzWilliam in 1752 (daughter of Earl Fitzwilliam) who died in 1776, and second to Elizabeth Jones. He had only daughters so on his death Welford Park and also the impropriatorship at Uffington passed to his grandson John Houblon (1773 to 1831) who changed his name to Archer-Houblon. He was later Tory MP in Essex, and inherited property, Hallingbury Place in Essex, from his father.

- Bartholomew **Tipping** of Woolley in the said county of Berks Esquire

- Lovelace **Bigg** of Chilton Foliat in the county of Wilts Esquire

- Reverend George **Watts** Vicar of Uffington in the said county of Berks

- Jeffry **Church** of Woolston in the said county of Berks Yeoman

- Joseph **Mayon** of the parish of Buckland of the said county of Berks Yeoman

- John **Stallard** of Uffington aforesaid blacksmith

- Edward **Warren** of Ashbury in the said county of Berks Yeoman (lessee

of said William Lord Craven)

- John William **Willaume** and Abraham **Chambers** Esquires trustees or assignees of the estate of Robert **Fettiplace** late of Swinbrook in the said county of Oxford Esquire

- Robert **Leaver** of Wallingford in the said county of Berks Gentleman

Figure G shows the signatures of the Commissioners and the landowners as they were appended to the Award document at the final meeting on 29th May 1778 at the Bear Inn in Wantage. Figure H shows an early 19th century painting of the Wantage Market Place which probably looked very similar some 30 years earlier. The Bear Inn still stands at the far end on the left its facade largely unchanged.

3.3 The Award Document and Maps

Our transcription of the full Award document including its financial table can be found in appendix 5 together with an index to names and places within the document.

We have also created a Map of Enclosures (at the end of this book) showing all the Allotments described in the Award document. An artist's impression of the enclosures is in figure E. No map was published as part of the Award. Later enclosures often have maps, but Uffington was among the earlier awards. We have been helped in our interpretation by two contemporary maps. The Craven estate prepared a map in 1785 showing all of the Uffington 'township' with the Craven and other holdings clearly identified (ref 6 and figure

K). Uffington 'township' differs from what we now call Uffington village in that it included the outlying fields and Hardwell (see figure B). In 1778 Reverend George Watts also had a map prepared of his holdings after all exchanges with Lord Craven had been completed and showing considerable detail of the area around St Mary's Church Uffington (ref 7 and figure L). This is precisely drawn and also very attractive as a work of cartography.

In section 4.7 there is a fuller description of other local 18th and 19th century maps.

We describe in the next section how we have prepared our map of the allotments.

3.4 Allotments

Before Parliamentary enclosure, the Open Fields of Uffington parish were divided into distinct areas. These are shown in figure C and their areas are displayed in figure J. The area available for enclosure

across the three parishes was 3670 acres or 57% of the total. The names of these areas are, in part, a reflection of their use, for example 'Meadow' for haymaking and grazing, 'Fields' for growing crops.

Reverend George Watts, Vicar of Uffington parish

The grandson of Henry Watts, vicar of Uffington from 1700 to 1712, George Watts was born in 1743. He was ordained priest in 1766 and became vicar of Uffington in 1769, aged 26, a post which he held until his death in 1810.

Watts would have played a major part together with the impropriator, John Archer, in negotiating compensation for tithes which were included in the Award. As vicar, he was entitled to tithes and under the Award he received land in lieu. Such property passed by law to subsequent vicars, in this instance his son-in-law and then his grandson. It was only in the 19th century that such property ceased to be owned by the incumbent vicar and was vested in the Ecclesiastical Commission following Acts of Parliament.

The photocopy of the 1776 Enclosure Act which is held at Tom Brown's School Museum in Uffington appears to be taken from a bound copy of the Act originally in the possession of Reverend George Watts. This copy of the Act has appended to it many pages of handwritten accounts and notes, which are almost certainly written by George Watts. They cover the period 1778 to 1799. These notes include:

- April 22 1778. A summary of payments made to William and Charles Briscoe, carpenters, and to Richard Aires, mason, for a barn to be erected at Sour Hill (now known as Sower Hill). Dimensions and other details are specified; and the 'work is left to the judgment of Thomas Salt.' See image within this box.

- A record of 'a tax for the relief of the poor in the parish' based on land value 'at quality price', payable by some 19 individuals including Archer and Watts himself.

- An account of window tax and land tax payable in 1778 by 24 individuals. George Watts himself had the most windows in the parish (18) followed by Angel Lockey (16) then Martha Mundy (15).

Richard Geering and William Noakes are named as assessors and collectors. We do not know why the vicar kept these records in this manner and whether he had a formal role in recording taxes.

- A record of residual tithes payable to Watts as vicar. This included tithes from the district of Hardwell, part of Uffington, but not covered by the enclosure Award, so tithes were still payable until they were extinguished in 1849, (see box 8). In his notes Watts refers to a page in the Act which refers to Hardwell and underlines on that page the statement that 'Hardwell was within the township of Uffington.'

- Watts let some of his land to tenants, and rents are recorded; interestingly, the main Church Yard he gives to a Mr Cooke rent free.

Between April and October 1778 Watts records that he made payments totaling £156 for fencing and new buildings. This was a substantial sum. There is a record of two loans in late 1778 taken to cover this expenditure and other costs. He borrowed £100 from Anne Drew and £110 from John Hillman of Craven St London. The former was a short term loan which then transferred to Hillman. In the 1776 Act the vicar was expressly empowered to raise a loan for such purposes.

Watts also made a sequence of notes analyzing the Award, presumably to ensure he received his legal entitlement. This must have been of considerable importance to him. For example he states: that in allotting lands to the vicar of Uffington mention is made of this being 'in lieu of tithes', but in the allotment (of land) to Mr Brown (vicar of Sparsholt) no mention is made of tithes but only as 'an equivalent for all land and rights over the said meadow called Oldfield'. He then identifies the hamlet of Baulking, and Oldfield in particular, not as being part of the parish of Kingston Lisle but only as part of the manor of Kingston Lisle.

In 1783 Watts declared to his bishop (ref 21) that he had spent the greater part of his time over the previous 3 years in Bath. He says: 'My sole reason for absence was want of health. I should be happy (God willing) to spend all my Days with my Parishioners.' He lived on for another 27 years.

George Watts was a JP for Berkshire and Wiltshire

SACRED TO THE MEMORY OF
GEORGE WATTS, MASTER OF THE TEMPLE CHURCH LONDON,
AND SON OF HENRY WATTS, VICAR OF THIS PARISH.
WHO DIED APRIL 19:1772, AGED 67.

ALSO OF HIS SON GEORGE WATTS,
VICAR OF THIS PARISH, AND MAGISTRATE
FOR THE COUNTIES OF BERKS AND WILTS.
WHO DIED FEBRUARY 2:1810, AGED 67.

LIKEWISE OF THOMAS HUGHES. DD.
SON-IN-LAW TO THE LATTER:
VICAR ALSO OF THIS PARISH, AND CANON
RESIDENTIARY OF St PAULS CATHEDRAL LONDON.
WHO DIED JANUARY 6:1833, AGED 77.

"THESE WERE MERCIFUL MEN, WHOSE RIGHTEOUSNESS"
"HATH NOT BEEN FORGOTTEN."
ECCLESIASTICUS. CH. 44. V.10.

The text of the Award describing each allotment states in which of these areas the allotment is situated. The 1785 map of Lord Craven's Uffington estate (figure K) also names these areas even though they had been enclosed when the map was drawn. So we can be confident about the boundaries of the separate Open Fields.

The unit in the Fields where crops were grown was typically a strip of 15 or so metres wide which, being ploughed up and down, resulted over time in soil being shifted towards the centre of the strip, creating a ridge. After enclosure, many areas were laid to grass for sheep and cattle grazing; this soil has, since then, remained largely undisturbed and hence the pattern of ridge and furrow has been preserved. Hoskins (ref 2) describes this as *'the fossilised remains of our ancient agriculture.'*

So there is evidence of the ridge and furrow pattern still visible locally, as indicated in our Map of Enclosures. The photograph in figure F shows this pattern in the area which was allotted to the Trustees of Uffington School (see TUS on the Map of Enclosures).

Although there is no map with the award document, the surveyors would probably have drawn working maps, as it would have been much easier to carry out their task with some sort of illustrations, but we have not found any such working documents. Possibly some may come to light as a result of this book. So we have had to reconstruct locations and boundaries as one might a jigsaw puzzle and we have succeeded in mapping all the 119 allotments in the Map of Enclosures. Here is how we have done this:

The Award text which defines an allotment follows a more or less standard structure and an example of such text is in **figure 2**:

allottee is Lord Craven	**To and for the said William Lord Craven** in lieu of and as a just and full recompense satisfaction and equivalent for all such of his lands and grounds rights of common and other properties in and over the said fields and commonable lands by the said
precursor lease of 1749	act directed to be divided and allotted **as were heretofore demised by the late Right Honourable Fulwar Lord Craven deceased by Indenture of Lease dated the twenty eighth day of March one thousand seven hundred and forty nine to Charles Garrard also deceased at the yearly reserved rent of one pound five shillings and eight pence.** One plot or parcel of land being **the second allotment**
2nd allotment of Lord Craven in the Meadow area 40.3 acres	to the said William Lord Craven situate in **Uffington Meadow** aforesaid containing **forty acres one rood and six perches** (exclusive of all roads and ways through and over the same) **bounded on the south east by the thirteenth and twelfth allotments to the said William Lord Craven on part of the south by an allotment to the said**
adjacent allotments etc	**John Archer exchanged by him with the said William Lord Craven as hereinafter mentioned on part of the west and remaining part of the south by the thirty third allotment to the said William Lord Craven on the remaining part of the west by the said inclosed Farm belonging to the said William Lord Craven and on the north by the sixth fifth fourth and third allotments to the said William Lord Craven** the fences for inclosing this allotment on the south against the said allotment to the said John Archer exchanged as aforesaid and on the south against the thirty third allotment to the said William Lord Craven the said Commissioners do award
maintenance of boundary fences	order and direct **shall be made and forever after maintained and repaired by the said William Lord Craven and the owners of this allotment for the time being.**

Figure 2 The text of the Award describing the second allotment to Lord Craven.   The key features are in bold with notes in the margin. The format of this text is typical of all allotments in the Award.

- the name of the landowner to whom the parcel is allotted: the 'allottee'

- details, but only where William Lord Craven is allottee, of any earlier lease, including date of lease, the lessee and the annual rent

- the allotment number, where the landowner has more than one allotment, the name of the Open Field where it is located and its area in acres, roods and perches. (A rood is a quarter of an acre and there are 40 perches in a rood.)

- a description of the adjacent allotments and other adjacent distinguishing features (such as roads, or parish boundaries).

- the name of the person (typically the landowner and his successors) who is responsible in the future for maintenance of each boundary fence, hedge or ditch.

There are 73 allotments in the Uffington township of which 48 were made to Lord Craven. Baulking had 22 allotments and Woolstone 24. The first allotment in each township or hamlet was to the Lord of the Manor (see box 1) in recompense for their respective 'rights of soil in and over the waste lands' within their Manor. Waste land was manorial land neither let to tenants nor part of the demesne; typically it included hedges, and verges.

We can help to identify the location of each allotment by using several other sources of information:

a) Contemporary **maps**:

- Craven estate map of 1785 (figure K)

- Reverend Watts map of 1778 (figure L)

- maps of the Queen's College Oxford holdings (ref 8) which were almost certainly prepared immediately after enclosure

- the Baulking Tithe map of 1839 (ref 9)

- a map of Craven Estate tenancies of 1860 (ref 10)

b) **Roads and paths** were defined as part of the Award as they traversed or bounded the new allotments. Since many of these roads and paths remain as public rights-of-way today, we can have some confidence about their route at the time of the Award which in turn increases our confidence in the position of the allotments traversed by them.

c) Particularly important for locating the boundary of an allotment is the measurement of the **area of the allotment** on the ground today which can be compared with the area given in the Award.

To measure the area of a given piece of land, whether it is two acres or 200 acres, we have used some free software called 'Daft Logic'. Using Google satellite images, this software allows the user to delineate the outline of a piece of ground, leading automatically to a calculation of the area within this boundary. We start by assuming that existing hedgerows and boundary features follow the lines of enclosure boundaries of 1778 (unless there is obvious evidence to the contrary). An example of this process is in figure M. The calculation of acreage using this method is usually within a few percent of the area specified in the Award. We expect some degree of error in the combination of the Google projection and in locating the boundary precisely. The original surveyors would have sometimes also made measurement errors as they used less sophisticated forms of measurement.

Of the larger allotments (over five acres) we find large discrepancies in just two cases (15 % or more); these are identified in the Map of Enclosures.

d) We also consider the wording of the Award regarding **'adjacencies'**, that is the allotments and other adjacent features like parish boundaries, roads, bridle- and foot-paths, farms, old enclosures, and distinctive features such as the Uffington White Horse. Such features can prove vital

Box7

Angel Lockey

The Lockey family had been in Uffington for several generations and at least since the 17th century. They lived at Moor Mill. Angel was a miller and he was born in 1726 and died in 1789 so at the time of enclosure was in his 50s, and a prominent member of the community. In common with others of his class and background he was active in various aspects of village life. His parents had lived at Moor Mill and he had been baptised in Uffington Church. In 1763 he inherited a dwelling called 'Pamphletts' from his uncle Edward – but we have not been able to locate this dwelling.

Not long after, he married Martha Taylor who had been born in 1742 and died in 1818, a widow for many years after Angel's death. Her family came from Filkins. The Lockeys had ten children between 1770 and 1783, of whom nine survived beyond infancy although Angel's monument in Uffington church records only eight living at the date of his death.

Angel Lockey occupied land which was owned by Lord Craven under a tenancy which had been granted to his brother John Lockey in 1754, for 99 years or lives. This land was in the area around Moor Mill and included rights of common (see sheet 16 of the Award and enclosure LC/AL on the enclosure map).

Although Angel and Martha appear to have been active members of the Church, in the 17th century several members of the Lockey family were Quakers at a time when to practice any other religion was an ecclesiastical and criminal offence. The strip of land including the present Quaker meeting house was owned by John Lockey at the time of the award (sheet 26). This would have been Angel's brother John who inherited a messuage or tenement in Fryday Street (possibly the same place) from his uncle Edward in 1763. The present Quaker meeting house was built about 1725-30 but by the 1760s there were many fewer Quakers and it became more or less redundant, being sold off in the early 19th century.

There are monuments to both Angel and Martha in Uffington Church. Angel's is shown in the photograph. In her memorial Martha is described as *'a sincerely pious Christian, and if there were any virtues that she did not practise, they could only be such as those with which she was unacquainted'*

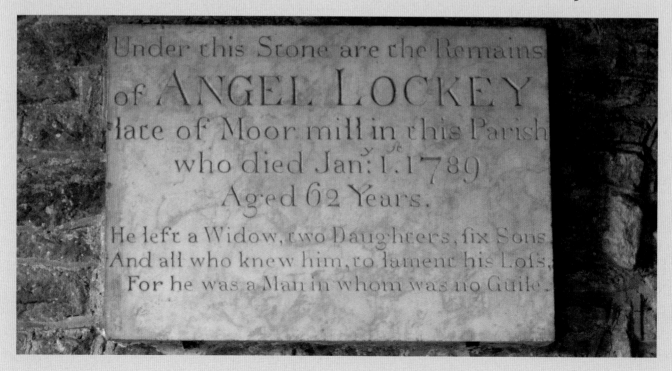

in locating the allotment in today's landscape since they usually remain unchanged.

Since an allotment is largely located by its adjacencies, mapping allotments is like solving a jigsaw puzzle. By initially locating a few key allotments we can work outwards from them. For example, an allotment on the east side of Broadway was made to the Trustees of Uffington School, (labelled TUS in the Map of Enclosures). This particular field is shown as 'Uffington School Land' in the Craven map of 1785. (This land was sold a few decades ago by the Saunders Trust, a local charity founded in the 17th century to support the first Uffington school.) The measured area of this field (17.3 acres) using the satellite view (see figure M) matches precisely that defined in the Award. So knowing exactly where this allotment is, we can analyse those allotments which identify the School Land as adjacent to them.

Usually we can align allotment boundaries with the hedgerows or roads we see today. Sometimes we may have to guess the route of the boundary between two allotments based on the best information we can gather. Where there is a significant level of uncertainty, this is shown with a dashed line on the Map of Enclosures.

Figure P illustrates how, in an area close to Uffington village, the pattern of the allotted parcels at the time of the Award remains visible today. Over two hundred years the boundaries of these have not changed and the hedgerows and fences remain on the same lines.

Appendix 2 gives information on each allotment: landowner, tenant, area and leases which predate enclosure but continue through and beyond it (see section 4.6).

The area of each allotment ranges from 0.08 to 186 acres. Some of the largest have complex shapes and may be the allocation of the residual area after all other allotments had been made; LB1 in Woolstone and LC14 in Uffington are examples.

Two allotments (JA2 and QC/RF2) straddle the Uffington/Woolstone boundary.

With one exception parish boundaries remained unchanged through the Enclosure process. The boundary of Uffington was altered on White Horse Hill at the expense of Woolstone, to allow Lord Craven to receive by allotment the part of the hill which includes the White Horse and castle – this was a requirement spelled out in the Act itself; Lord Craven wanted the ancient monument from the outset and will have negotiated this arrangement before the Act was drafted.

3.5 Exchanges and sales

Sheets 28 to 32 of the Award cover exchanges between landowners which occurred after allotments had been initially allocated. The Act directs some of these exchanges. Exchanges sometimes involved property outside the Uffington parish, for example in Kingston Lisle. Some exchanges involved property which was not part of the Parliamentary enclosure of the Open Fields but was part of an old enclosure; in one case a building was part of an exchange.

Exchanges would have been motivated by the desire of landowners to further de-fragment their holdings and also to consolidate their holdings closely around their dwelling. We can see this in the exchanges between Lord Craven and George Watts. The former owned old enclosures around the vicarage and the church, land from which the vicar could benefit and could manage more easily. The vicar's final holdings are shown in his map of 1778, (see figure L). The land he gave up to Lord Craven in exchange (GW3 and GW4) was adjacent to other Craven lands below Ickleton Way.

Some of the smallest allotments were no doubt part of a pre-agreed package of exchange or sale with the landowner of a larger adjacent allotment. That is they were located at the edge of this larger allotment and were subsequently transferred as part of the Award. Two examples in the Woolstone parish are LB6, JC3 and BT7 transferred to JM, and LB5 and BT6 transferred to JC1. This arrangement would have allowed the commissioners conveniently to deal with a small residue of land allocation owing to an individual and for whom a subsequent sale to the neighbouring landowner was an acceptable outcome.

Future historians may wish to analyse in further detail the large number of exchanges and sales described in the latter part of the Award. We hope our researches will facilitate this activity.

Figure 3 A sketch of the old vicarage in Uffington by Rev Charles Lord, vicar 1831 – 1846.

TBSM archive.

IV. Villages, Roads and other aspects

4.1 The Villages

The boundaries of the three parishes today have probably remained largely unaltered for at least a thousand years. Apart from some new housing in the last 60 years, the general shape of the three villages has remained unchanged since the time of Enclosure, although inevitably some old buildings have disappeared. Uffington was the largest of the three communities and is described as a 'township' in the Award while Woolstone and Baulking are 'hamlets' (yet interestingly the name 'Town Street' describes a place in Woolstone in the Award – sheet 31) In ecclesiastical terms Woolstone and Baulking were chapelries within the parish of Uffington; they only became separate parishes in the mid 19th century. To complicate matters further Baulking was part of the Manor of Kingston Lisle while Uffington and Woolstone were each within different Manors (see figure B).

Uffington village

The names of streets and paths at the time of enclosure are shown in figure Q which also gives some names of landmarks which we may not recognise today. Most houses, cottages and their gardens were clustered along Broad Street, High Street (then known as Friday Street), Upper and Lower Common and Town Street, which was the continuation of Friday Street, running south from Garrards Farm and may have continued all the way round the village to the house now known as 'The Manor' which was previously the Agent's house of the Craven Estate (ie over what is known today as Woolstone Road). Chapel Lane was called Little Lane, Packers Lane was Grays Lane and Green Lane was Lockey Lane.

The village was surrounded by 'old enclosures', that is closes and small fields enclosed informally over a long period and years before 'official' enclosure through the Award in 1778. The Open Fields, which were the subject of the Parliamentary enclosures, were generally further out. However, what is now the recreation ground was part of Uffington Common reaching into the built-up part of the village, and was the first allotment made to Lord Craven to compensate for his loss of 'wastes'.

As we have seen in the last chapter (under 'exchanges') George Watts, the Vicar, received land from Lord Craven in exchange for some of his outlying landholdings. The field lying between Chapel Lane and the footpath extension to Packers Lane was one of these. At the time it was called Puzey's Field and was divided into smaller parcels. The family Puzey's records go back to 1617 and it was an Anne Puzey who, though living in London, built in 1835 what is now Willow Cottage on Packers Lane. The land to the north between Chapel Lane and Broad Street would have been mainly orchard and pasture closes but with a handful of dwellings and barns, (see figure L).

Near the church, on Broad Street, was the vicarage, the largest house in the village (see Box 6 and **figure 3**). We do not know its precise location, but an area opposite the present school site is a likely candidate.

Many of the old enclosures and the later Parliamentary enclosures were let by Lord Craven to tenants who farmed them – see section 5.5.

Woolstone village:

Woolstone comprised then, as now, Upper and Lower Woolstone. There were a few 'old enclosures' clustered along the bridle path between them. The Open Fields came close to the village and so the new enclosures abutted the village. Apart from the Queen's College maps showing

Box8

Hardwell

Hardwell Lane is mentioned by name (as 'hordwelles weg') in Anglo-Saxon charters which are on 12th-century manuscripts. There are the remains of a moat at Hardwell Farm suggesting a building of some significance was located here in the past.

Though separated physically from Uffington parish, Hardwell was at the time of the enclosure Award part of the township of Uffington. Indeed Reverend Watts made a handwritten note in his copy of the Act of 1776: 'p21 Hardwell farm expressly said to be in the township of Uffington'. But Hardwell was not subject to enclosure, and therefore its tithes remained payable to the vicar and impropriator.

Seventy years later the somewhat ambiguous relationship between Hardwell Farm and nearby parishes remained. In a scrawled handwritten report (ref 12), the commissioner responsible for finally commuting the tithes in 1849 observed:

"[The vicar] appears to think that, if Hardwell is within the Village or Township of Uffington as well as the Parish, the vicar's claim is secure. Baulking and Woolstone are Townships in Uffington but maintain their own poor [rates].

Mr Bennetts' land, which constitutes the whole of Hardwell Farm, pays poor rate to Uffington and highway rate to the adjoining parish of Compton. The Impropriate Tithes on [Hardwell] pay poor and highway rate to Woolstone and the Vicarial Tithes pay these rates to Uffington.

Such a confusion of rating I never before heard of!'

their own allotments around Lower Woolstone, we have been unable to find other contemporaneous maps, which has made the assignment of allotments in Woolstone parish less certain.

John Hadow (1975) in his booklet on the history of Woolstone (ref 11) provides a sketch map of the village around the time of enclosure, showing the larger dwellings, roads and paths; (though we do not know from where he obtained all his information). Interestingly he shows a path or road connecting directly the southern end of Marsh Lane with Icknield Way. This is shown on the Rocque map of 1761 and on a map of 1811 (see section 4.7). But this road or path is not defined in the Award, although it crosses allotment BT3; so unless it was a private road it remains a puzzle to us.

Baulking Village and Hardwell:

In contrast to the situation in Uffington and Woolstone, the Enclosure Award did not extinguish tithes in Baulking, nor in Hardwell, the small isolated outpost of Uffington parish to the west of Woolstone. The hamlet of Baulking was part of the Manor of Kingston Lisle and perhaps that is why it was treated differently from Uffington and Woolstone. We do not know why tithes in Hardwell were not commuted like the rest of the Uffington township at the time of enclosure. Tithes in Baulking and Hardwell were commuted in the years following the Commutation of Tithes Act of 1836.

The Baulking tithe map (1839) and its table of landowners and tenants (ref 9) have been useful in defining landowners, and so help confirm the location of enclosures. Many lands remained in the same ownership over the 60 year period after enclosure. The Queen's College map of their allotment on Portway (ref 8) also helpfully indicates adjacent landowners. The houses and farms of Baulking in 1839 surrounded the Green with many of those which remain today clearly shown. The table of land areas, prepared as part of the tithe commutation process, also gives an insight into the use of land at that date.

An extract from the 1849 report by the Tithe Commissioner on Hardwell (ref 12) is given

in Box 8. He must have found it frustrating trying to sort out the confusing relationship between Hardwell and its neighbours!

4.2 Roads, Bridle-Roads and Foot-Roads

The routes of roads and of many paths have remained the same since enclosure, even though some paths and bridle paths have been upgraded into roads. For example the direct road from Uffington to Woolstone was a bridle path and the normal route for carts between the villages would have been along Claypits Road (now also known as The Hams) and Marsh Lane. One or two paths have completely disappeared or moved. The route of some streams have been diverted since the 18th century; in some cases evidence of the old watercourse route can be seen on the ground or in aerial views.

Public access was needed across or alongside new allotments. Provision was made for carts and carriages (on roads), horses (on bridleways) pedestrians (on foot roads) and animals (on drove roads). Some land owners or occupiers were granted private rights of access. After delineating the allotments, the Commissioners defined these rights of way in the Award. Frequently such roads or paths already existed and usage was informal, but it was important to ensure public rights of way were legally binding so that owners or occupiers of the new enclosures could not stop them up at will.

Appendix 3 tabulates the roads and paths defined in the Award. These roads were only defined where they traversed enclosures and that is how they are shown on the Map of Enclosures. Of course they continued beyond the boundaries of the enclosures - this can be seen on the map - since in most cases the road aligns with a modern road or path which is recorded in the underlying 1960 ordnance survey base-map.

Two roads cannot be confidently identified.

The widths of each category of road are defined in the Award and are typically:

- roads: 40 feet between the ditches
- bridle-roads: 15 feet
- foot-roads: four feet

The wheel span of a cart or carriage was probably no more than seven feet so the width of public roads might seem generous. But the widths had to allow for the poor conditions which could pertain in wet weather when parts of the road would become impassable due to deep ruts.

Enclosure roads often have long straight sections and wide verges. This is the case with all of the five roads leading out of Uffington. We cannot say whether these roads had been less straight before enclosure. Indeed, in the financial reconciliations at the end of the Award document (see 4.5) there is no provision for work on roads while costs of boundary fencing, hedging etc is accounted for; we can assume that road-work was only minor feature of the post-allocation expenditure.

There are two examples of the route of foot roads being defined to run directly alongside the 40 foot roads. This may seem curious, but presumably these allowed pedestrians to pass without having to negotiate muddy and rutted cart tracks which might have become impassable in wet weather. This feature occurs elsewhere in Oxfordshire, (ref 13).

The pattern of footpaths in and around the villages reflects the routes which people in the late 18th century would take as they carried out their various activities, walking from their homes and farms, to school, pubs, shops and church. Uffington footpath number one from Moor Mill to Uffington (appendix 3) is described in the award as 'burying and church way'. We do not know why only this particular footpath carries this description.

Gates were authorised across roads by the Award, so that animals could be left to graze the verges. The width of such gates was also defined. The Watts map (figure L) shows two such gates across the road leading from Uffington village towards Fernham. The Kingston Lisle Award document includes a detailed schematic of the construction

of a gate (ref 14) no doubt to illustrate the detail and standard required by the Commissioners.

Notably these early, legally defined, rights of way retain their status and route today, unless changes have been determined formally by the local authority or under statute. Hence the saying: 'Once a Road always a Road'. So for example, when the so-called Definitive Map of foot-paths was set up nationally in the 1950s, in Uffington, the then Chairman of the parish council recorded a number of footpaths with specific reference to the Enclosure Award.

4.3 Commutation of Tithes and other Rights

The Commissioners' core activity was allotting land. But they also had power to rationalise and formalise traditional rights and agreements which had evolved over time. Chief among these was tithes. Tithes were a tax of one tenth of the produce of a particular parcel of land paid to the vicar. After the dissolution of the monasteries when land passed from the Church to lay ownership, tithes were also paid to a private landowner, who was known as the impropriator or lay rector. In Uffington at the time of Enclosure this was John Archer (see Box 5) and the Vicar was George Watts.

Archer and Watts were compensated for the loss of tithes in Uffington and Woolstone (see figure J) by allotments of additional land, at the expense of tithe payers (who would have lost some land); but then they would not have had to pay tithes, so it was all fair, or so it was intended. This process is called commutation of tithes. Those who were tithe payers but who did not

own land in the Open Fields continued to make an annual payment of money in lieu of tithes. As with many matters relating to Parliamentary Enclosure formulas would have evolved for use by Commissioners acting in different districts.

Baulking and Hardwell retained the old tithe arrangements.

Other arrangements which were terminated as a result of enclosure included the right to pasture one ox by Queen's College, or their tenant, at Oxlease farm between Whitsun and Michaelmas each year. The two vicars, Watts and Brown were relieved from the obligation to keep a bull and a boar, for the use by the inhabitants of their respective parishes for serving their cows and sows; this last change seems to us to exemplify the transition from the old communal agricultural methods to the new self-contained each-for-himself approach.

4.4 Fences, Hedges, Boundary Markers and Stone Pits

Within the text describing each allotment is a statement describing who would be responsible for the creation and maintenance of the new boundaries, whether hedges, fences or ditches. Following publication of the Award in May 1778, such landowners were required, within 12 months,

to plant 'quicks' (young hawthorn hedge plants) or make fences along their boundaries. The source of the very large number of young quicks needed and timber for the fencing is unknown, but must have required significant organisation and forward planning. These miles of new hedgerow would, over time, have increased and changed wildlife in the area.

In contrast with other landowners, the vicar, George Watts, and the Trustees of Uffington School land did not have to plant and maintain their boundaries for the next seven years. This was the responsibility of the other landowners. We do not know why.

No hedgerows were planted on the downland, south of Icknield Way. There the new boundaries were marked by large stones, perhaps because of the scale of the task coupled with the difficulty of successfully cultivating hedging on the downland soil. Ordnance survey maps still show boundary stones (marked BS) on the downs. It would have been particularly important to record the corners of land areas using markers which would be permanent (figure T).

While the hedges were growing and crops were planted in the new landholdings, the Commissioners managed the transition so that order was maintained ensuring continuity in harvesting of crops and animal husbandry.

Before enclosure the maintenance of boundaries with bounds, mounds, or meer stones was carried out each year under the Manor court system (see Box 9). They also kept watercourses clear. Transitioning from the shared arrangements in the Open Fields, to a situation where a single landowner was responsible simplified this task.

The Award defined and allotted stone pits for the materials necessary for the building and upkeep of roads in each parish. Each was three acres and therefore more a 'quarry' rather than a 'pit'. They were *'to be used in common'* by owners or tenants. There was one Uffington stone pit, two in Woolstone and none in Baulking; they are shown on the Map of Enclosures. We do not know whether these stone pits were created at the time of enclosure or existing pits merely given a new status.

4.5 Financial Reckoning

Enclosure was expensive, £2198 in total, and this was paid by landowners in proportion to the quantity and value of the land each was allotted. These costs included:

- surveying the ground and assigning and marking out allotments

- analysis of the tithes and their commutation

- overseeing exchanges and sales

- preparing and enrolling the Award document

- paying for the boundary fencing of the Watts and School allotments and its maintenance

- the commissioners' remuneration and reimbursement for their 'time and trouble'

Two schedules at the end of the Award (see Appendix 5) provide figures.

The first schedule shows the amount owed by each landowner. There is an adjustment for the cost of 'mounds and fencing' which would have fallen more lightly on those landowners with large area allotments.

The second schedule shows compensation, relating to the planting and gathering of wheat by certain landowners, payable to other landowners who, in the process, lost some crops to which they were entitled.

4.6 Craven Tenancies Before and After Enclosure

At the start of the Commissioners' work, landowners would have been invited to submit claims to the area of land or rights to use land for which they would hope to receive a compensating allotment. We have been unable to find documentary evidence of these negotiations though some might exist in letters and estate documents.

Allotments to Lord Craven usually make reference to earlier leases. Of course much of his land if not all of it, was let and those leases continued over the period of Enclosure. They did not automatically terminate on Enclosure. Thus the rights of the individual tenants or leaseholders under each particular lease had to be defined and protected despite Enclosure. As a result Lord Craven received many relatively small separate allotments rather than a few large ones. These follow the pattern of existing leases.

We call these pre-existing leases 'precursor leases'. There are two categories. One group gives the name of the tenant, the date of the lease and the annual rent (probably a tenancy at rack rent - see Box 2). The second gives the name of the tenant, the date and the period of the lease which in all cases is 99 years. The earliest lease dates from 1720. As we have not found any copies of such leases we do not know their detail. They are most likely to have been for a defined area of land in the Fields with associated rights on the Common and possibly also use of the Meadow. However in one case (LC/AL) the text describing the precursor lease shows a combination, making specific reference to both an area of land and rights of common.

We show in Table 2 details of these precursor leases with our calculation of the annual rent per acre for each allotment (this is approximate, since the rent is taken from the precursor lease, but the area from the Award.) While there are a few cases in which this figure is well above the average, many are between 7 and 15 pence per acre per year. After Enclosure the annual rent per acre recorded for Craven tenants was around £1 per acre. The reason for this tenfold increase may result simply from improved productivity but there may be other reasons as well.

In the second category, 99 year leases, the tenant associated with the precursor lease is usually from the family of the present tenants, so that continuity of occupation was maintained across the potentially disruptive enclosure period.

There exists a handwritten list of Craven tenants in 1785 immediately following enclosure (ref 15) and the field/close/household can be linked to the Craven map. We show in figure R the holdings of the major Craven tenants in and around Uffington village. This map of the village area shows how usually tenants were assigned adjacent lots. Most of those named also rented larger parcels of land outside the village.

4.7 18th and 19th Century Maps

Immediately following enclosure, the larger landowners presumably would have drawn maps showing their holding, not only for practical reasons but also for display to demonstrate the scope of their estate (ref 16) - hence the decorative nature of these maps. Those maps linked to the Uffington Enclosure (Craven and Watts, figures K and L) were drawn by George King, who was also the surveyor for the Commissioners. As well as the Craven and Watts maps covering the Uffington parish, there are, for example, in the Berkshire Record Office similar maps of Kingston Lisle and of Sparsholt, (ref 17). Some landowners associated with the Uffington award held land in these parishes.

The British Library holds a map of the Vale of White Horse drawn by William Stanley in 1811 (ref 18). It does not show much detail of individual field boundaries but shows roads and the outlying farms with their names, many still in use today. This map gives emphasis to features and conventions being developed for the Ordnance Survey which was the major national mapping project of the early 19th century (ref 19). The canal, but not of course the railway which postdates it, is shown on this map.

For those parishes and hamlets where tithes were not commuted, including Baulking and Hardwell, maps were produced as part of the later commutation under statute. These maps were generally more professional looking and probably more accurate, though less decorative, than those produced 60 years earlier.

In 1860 the Craven Estate produced a set of maps (ref 10) showing their tenanted farms in the Uffington and Woolstone parishes. The estate had expanded since 1778 mainly through the acquisition of land in Woolstone.

The Uffington museum holds a copy of an Ordnance Survey map of Uffington prepared by a Captain Archer (possibly a descendent of John Archer, see box 5) and dated 1878.

Uffington Parish Jury: presentments

During the time of the Award there was a parish jury, which looked after the maintenance of the village and could impose fines. It also appeared to act on behalf of the Lord of the Manor or his Steward for example in approving new tenancies. Here are some examples from the book of jury presentments, or court book as it was later called (ref 21) [our comments in square brackets].

1740 No pigg shall go into the Common from 1st November next till after harvest next and each pigg shall be ringed on the penalty of 1/- a pigg.

1740 We present that all ye Jurymen shall meet at ye Church Gate on 8th November by 8 of ye clock in the forenoon to go and view the mounds as be presented and to sett mearstones if required and that all ye Jurymen shall attend until the same be done on ye penalty of 10/-.

1741 We present that a wash pool be made at Moor Mill for washing all the sheep that depasture in the common fields and other commonable places in Uffington and not elsewhere and that the person that shall wash the said sheep shall have four pence for washing every sheep by the respective owners thereof.

1751 We present that all the necessary houses [ie privies] in the Row that stand over the ditch which run into the stream …. on the penalty of 5/- for each house not being removed by the 1st day of June.

1788 No horse or cow shall feed upon the highway before sun rising or after sun setting under penalty of 5 shillings and not then without a keeper to follow them.

1791 No sheep upon the highway except they be in drift from one place to another
No piggs out of their own liberty
No horses ass or cow out before sun-up

1795 William Pauling came to this court and craved to be admitted tenant to a copyhold cottage and garden now in the tenure of him the said William Pauling which by the death of Mary the widow of John Pauling came into the hands of the Lord of this Manor to which the said copyhold cottage and garden the Lord of this Manor by William Budd, Gentleman, his Deputy Steward, granted siezen thereof by the Rod to hold the same unto the said William Pauling and his heirs. For and during the life of him the said William Pauling now aged 36 years, George Pauling his son aged 7 years and William Pauling his son aged 6 years at the yearly rent of [space]. He paid 1d for a fine and was admitted tenant. [This new copyhold tenancy appears to be an example of a 'rolling' copyhold referred to in box 2]

1810 Any person who shall, by stopping the water in the current in or near Friday street, turning the same over the road, shall be liable to payment of a penalty of not more than 40/- and not less than 2/6.

V. Conclusions

We have told the story of enclosure in Uffington, Baulking and Woolstone from the perspective of the landowners.

In the preface we referred to a dispute concerning a path which the Berkshire County Surveyor in 1967 had stated was defined in the Enclosure Award. In fact we discovered that, while this path is referred to within the Award, such reference is only as a landmark in defining the southern boundary of Puzey's field, not as an enclosure path as such, that is one crossing allotments. So even County Surveyors can be wrong!

Our annoyance regarding the use of this path by motor vehicles was nothing by comparison with the anger and frustration which we assume poorer residents of the parish would have felt when they saw the modest perks available to them within the open field system (gleaning, gathering wood, grazing their animals on the waste lands etc) extinguished by the actions of large landowners. There were strong voices opposed to enclosure generally including John Clare:

'Inclosure came and trampled on the grave
  Of labours rights and made the poor a slave'

That side of the Uffington enclosure story is not revealed in the records which we have seen; but that does not mean it was welcomed by everyone. Surely it was painful for some.

We hope that the data we have assembled in this book will form a useful stimulus for further research into family and local history and other aspects of our rich and beautiful landscape.

Figure A A black poplar in the area called East Coppice Close in 1778. This tree was probably growing at the time. Black poplars are a rare English tree but with a long history; they grow in flood plains and meadows but since 1800 have declined to a few thousand countrywide (ref 4).

Photo Muriel Lindo

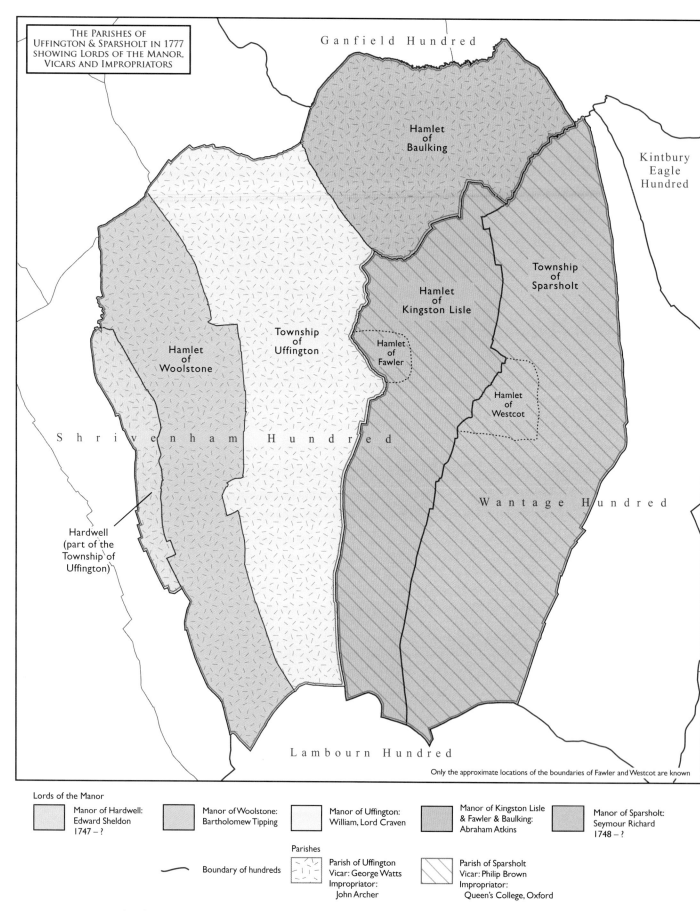

THE PARISHES OF UFFINGTON & SPARSHOLT IN 1777 SHOWING LORDS OF THE MANOR, VICARS AND IMPROPRIATORS

Ganfield Hundred

Hamlet of Baulking

Kintbury Eagle Hundred

Township of Sparsholt

Hamlet of Kingston Lisle

Hamlet of Woolstone

Township of Uffington

Hamlet of Fawler

Hamlet of Westcot

S h r i v e n h a m   H u n d r e d

W a n t a g e   H u n d r e d

Hardwell (part of the Township of Uffington)

Lambourn Hundred

Only the approximate locations of the boundaries of Fawler and Westcot are known

Lords of the Manor

Manor of Hardwell: Edward Sheldon 1747 – ?

Manor of Woolstone: Bartholomew Tipping

Manor of Uffington: William, Lord Craven

Manor of Kingston Lisle & Fawler & Baulking: Abraham Atkins

Manor of Sparsholt: Seymour Richard 1748 – ?

Parishes

Boundary of hundreds

Parish of Uffington Vicar: George Watts Impropriator: John Archer

Parish of Sparsholt Vicar: Philip Brown Impropriator: Queen's College, Oxford

Figure B Hundreds, parishes, townships, hamlets and manors at the time of the enclosure award. The Uffington Award covered the Uffington parish but excluding Hardwell, and also, in a separate Award document, the hamlets of Kingston Lisle and Fawler in the parish of Sparsholt. Details of Hundreds are taken from ref 1 and of the Lords of the Manor are taken from ref 20.

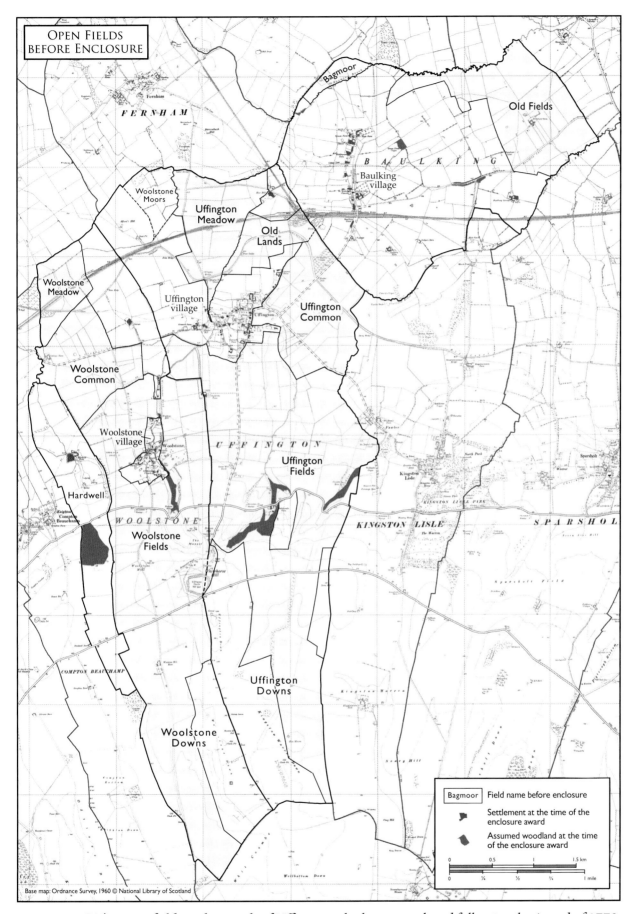

Figure C The open fields in the parish of Uffington which were enclosed following the Award of 1778.

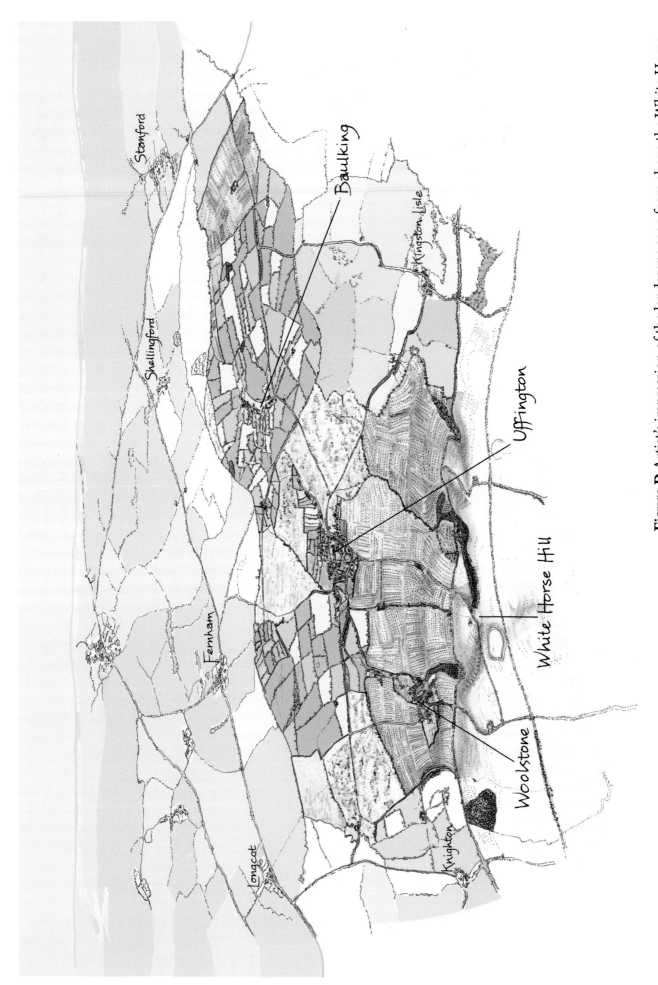

Figure D Artist's impression of the landscape seen from above the White Horse Hill before enclosure, showing the pattern of cultivation in the common fields, including grazing on the common and ridge and furrow strips in the arable fields.

Art work by Bronwen Thomas.

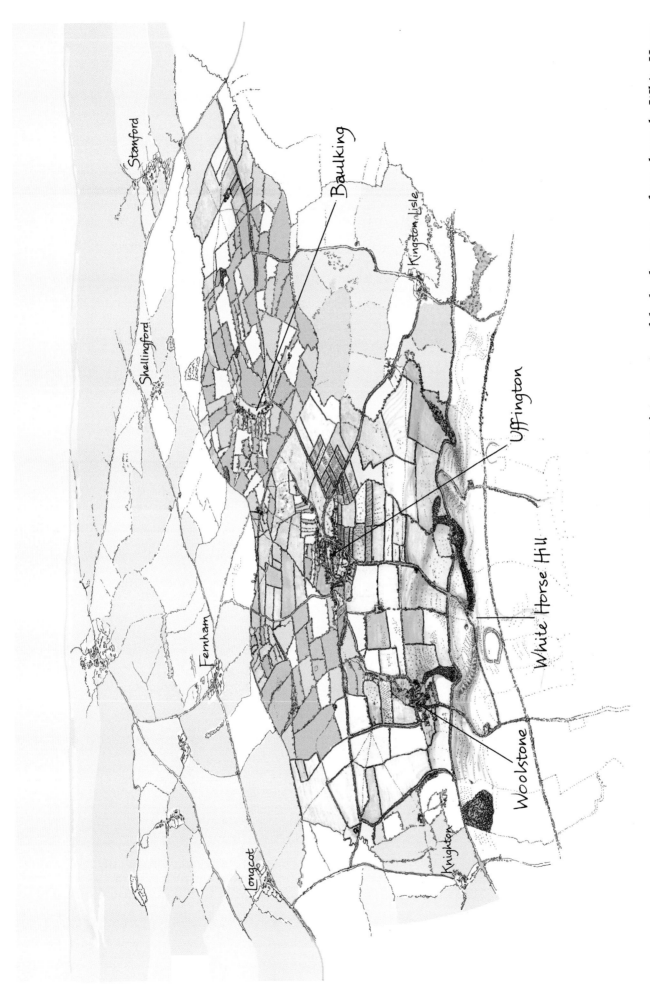

Figure E Artist's impression of the landscape seen from above the White Horse Hill about 10 years after enclosure showing how the open fields have been divided into individually owned areas.

Art work by Bronwen Thomas.

Figure F The School field (TUS on the main map) showing the ridge and furrow pattern which has survived since the time of enclosure.

Figure G The signatures and seals of the five Commissioners, major landowners and others on the completed Award document.

Image reproduced courtesy of the Berkshire Record Office.

Figure H The market place in Wantage from an early 19th century painting. The Bear Inn, where the Uffington Enclosure Award was signed at a public meeting on 29th May 1778, is at the far left hand end.

Image reproduced courtesy of the Vale and Downland Museum, Wantage.

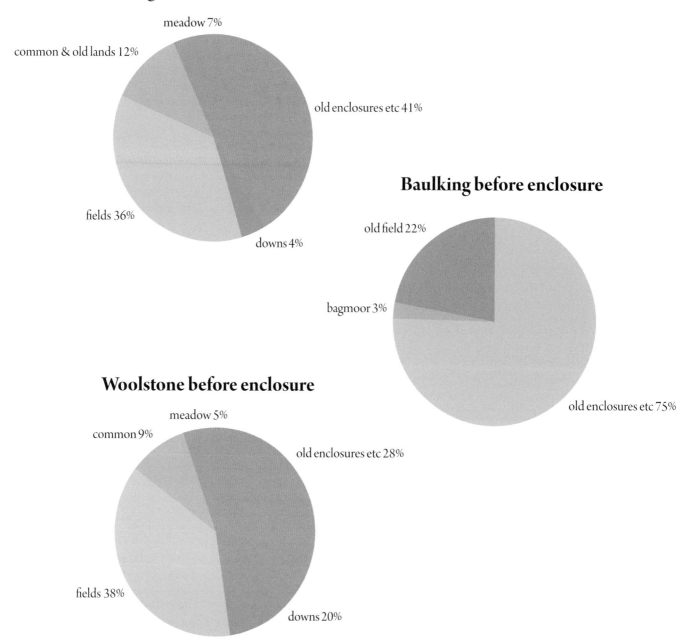

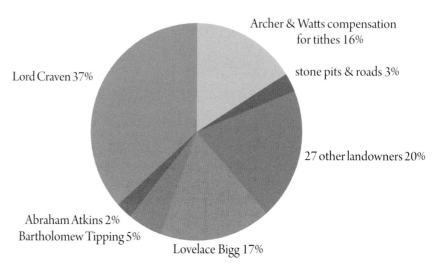

Figure J A breakdown of the areas of open fields before enclosure and a breakdown of allotted areas following enclosure.

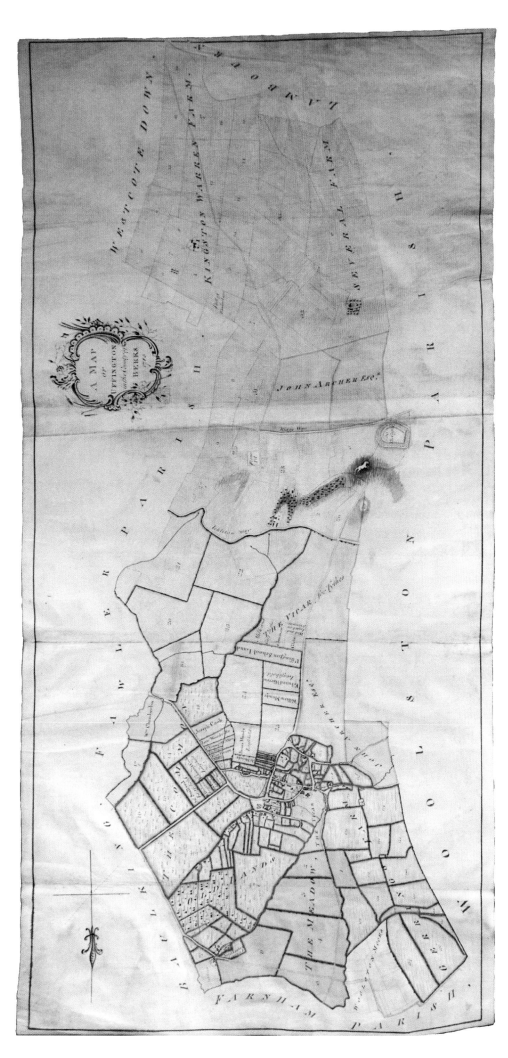

Figure K The 1785 map of the Craven estate in the Township of Uffington. The Craven holdings reflect the allotments and exchanges recorded in the 1778 Award. The tenant leasing each area is recording via a number and a contemporary handwritten table (copy in the TBSM) shows the name of the tenant against the number on the map.

Image reproduced courtesy of the Berkshire Record Office.

Figure L(a)

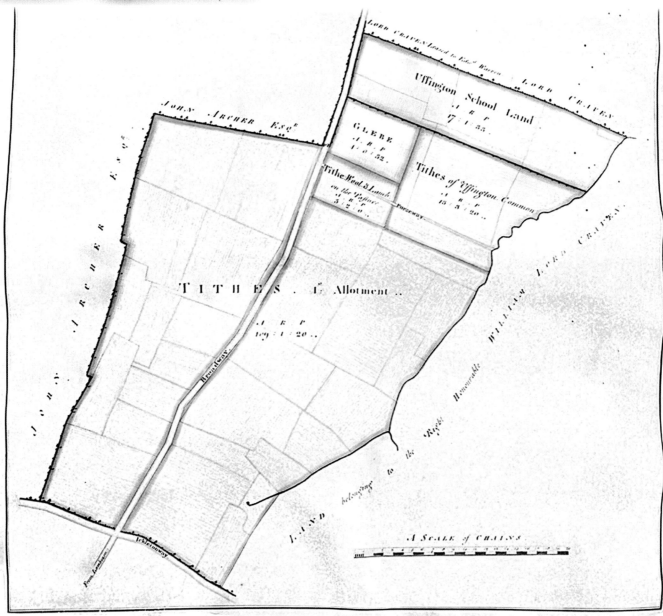

Figure L(b)

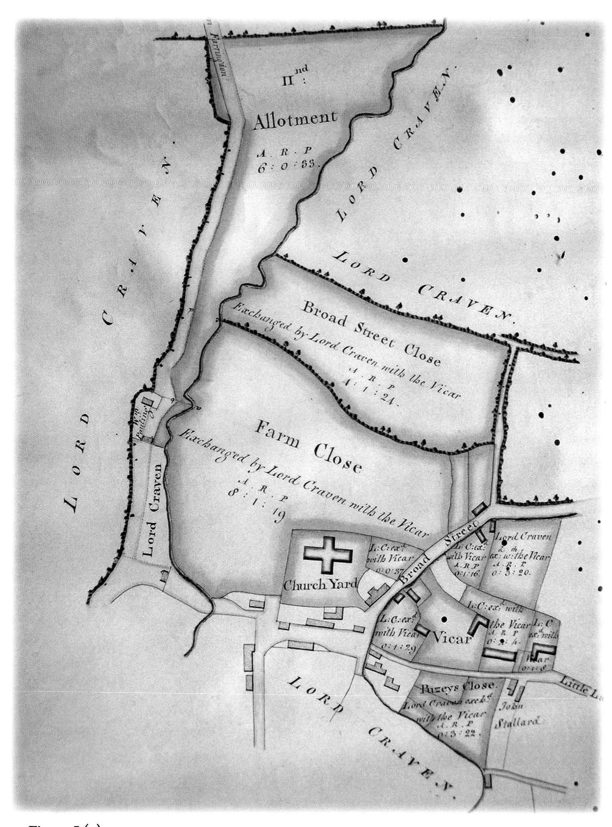

Figure L(c)

Figure L(a-c) The 1778 map of Reverend George Watts' holdings showing allotments he received in lieu of tithes as well as the land he received from Lord Craven in the exchanges recorded in the Award.

Images reproduced courtesy of Mrs Elizabeth Rosser.

Figure M The School field (TUS on the main map) in a Google satellite view showing the technique used to measure the area using Daft Logic software. This measured area of the modern field can be compared with the area of the corresponding enclosure allotment as recorded in the Award document. In this example the area is 17.4 acres in both cases. *[Copyrights to satellite image acknowledged on image itself.]*

Figure N Enclosure roads: (a) 19th century photograph from the White Horse showing Broadway in the distance and the road leading past Dragon Hill in the foreground, described in the Award as '*a road leading from Uffington to Ashdown Park and Baydon*'. *TBSM archive.*
(b) A track across the downs in Woolstone described in the Award as '*part of the road from Woolston towards Lamborne*'.

Figure P An area east of Uffington village shown on the 1785 Craven map and the satellite view of the same area today. This shows how little the boundaries have changed over 230 years.

Image of the Craven map reproduced courtesy of the Berkshire Record Office. [Copyrights to satellite image acknowledged on image itself.]

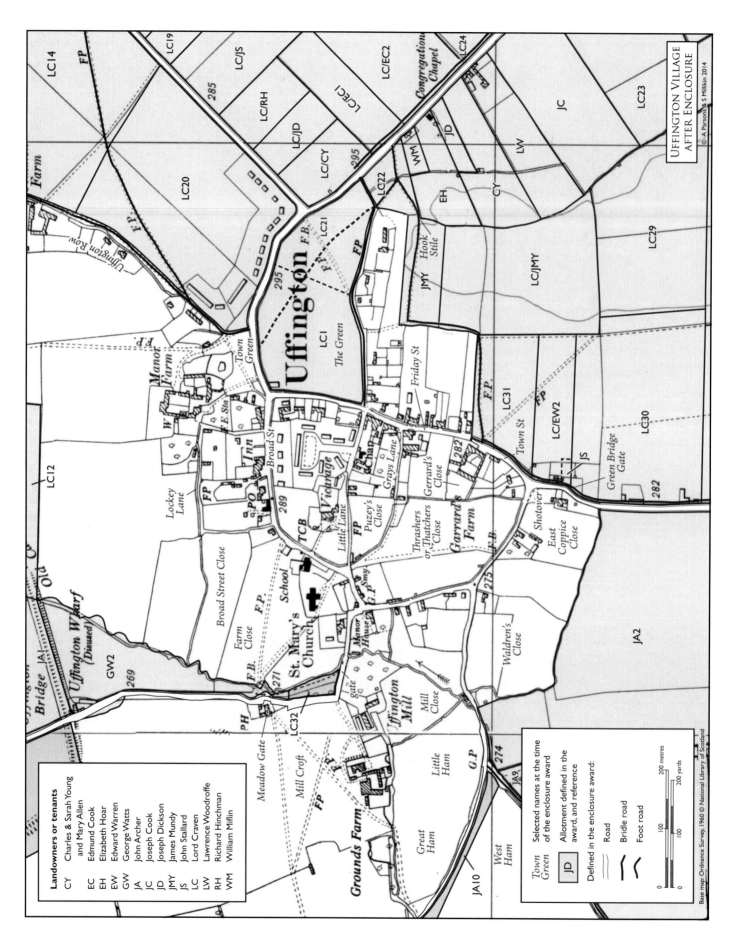

Figure Q Uffington village after enclosure showing the nearby allotments, roads and paths within the village and a selection of names of roads and other features in use at the time of enclosure.

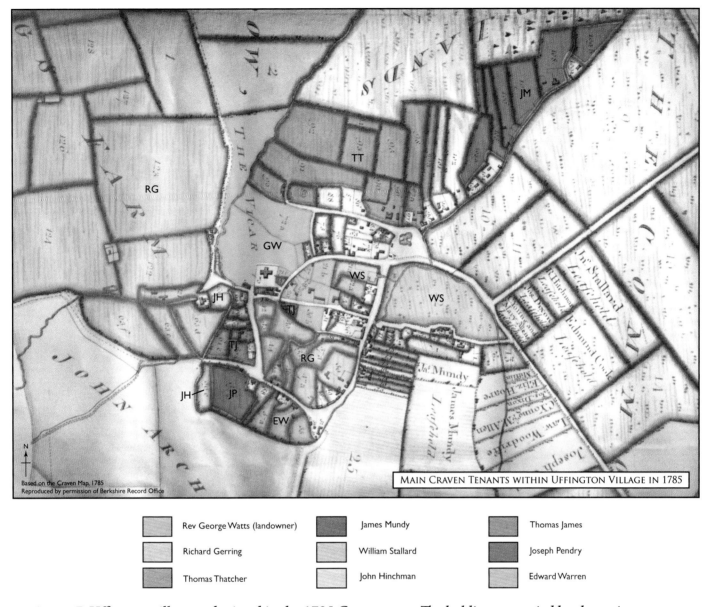

MAIN CRAVEN TENANTS WITHIN UFFINGTON VILLAGE IN 1785

Based on the Craven Map, 1785
Reproduced by permission of Berkshire Record Office

▨	Rev George Watts (landowner)	▨	James Mundy	▨	Thomas James
▨	Richard Gerring	▨	William Stallard	▨	Joseph Pendry
▨	Thomas Thatcher	▨	John Hinchman	▨	Edward Warren

Figure R Uffington village as depicted in the 1785 Craven map. The holdings occupied by the main tenants at the time are shown.

Image of Craven map reproduced courtesy of the Berkshire Record Office.

Figure S An old hedgerow possibly planted at the time of enclosure and showing evidence of having been laid in the distant past.

Figure T Two boundary stones on the downs on the boundary between Uffington and Woolstone.

Appendices

Appendix 1: Glossary

A glossary of certain terms used in this book [some are taken from the Berkshire Record Office website (ref 5) where additional words relevant to enclosure may be found]

Advowson (*or patronage*)   The right of a patron (advowee) to present to the diocesan bishop a nominee for appointment to a vacant church living, a process known as presentation

Allotment   A parcel of land allocated by Enclosure Commissioners in exchange for rights held in the open field system

Award   The legal document produced by the Commissioners recording their decisions

Bridle road   A right of way for horses

Carriage road   A right of way for carriages

Chapelry   See hamlet

Close   A small parcel of land enclosed by hedges or fences often near a house or cottage

Common rights   Rights enjoyed by manorial tenants over the commons and open fields

Copyhold   A type of landholding so named because the tenant held a copy of the court roll as a title deed recording his/her possession of the holding on agreed terms

Drove or drift road   A road for driving livestock on foot

Fields (*as defined before enclosure*)   A large area of open arable land, subdivided into strips and typically used for growing crops

Foot road   A right of way for people on foot but without horses or carriages

Glebe   Land held by the vicar

Hamlet or chapelry   Village or settlement that does not have its own church and belonging to a parish of another village or town

Homestead   A larger dwelling, in contrast to house/cottage, and with more land

Hundred   A subdivision of a shire or county for judicial purposes. However a hundred could be split between counties and a parish split between hundreds.

Impropriator (*or lay rector*)   Person with a right to receive tithes from parishioners and an obligation to repair and maintain the chancel of the parish church. Usually the impropriator also held the advowson (see above)

Lord of the manor   The owner of the manor

Manor   Historically the nucleus of English rural life. An estate comprising an area of land and other rights originally held by an individual as 'tenant of the Crown'

Messuage   A dwelling including its surrounding buildings and grounds

Moor stones   Stones used to mark boundaries

Mounds   Spoil forming a ridge of soil alongside a ditch

Open fields (*as defined before enclosure*)   Large fields for growing crops and managed communally. Individuals farmed strips within the open fields

Parish   The basic territorial unit of the church under the care of a vicar or rector. Within a parish there may be chapelries or hamlets with their own places of worship.

Perch   An area of land equal to 1/40th of a rood (or rod) or about 30 square yards

Quicks or quickthorn   Hawthorn plants used for making stockproof hedges

Rack rent   The full market rent of a property

Rod   See rood

Rood   An area of land equal to quarter of an acre

Severalty   Land held in one's own right rather than jointly with others

Tithes   Payments by parishioners to the vicar or rector usually originally "in kind" and taking its name from a tenth of the income of the payer

Township   An area associated with a larger village.

Vicar   Parish priest who received 'small' or lesser tithes ie within a parish in which other tithes are in lay hands (as opposed to a rector who received all tithes)

Waste   Uncultivated or unuseable land of a manor often subject to rights of common, effectively "leftover land"

Appendix 2: Allotments

A list of all allotments in the Uffington township and the hamlets of Baulking and Woolstone with codes used to identify each on the Main Map of allotments. The area of each allotment is taken from the Award document to the nearest rood (0.25 acre). The final column, showing pence per acre for Craven allotments, is calculated from the rent quoted for the precursor lease and the area of the associated (ie compensating) allotment in the Award.

a) Uffington allotments

Award sheet	allot code	allottee	acres	date of precursor lease	lessee	annual rent (-/)	pence ** per acre
5	LC1	Lord Craven as Lord of the Manor	8				
6	JA1	John Archer	15				
6	JA2	John Archer *	157.25				
7	GW1	Rev George Watts	109.25				
7	GW2	Rev George Watts	6				
7	GW3	Rev George Watts	12.5				
7	GW4	Rev George Watts	18.5				
7	JA4	John Archer	81.25				
7	JA5	John Archer	75				
8	GW5	Rev George Watts	13.75				
8	GW6	Rev George Watts	3.5				
8	JA6	John Archer	1				
9	JA8	John Archer	17.2				
10	LC2	Lord Craven	40.25	1749	Chas Garrard	25.66	7.65
10	LC3	Lord Craven	7.5	1752	Jane Brooks	6.75	10.80
10	LC4	Lord Craven	2	1744	John Alder	2.83	16.98
10	LC5	Lord Craven	16	1742	Joseph Brooks	14	10.50
11	LC6	Lord Craven	8	1726	John Clarke	10	15.00
11	LC7	Lord Craven	17	1733	Wm Chamberlain	13.33	9.41
11	LC8	Lord Craven	33.5	1722	Chas Garrard	30	10.75
11	LC9	Lord Craven	30.25	1754	Joseph Green	34.66	13.75
11	LC10	Lord Craven	7.5	1755	Angel Lockey	6.66	10.66
11	LC11	Lord Craven	3.5	1737	Anthony Shilton	6.83	23.42
11	LC12	Lord Craven	29.75	1742	George Watts clerk	41.5	16.74
12	LC13	Lord Craven	16	1731	Oliver Lockey	39.15	29.36
12	LC14	Lord Craven	106.75	1724	John Green	240	26.98
12	LC15	Lord Craven	10.75	1746	Lawrence Woodroff	6.5	7.26
12	LC16	Lord Craven	21.25	1744	Henry Cook	32.85	18.55
12	LC17	Lord Craven	17	1753	Elizabeth Puzey	20	14.12
12	LC18	Lord Craven	7.25	1723	Wm Moss	4.5	7.45
13	LC19	Lord Craven	4.5	1731	Thomas Taylor	3	8.00
13	LC20	Lord Craven	22.75	1756	Henry Cook	37	19.52

Award sheet	allot code	allottee	acres	date of precursor lease	lessee	annual rent (-/)	pence ** per acre
13	LC21	Lord Craven	3.5	1723	Wm Smith	7.5	25.71
13	LC22	Lord Craven	2	1726	Richard Dean	10	60.00
13	LC23	Lord Craven	27.5	1731	John & Oliver Lockey	11	4.80
13	LC24	Lord Craven	5	1744	Wm Stallard	5.5	13.20
13	LC25	Lord Craven	12	1737	Wm Stallard	9.58	9.58
14	LC26	Lord Craven	19	1742	Chas Garrard	14.42	9.11
14	LC27	Lord Craven	37	1754	John Garrard	20.66	6.70
14	LC28	Lord Craven	57.5	1742	John Isles	37	7.72
14	LC29	Lord Craven	9.75	1753	Mary Saunders	13.33	16.41
14	LC30	Lord Craven	17.25	1755	John Garrard	15.66	10.89
14	LC31	Lord Craven	5				
15	LC32	Lord Craven	0.25				
15	LC33	Lord Craven	12.5				
15	LC34	Lord Craven	215.5				
15	LC35	Lord Craven	181.75				
15	LC36	Lord Craven	186.25				
15	LC37	Lord Craven	24.5				
16	LC/AL	Lord Craven and Angel Lockey his Lessee	4.5	1754	John Lockey	99 year lease	
16	LC/RH	Lord Craven and Richard Hinchman his Lessee	3	1753	Richard Hinchman	99 year lease	
16	LC/JD	Lord Craven and Joseph Dickson his Lessee	1.75	1748	Wm Stallard	99 year lease	
16	LC/CY	Lord Craven and Charles Young and Mary Young his wife, and Mary Allen his Lessees	2.75	1744	Joseph Cook	99 year lease	
16	LC/JS	Lord Craven and John Stallard his Lessee	10.75	1742	Jonathon Stallard	99 year lease	
17	LC/EC1	Lord Craven and Edmund Cook his Lessee	4.25	1744	Henry Cook	99 year lease	
17	LC/EC2	Lord Craven and Edmund Cook his Lessee	8.25	1756	Henry Cook	99 year lease	
17	LC/JM	Lord Craven and James Mundy his Lessee	12.25	1748	Wm Mundy	99 year lease	

Award sheet	allot code	allottee	acres	date of precursor lease	lessee	annual rent (-/)	pence ** per acre
17	LC/WM	Lord Craven and William Mundy his Lessee	9.25	1738	Wm Mundy	99 year lease	
17	LC/EW1	Lord Craven and Edward Warren his Lessee	16.5	1753	Edward Warren	99 year lease	
17	LC/EW2	Lord Craven and Edward Warren his Lessee	4.3				
19	JA9	John Archer	19.25				
19	JA10	John Archer	3.5				
22	WC	William Chamberlain	32.5				
23	GW8	George Watts	4				
23	TUS	Trustees of Uffington School	17.25				
23	JS	John Stallard	0.1				
23	Jck	Joseph Cook	9				
23	LW	Lawrence Woodroffe	4.75				
23	CY	Charles Young and Sarah Young his wife and Mary Allen	4				
23	JD	Joseph Dickson	0.75				
23	EH	Elizabeth Hoar	2.75				
24	WM	William Miflin	0.5				
24	JMY	James Mundy	2.25				

Notes: * allotment JA2 lies in both Uffington (79.3 acres) & Woolstone (77.9 acres)

** pence per acre taken from rent for earlier lease and area of allotment which replaced it in 1778

b) Baulking allotments

Award sheet	allot code	allottee	acres	date of lease	lessee	
5	AA1	Abraham Atkins as Lord of the Manor	0.25			
15	LC38	Lord Craven	83.75			
15	LC39	Lord Craven	0.25			
15	LC/GR	Lord Craven and George Read his Lessee	2.25	1768	George Read	99 year lease
16	LC/RQ	Lord Craven and Robert Quarme his Lessee	11.75	1768	Robert Quarme	99 year lease
17	SPEN	Earl Spencer	7.75			
19	JH1	John Hippesley	26.75			
19	JH2	John Hippesley	18.75			
20	PSQ/PB	Queen's College Oxford, and Philip Brown their Lessee	2			
20	AA2	Abraham Atkins	93.5			
20	ET	Edward Thornhill and Collier Thornhill his wife	15.5			
20	JHYD1	John Hyde	26.25			
20	JHYD2	John Hyde	10.5			
20	HA	Henry Aston	9.5			
20	PSW	Trustees of Presbyterian Society, Wantage	5			
20	DCW/JM	Dean and Chapter of Westminster and John Merest, their Lessee	1.75			
21	RL	Robert Leaver	4.25			
21	JWLL	John Williams	0.75			
21	JWIR	Joseph Wirdnam	3.25			
21	RS	Roger Spanswick	0.75			
21	RF	Trustees of Robert Fettiplace	11.25			
21	QC/RF1	Queen's College Oxford, and Trustees of Robert Fettiplace as Lessees	12.75			

c) Woolstone allotments

Award sheet	allot code	allottee	acres
5	BT1	Bartholomew Tipping as Lord of the Manor	1.75
9	GW7	Rev George Watts	70.75
9	JA7	John Archer	25.75
18	BT2	Bartholomew Tipping	13
18	BT3	Bartholomew Tipping	5
18	BT4	Bartholomew Tipping	146.25
18	BT5	Bartholomew Tipping	28.5
18	BT6	Bartholomew Tipping	3.5
18	BT7	Bartholomew Tipping	0.6
18	LB1	Lovelace Bigg	196
19	LB2	Lovelace Bigg	17.5
19	LB3	Lovelace Bigg	41.5
19	LB5	Lovelace Bigg	2
19	LB6	Lovelace Bigg	0.9
19	LB7	Lovelace Bigg	4.75
19	LB4	Lovelace Bigg	384
21	QC/RF2	Queen's College Oxford, and Trustees of Robert Fettiplace as Lessees	13.5
22	QC/RF3	Queen's College Oxford, and Trustees of Robert Fettiplace as Lessees	19.75
22	JC1	Jeffry Church	34.5
22	JC2	Jeffry Church	60.75
22	JC3	Jeffry Church	0.5
22	JM	Joseph Mayon	92.5
22	WT1	William Thatcher	15.25
22	WT2	William Thatcher	70.5

Note: allotment JA2 is in both Uffington and Woolstone but is listed in Uffington only

Appendix 3: Roads and Paths

Roads, bridleways and footpaths defined in the Uffington Enclosure Award.

These are public roads which pass over, or run alongside, defined enclosures and are shown on our Main Map.   BW and FP refer to rights of way in the local 'Definitive Map'. WP refers to observation made by Parish Council chairman when Definitive Map was being drafted.

Public roads in Uffington

road no	description in Award	from	to	comment e.g. as road is known today
1	part of ancient way called Ickleton Way	Fawler Foredown Field N side LC35	Woolstone Fields	Icknield Way
2	part of ancient way called Ridgeway	Several Farm E side Uffington	into Several Farms	Ridgeway
3	Uffington towards Ashdown Park & Baydon	S part Uffington called Green Bridge Gate	Woolstone Fields	Broadway
4	towards Lambourne	Icknield Way (guide post)	Kingston Warren Farm	see 1785 Craven map
5	part Uffington to Fawler	end Broad St	White Foot Lane	Uffington to Fawler road
6	Broad St to Friday St	Broad St	Friday St	N end High St to Upper Common Lane
7	part road Uffington to Baulking	#5	Baulking gate	Uffington to Baulking road
8	part road Baulking to Moor Mill	#7	SE side Moor Mill Lane	road past Uffington station
9	from Baulking & Moor Mill to Longcot	NW end Moor Mill Lane	E end of lane called Moor Lane	former Longcot road – see Craven map
10	part road Uffington to Faringdon	lane W side Uffington	road Moor Mill to Moor Lane	Uffington to Fernham road
11	part road Fernham to Woolston	#10 opp gate called Morrell Leaze gate	Morrell Leaze gate	not identified
12	part road Uffington to Shrivenham	another lane W side of Uffington	gate leading to Oxleaze farm	Claypit road

Bridle roads in Uffington

road no	description in Award	from	to	comment
1	Uffington to Moor Mill	public road Uffington to Fawler	public road Baulking to Moor Mill	Lower Common Lane
2		public road Broad St to Friday St	public road Uffington to Fawler	Upper Common Lane
3	part bridle road Uffington to Woolstone	public road Uffington to Shrivenham	bridle road in Woolstone	direct metalled road to Woolstone
4	part bridle road Uffington to Faringdon	public road Moor Mill to Longcot	bridle bridge across brook leading into Fernham Lane	not identified

Foot roads in Uffington

road no	description in Award	from	to	comment
1	Moor Mill to Uffington	stile in Moor Mill Close	stile in old enclosure (LC/John Forty)	Award ref: "burial & church way" FP4
2	Uffington & Moor Mill to Shellingford	Public road Moor Mill to Longcot	foot plank across brook between Uffington Meadow & Fernham	Moor Mill towards Fernham/Shellingford BW2
3	E Uffington to Fernham	#1	public road Moor Mill to Longcot	WP quote 'see early 1" o/s map'
4	Uffington & Moor Mill to Shellingford	#3 at Mond Plank	foot plank across.... see #2	FP1
5	Uffington to Baulking	Uffington near pond	Baulking stile	FP12
6	easy communication between parts of Uffington	Town St	public road Uffington to Fawler opposite pond on Green	FP17,19
7	part road Uffington to Fawler	foot road Uffington to Fawler	SW corner of place called Hitchins	alongside road Uffington to Fawler
8	part road Uffington to Lambourne	Town St SW enclosure J Lockey	Lime Kiln Way at Several Farm	alongside Broadway
9	part road Fawler to Woolstone	stile in old enclosure in Fawler	Woolstone	FP20

Public roads, bridle roads & foot roads in Baulking

road no	description in Award	from	to	comment
1	Portway: public road Baulking to Standford	SW corner of Old Field at Fortisons Gate	Standford Gate	existing road Baulking to Standford
2	part bridle road Standford to Baulking	out of #1	gate leading into old enclosure (JHyde)	BW7
3	part bridle road Baulking to Shellingford	across Bagmoor		BW2
4	part foot road Baulking to Standford	stile W Old Field	stile Standford Grounds	FP5
5	part foot road Kingston Lisle to Standford	stile SW Old Field	stile Standford Grounds	FP11
6	part foot road Sparsholt to Standford	S part Old Field called Sparsholt corner	stile Standford Grounds	FP10

Public roads in Woolstone

road no	description in Award	from	to	comment
1	Ickleton Way	Ickleton Way in Uffington township	Hardwell Farm	Icknield Way
2	Ridgeway	Ridgeway in Several Farm Uffington	entrance to same road on Hardwell Farm	Ridgeway
3	part road Woolstone to Lambourne	lane on S part Woolstone village	Lambourne Downs	road/track Woolstone to Upper Lambourne
4	part road Uffington to Ashdown & Baydon	#3	into road Uffington to Ashdown/Baydon	road from #3 to Dragon Hill
5	part road Uffington to Shrivenham	Claypit Gate E side Woolstone Common	Longcot Common	Claypit Lane
6	Hardwell to Longcot	Hardwell gate W side Woolstone Common	road Uffington to Shrivenham	Hardwell Lane
7	part road Woolstone to Longcot	lane W side Woolstone town	road Uffington to Shrivenham by Claypit Gate	Marsh Lane

Bridle & foot roads in Woolstone

road no	description in Award	from	to	comment
1	public bridle road Woolstone to Uffington	lane E side Woolstone village	bridle road in Uffington	existing metalled road
2	part foot road Woolstone to Fawler	#1	foot road Fawler Uffington towards Woolstone	FP13
3	Woolstone to Hardwell	public road Woolstone to Longcot	Hardwell stile	FP14
4	part foot road Lower Town to Hardwell & Knighton	houses in Woolstone called Lower Town	stile in hedge between Woolstone Fields and Hardwell Farm near SW corner of W Common	FP10
5	part foot road Woolstone to Longcot	public road Uffington to Shrivenham near Claypit Gate	stile entering Longcot Common NE corner Woolstone Meadow	FP7
6	not defined	public road Woolstone to Longcot	public road Woolstone Common at NE corner Vicar's allotment	FP9

Appendix 4: References

Ref 1:   An Historical Atlas of Berkshire, Joan Dils (ed) 1998 Berkshire Record Society *

Ref 2:   The making of the English Landscape, WG Hoskins 1955 Penguin

Ref 3:   Fields in the English Landscape, Christopher Turner 1975 Dent

Ref 4:   The History of the Countryside, Oliver Rackham 1986 Dent *

Ref 5:   for a comprehensive bibliography see the website of the Berkshire Record Office:
          http://www.berkshireenclosure.org.uk/

Ref 6:   Craven map 1785, Berkshire Record Office ref D/EC/E13 *

Ref 7:   Watts map 1778, private collection *

Ref 8:   Queen's College Oxford archive, ref Fettiplace estates

Ref 9:   Baulking tithe map, Nat Archives Kew ref IR30/2/13*

Ref 10:   Craven estate1860 maps, TBSM ref M/F4*

Ref 11:   The Village of Woolstone in the Vale of the White Horse, John Hadow 1975 *

Ref 12:   Hardwell Tithe Commissioner's Report, Nat Archives ref IR29/2/69;
          and map, Nat Archives ref IR30/2/69

Ref 13:   private communication David Godfrey, Oxfordshire Field Paths Society

Ref 14:   BRO Sparsholt (Kingston Lisle & Fawler) award, Berkshire Record Office ref D/EFH/E1

Ref 15:   list of Craven tenants, Berkshire Record Office re D/EC/E13*

Ref 16:   private communication Dr Durant, Berkshire Record Office

Ref 17:   Kingston Lisle map, Berkshire Record Office ref D/EC/E11/2 map 13 *

Ref 18:   map of Vale of the White Horse (Wantage) 1811, William Stanley, British Library OSD160/9

Ref 19:   Map of a Nation, Rachel Hewitt 2010 Granta

Ref 20:   Victoria History of Berkshire Vol 4, W Page & PH Ditchfield (eds) 1924

Ref 21:   Visitation – Presentments for Uffington, Baulking & Woolstone, Ivy Curzon 1970 Berkshire Tracts*

* Copies of these items can be found in the Tom Brown's School Museum, Uffington [TBSM]

Appendix 5: The Award

Transcription of the Uffington Enclosure Award 1778 followed by its two financial schedules and an index of names. The original Award is available via the Berkshire Record Office: website www.berkshireenclosure.org.uk or ref Q/RDC/84A and our sheet numbers reflect these original 33 manuscript sheets. The Record Office also holds a handwritten 19th century version.

The words in bold in our transcript are as shown in the original manuscript. We have used margin notes and line numbers to guide the reader. Inevitably we will have made transcription errors in this document. We have placed question marks in the few places where there are self-evident errors in the original (eg 'west' for 'east' etc).

Contents

Appendix 5a

Appendix 5b:

Appendix 5c

Commissioners

1

1

To all people to whom this present writing or instrument of award division appointment or allotment shall come **James King** of Daventry in the county of Northampton William Fillingham of Newark upon Trent in the county of Nottingham John Brothers of Hungerly in the parish of Wykin in the county of the city

5   of Coventry John Watts of Sulgrave in the said county of Northampton and John Mitchell of South Weston in the County of Oxford gentlemen Commissioners named and appointed in and by virtue of the Act of Parliament from hereinafter inscribed and also the Rt Honourable **William Lord Craven** Baron Craven of Hampstead Marshall in the county of Berks Abraham Atkins of Kingston Lisle in the said county of Berks

*landowners
& signatories
to the award*

10   Esquire John Archer of Welford in the said county of Berks Esquire impropriator of the rectory or parsonage of Uffington in the said county of Berks Bartholomew Tipping of Woolley in the said County of Berks Esquire Lovelace Bigg of Chilton Foliat in the County of Wilts Esquire the Reverend George Watts Vicar of Uffington in the said County of Berks Jeffry Church of Woolston in the said County of Berks Yeoman Joseph

15   Mayon of the parish of Buckland of the said county of Berks Yeoman John Stallard of Uffington aforesaid blacksmith Edward Warren of Ashbury in the said county of Berks Yeoman (lessee of said William Lord Craven) John William Willaume and Abraham Chambers Esquires trustees or assignees of the estate of Robert Fettiplace late of Swinbrook in the said county of Oxford Esquire Robert Leaver of Wallingford in the

20   said county of Berks Gentleman (owners and proprietors of certain lands and premises hereinafter mentioned to be exchanged) send greeting whereas by an **Act of**

reference to Act

Parliament passed in the seventeenth year of the reign of his present majesty King George the Third instituted an Act for dividing allotting and inclosing certain open and common fields common meadows common pastures downs commons and other

25   commonable lands within the Township of Uffington and the hamlets of Balking and Woolston otherwise Wolverston and within the hamlets of Kingston Lisle and Sparsholt in the county of Berks after writing as therein is inscribed It was amongst other things enacted that the said James King William Fillingham John Brothers and John Watts together with Francis Burton late of Aynho in the said county of

30   Northampton Gentleman since deceased and their successors to be alerted in manner thereinafter mentioned should be and they were thereby appointed **Commissioners**

*role of
commissioners*

for dividing and allotting the said open and common fields common meadows common pastures downs commons and commonable lands within the township of Uffington and the hamlets of Balking and Woolston otherwise Wolverston and for

35   putting the said Act into execution touching the same Township and hamlets and that all and every of the powers authority directions matters and things by the said Act given to or vested in or directed to be done and executed by or before the said Commissioners should and might be done and executed by or before any of the five Commissioners touching or concerning the Township of Uffington and hamlets of

40   Balking and Woolston otherwise Wolverston (except in such cases where any smaller or other number of Commissioners is appointed by the said Act so that the act and acts of any three of the said commissioners should be of as full force and effect as if done or executed by or before the said Commissioners (except as before excepted) any thing therein contained to the contrary thereof in any wise notwithstanding and it was

45   thereby further enacted that no person should be capable of acting as Commissioner in

the execution of the said Act so far as the same concerns any lands or tithes within the *46*
parish of Uffington (unless it be the power thereby given of administering the oath and
of appointing and giving Notice of the first meeting of the said Commissioners) until he
should have taken an oath to the effect therein set forth which oath it should be and
might be lawful for any one of the said Commissioners to administer to the others and *50*
other of them and they were thereby required to administer the same and the said oath
so taken and subscribed should be enrolled at the same time and place as this Award is
in and by the said Act directed to be enrolled And for the more just and regular
division and distribution of the said open and common fields common meadows
common pastures down commons and commonable lands thereby directed to be *55*
divided and allotted as aforesaid and for the better ascertaining the same it was enacted
that the quantity and value of the said open and common fields common meadows
common pastures downs commons and commonable lands should be ascertained by
the said Commissioners or their successors by such person or persons as they should by
any writing under their hands for that purpose nominate and appoint and that true and *60*
perfect surveys and admeasurements of all the said open and common fields common
meadows common pastures downs and commonable lands so intended to be divided
and allotted and also of such of the Old Inclosures within the Township of Uffington
and within the hamlets of Balking and Woolston otherwise Wolverston as should
thereinafter be directed to be discharged from tithes or to accommodate any exchange *65*
in the manner thereafter mentioned should be sometime before the first day of July one
thousand seven hundred and seventy seven or as soon after as conveniently might be
laid before them by George King of Daventry aforesaid or by such person or persons as
should for the purpose be appointed by the said Commissioners and such survey and
admeasurement should be reduced into writing and the number of acres roods and *70*
perches belonging to each proprietor should be specified declared and set forth and
should be laid before the said Commissioners at their next and every other meeting
held subsequent to the making the same and it was thereby further enacted that the said
Commissioners should have full power and authority and they were thereby required at
any time or times after the said survey should have been laid before them but before the *75*
tenth day of October one thousand seven hundred and seventy seven or as soon after as
conveniently could be done to set out divide ascertain and allot all the same open and
common fields common meadows commons pastures downs commons and other
commonable lands unto and amongst the several persons entitled to and interested
therein in proportion to their several and respective shares rights interests of common *80*
tithes and other properties in and over the same but subject to such rules orders and
regulations as are thereinafter particularly declared and set forth and after divers special
orders and directions therein contained respecting the manorial and tithe allotments
and the land to be laid out for public stone pits it was thereby further enacted that from
immediately after the said Commissioners should have made the said several allotments *95*
thereinbefore mentioned and should also have deducted a sufficient quantity of the said
lands and grounds directed to be allotted and divided for the purpose of setting out
roads and highways as therein mentioned then the said commissioners should set out
divide assign allot and award all the residue and remainder of the said open and
common fields common meadows common pastures downs and other commonable *100*

*principles &
practice of
enclosure*

101 lands lying within the township of Uffington and the hamlets of Balking and Woolston otherwise Wolverston (except as before excepted) unto and amongst the said William Lord Craven the Rt Honourable John Earl Spencer the said Bartholomew Tipping Lovelace Bigg John Hippesley John Archer and to the other persons entitled to and

105 interested in the same in such quantities shares and proportions as by the said Commissioners should be adjudged and determined to be just recompense and satisfaction for and equal to their several and respective lands and grounds rights of common and other properties therein (except Tithes aforesaid) and it was by the said Act provided and thereby further enacted and declared that the said Commissioners in

110 making the said allotments should have due regard to the quality situation and convenience as well as quantity both of the lands and growths then belonging to each proprietor and of the lands and grounds by the said Act directed to be allotted in lieu

disputes

thereof and if any **disputes** should arise between the parties interested in the said division or allotment or any of them touching and concerning the respective shares

115 rights and interests which they or any of them should claim in the said lands and grounds so directed to be divided and allotted or touching or concerning the respective shares and proportions which they of any of them ought to have on or in the said division and allotment it should and might be lawful for the said Commissioners and they were thereby authorised and required upon examination of a witness or witnesses

120 upon oath (which oath any one of the said Commissioners was thereby authorised or empowered to administer) or upon other proper and sufficient evidence and inquiry to hear and finally determine the same and it was thereby provided that nothing therein contained should authorise the said Commissioners to hear and determine any differences or disputes which might arise touching the right or title to the lands or other

125 rights that might be claimed in the said open and common fields for which the parties might comment and propound such suits and remedies as they should be advised and think proper and that no difference or suit touching the title to any lands or rights should impede or delay the Commissioners in the execution of the powers vested in them by the said Act and that the division and inclosure should be preceded in

130 notwithstanding such differences or suits and after reciting The Provost and Scholars of Queens College in the University of Oxford and Robert Fettiplace Esquire their lessee

compensation for right to depasture ox

his assignees or undertenants had a **right to the feeding** or depasturing of one ox from Whitsun Eve until the Feast of Michael the Archangel yearly in a certain pasture ground called the Oxleaze in Woolston otherwise Wolverston aforesaid then in the occupation

135 of James Mattingly as lessee of the said Bartholomew Tipping. **It was therefore enacted** that the said Commissioners and their successors should and they were therefore required by this Award to be made touching the same hamlets in pursuance of the said Act to allot and appoint unto and for the said Provost and Scholars of Queens College their lessee or assigns from and out of the allotment to be made to the said

140 Bartholomew Tipping in pursuance of the said Act such parcel of land as in the judgement of the said Commissioners should be a just full and adequate

2 **Satisfaction** for such right of feeding or depasturing of the said ox as aforesaid and from and immediately after the said award should be so made all rights of the said Provost and Scholars their lessees or assigns to feed or depasture the said ox in manner aforesaid should cease determine and so utterly extinguished any usage to the contrary notwithstanding **And it was** by the said Act further **enacted** that the said Commissioners should and might and they were thereby authorised and required to ascertain **set out and appoint** private roads and also before any allotment should be made to any proprietor or other persons (together with two of his Majesty's Justices of the Peace for the hundred or hundreds wherein the township of Uffington and the hamlets of Balking and Woolston otherwise Wolverston respectively are situate if the said Justices should think proper to attend ten days notice being given to them by the clerk to the said Commissioners of the time of the Commissioners' meeting for that purpose) to ascertain set out and appoint public roads and ways through and over the said now intended allotments with the sizes and breadths thereof so as such public roads and ways should be and remain of the breadth of forty feet at least between the ditches (except bridle and footways in case any such should be set out by the said Commissioners) **And it was** thereby further **enacted** that the said Commissioners should have power and authority and they were thereby authorised and required to **direct good** and sufficient fences to be made for separating and dividing all such of the now intended allotments as should lie or be allotted in any of the said lands and grounds commons and meadows by the said Act directed to be allotted and divided on the north or lower side of a certain ancient way or road called Ickleton Way and they were required to apportion the said fencing and the expenses thereof amongst the several owners or proprietors of such now intended allotments in such manner shares and proportions as to them should seem reasonable and just. **And it was** by the said Act **provided** that such of the allotments to the said George Watts and his successors Vicars of Uffington and to the Trustees of certain commonable lands given by Thomas Saunders deceased for maintaining a schoolmaster at Uffington which should lie on the north or lower side of the road called Ickleton Way should be inclosed and ring fenced by ditches and quick set hedges or other proper mounds and fences already made or to be made in or upon such allotments or in or upon the next adjoining allotment or allotments or on other lands or ancient inclosures and in case the fences for inclosing the said allotments or any of them to the said George Watts and his successors Vicars of Uffington and the said Trustees or any or either of them should be directed to be made upon the same allotments or any of them the same should be made and for the term of seven years supported by and at the expense of such of the other proprietors in such proportions and in such manner as the said Commissioners should award direct and appoint and from and after the expiration of the said term of seven years the fences so made on the said allotments to the said George Watts and his successors and the said Trustees respectively should be forever supported by and at the expense of and be the property of the said George Watts and his successors and the said Trustees respectively but in case the ring fences of the said allotments should be made in or upon the next adjoining allotment or allotments the same should be made by and at the expense of such other of the said proprietors of the said open fields lands and grounds thereby directed to be divided (except the said George Watts and the said Trustees) in such manner and proportions as the said

roads & paths role of Justices of the Peace

expense of fencing

1

5

10

15

20

25

30

35

40

45

46 Commissioners should direct which said fences should be of substantial posts and three rails on one side and substantial posts and two good rails on the other side for the security of good quick plants to be planted at the expense of the proprietors of lands to be inclosed according to their respective interests herein **And it was thereby provided**

compensation for tithes & glebe

50 that nothing in the said Act contained should empower the said Commissioners or any of them to **allot** to the said George Watts and his successors or the said Trustees any more or any larger proportion of land on the north or lower side of the said Ickleton Way than their just proportion arising out of the lands commons and meadows lying on the same side of the said Road or Way without the consent of the said George Watts and

55 his successors or the said Trustees signified in writing to the said Commissioners on or before the tenth day of October one thousand seven hundred and seventy seven but for and in lieu of such tithes and glebe arising to the said George Watts and his successors and the said Trustees out of the downs and lands on the south or upper side of the said Ickleton Road or Way for which any allotment of land should be made in pursuance of

60 the said Act lands should be allotted to them respectively on the said Upper or South side thereof unless such consent was so had and obtained **And it was** by the said Act further **enacted and declared** that the said Commissioners were thereby fully authorised and empowered in all cases where they should think fit and proper to lay the several allotments of the several owners of any of the commonable lands or common

65 rights before mentioned within the parish of Uffington in one or more plot or plots in any one or more of the said Townships or hamlets of Uffington, Balking or Woolston otherwise Wolverston whether the open field estates lands or commons in lieu whereof such allotments respectively were made in their present state were in either or all of the said Townships or hamlets. **And it was thereby enacted** that all the allotments made by

70 the said Commissioners within the parish of Uffington by virtue of the said Act should be taken and deemed to be within the Township of Uffington or within such of the hamlets of Woolston and Balking in which the same were or should be allotted notwithstanding the lands or commons in lieu of which such allotments were made were then in either or any other of the hamlets or places **And it was thereby provided**

assigment of White Horse & castle to Lord Craven

75 that the said commissioners should in and by their said **award allot** to and for the said William Lord Craven and as part of the allotments to be made to him in pursuance of the said Act a certain part of the said downs in the parish of Uffington aforesaid on which were marked out the figure and form or representation of a horse commonly called The White Horse and of a castle near to the same and that such allotment should

80 forever thereafter be deemed and considered as lying within and part of the Manor of Uffington **and** that for and in lieu of so much of the said allotment last mentioned as is situate and being within the Manor of Woolston otherwise Wolverstone aforesaid the said Commissioners or their successors should and were thereby required to mark out and describe so much of the land belonging to the said William Lord Craven within the

95 manor and township of Uffington then in the occupation of Joseph Lousley as should in the judgement of the said Commissioners be deemed equivalent thereto which said last mentioned parcel of land should forever thereafter be deemed and considered as lying within and part of the Manor of Woolston otherwise Wolverstone aforesaid **And it was** amongst other things **provided** that in case any hedges then standing upon the premises

100 should be assigned or appointed by the said commissioners as or for a boundary or

subdivision fence for any allotments to be made as aforesaid all hedges should be left *101*
uncut for the benefit of such person or persons to whom such new allotments should
belong by virtue of the said Act he she or they making such allowance or consideration
to the former owners and proprietors of such hedges respectively as the said
Commissioners should by any writing under their hands in that behalf order and appoint *105*
And for preventing differences and disputes relating to the said division of allotments
and Inclosures **it was thereby enacted** by the authority aforesaid that as soon as
conveniently might be after the said Commissioners should have completed and finished
the said partitions and allotments of the said open and common fields common pastures
common meadows downs and other commonable lands thereby intended to be divided *110*
and allotted as aforesaid pursuant to the purport and directions of the said Act they the
said Commissioners should form or **draw up** or cause to be formed and drawn up two
awards or Instruments in writing one of the said Awards to contain all such matters and
things as relate to or concern the Township of Uffington and hamlets of Balking and
Woolston otherwise Wolverston the other of the said Awards to contain all such matters *115*
and things as relate to or concern the hamlets of Kingston Lisle and Fawler which said
several awards should express and contain the quantity of acres roods and perches
contained in the said open and common fields common meadows common pastures
downs and other commonable lands so directed to be allotted and divided as aforesaid
and which should be comprised in the said awards respectively and the quantity of each *120*
and every part and parcel thereof should be assigned and allotted to each and every of
the proprietors entitled to and interested in the same and a description of the situation
buttals and boundaries of the same parcels and allotments respectively and proper
orders and directions for mounding such of the said allotments as should be laid or
allotted on the north or lower side of the said Ickleton Road or Way and for ascertaining *125*
and fixing the boundaries of the respective allotments on the south or upper side of the
said Ickleton Road or Way and for keeping in repair and supporting maintaining
ascertaining and distinguishing the said mounds and fences boundaries divisions and
allotments and also for laying out proper roads ways and passages in and through the
same premises thereby intended to be allotted or inclosed and should also express and *130*
contain such other orders regulations and determinations as should be proper and
necessary to be inserted therein conformable to the tenor and purport of the said Act
which said Instruments respectively should be fairly engrossed or written on parchment
and signed and sealed by the said commissioners and should within six calendar months
next after the same should be so respectively signed and sealed as aforesaid be **enrolled** *135*
by the clerk of the Peace for the said County of Berks or in one of his Majesty's Court of
Record at Westminster to the end recourse might be had to the same by any person or
persons interested in the   said intended division allotting or inclosing and the said
several awards so executed and enrolled should be binding and inclusive unto and upon
all persons interested in the said premises respectively to all intents and purposes *140*

records of awards for: Uffington, Woolstone, Baulking & for Kingston-Lisle & Fawler

places where document are to be filed

*exchanges
between Rev
Watts & Lord
Craven*

3 **Whatsoever and** after reciting that a piece of inclosed land in the Township of Uffington aforesaid then in the occupation of Richard Geering the **property** of the said William Lord Craven called Farm Piece lies near to the Vicarage House at Uffington containing eight acres or thereabouts and the site of two cottages lately taken down or intended so to be late in the possession of William Wheeler and Henry Smith and the gardens and orchards thereto belonging and part of a close containing one acre one rood and nine perches in the possession of Widow Isles and part of an Orchard called Taylors Orchard containing two roods and twenty perches with a barn and stable thereon erected also lie near to the said Vicarage house and are the property of Lord Craven and it would be convenient for the said George Watts and his successors vicars of Uffington that the same should be held and enjoyed with the said Vicarage **it was therefore enacted** that from and after the date and execution of the Award to be so made touching the Township of Uffington as aforesaid the said several pieces of parcels of inclosed land last mentioned and also the said barn and stable should be vested in and forever enjoyed by the said George Watts and his successors vicars of Uffington and in exchange for the same the said Commissioners were thereby authorised and required to assign and allot unto and for the said William Lord Craven so much of the said open and common fields or other commonable lands within the Township of Uffington or hamlet of Balking to be allotted to the said George Watts and his successors vicars as aforesaid as in the judgement of the said Commissioners should be of equal value with the said lands grounds barn and stable **And it was** by the said Act further **enacted** that for the more convenient situation and disposition of the several farms lands and grounds of the several land owners within the fields liberties territories and precincts of the township of Uffington and hamlets of Balking and Woolston otherwise Wolverston within the fields liberties territories and precincts of the hamlets of Kingston Lisle and Fawler aforesaid upon the said intended division and inclosure it should and might be lawful as well to and for the said John Archer and to and for the said George Watts and his successors as also to and for the said William Lord Craven and all and every of the **owners and proprietors** of messuages lands or tenements within the parishes of Uffington or Sparsholt or either of them being seized of an estate for life or for any term or terms of years originally granted for ninety nine years determinable on one or more life or lives with the consent of the owner of the inheritance or any greater interest to exchange all or any of his her and their messuages farmhouses and tenements old inclosures new allotments or any other lands and grounds or any tithes or moduses in lieu of tithes not directed or intended to be discharged under or by virtue of act situate or arising within the said parishes of Uffington and Sparsholt for any other messuages tenements farmhouses old inclosures or any other lands or grounds within the same parishes so as all and every such exchange and exchanges be made by and with the consent and approbation of the said Commissioners to be ascertained and declared in the awards or instruments respectively so directed to be made and executed as aforesaid or by some other Act or instrument to be enrolled as aforesaid and that all and every exchange or exchanges so as to be made as aforesaid should be good valid and effectual to all intents and purposes whatsoever. **And it was** by the said Act **provided** and thereby further **enacted** amongst other things by the authority aforesaid that in case the said Francis Burton should die or refuse to act in the Trusts thereby reposed in him then and in such

*exchanges with
landowners
in Sparsholt*

case the said **Provost and Scholars** of Queens College in Oxford and the said Philip
Brown and his successors Vicars of Sparsholt should and might upon such death refusal
or neglect or as soon after as occasion might require by writing or writings under the seal
of the said College and under the hand of the said Vicar Elect any other person (not
interested in the said intended division or inclosure) to be a Commissioners in the stead
and place of the said Francis Burton and every commissioners so to be elected or chosen
as aforesaid should after he had taken and subscribed the aforesaid oath have the same or
the like powers and authorities as the commissioners named in and appointed by the
said Act were thereby invested with and in the said Act are contained powers for certain
other persons to elect new commissioners in case of the death of any other of the
Commissioners named in the said Act. **And it was** by the said Act further **enacted** that
in case through the necessity of situation or **that any** other unavoidable accident or
circumstances it should so happen that any one or more of the said proprietors should
not have an equal quantity of boundary mounds or fences allotted to him her or them on
the said inclosure it should and might be lawful for the said Commissioners and they
were thereby authorised and required where they should judge it necessary and
reasonable first taking into consideration the interior mounds necessary to be made to
award order ascertain and appoint what sum or sums or money such proprietor or
proprietors should respectively pay and contribute towards making the mounds and
fences of such other of the said proprietor or proprietors who might have too great a
proportion of mounding according to the quantity and value of the land and grounds
allotted to him her or them by virtue of the said Act in order that the same boundary
mounds and fences might be brought as near as might be to a just and equal proportion
to be settled by the said Commissioners and as they should deem reasonable and just
and should award order direct and appoint. **And it was** by the said Act further **enacted**
that all the charges and expenses incident to and attending the obtaining and passing of
the said Act and of the surveying admeasuring planning valuing dividing and allotting
the said common fields common meadows common pastures downs and other
commonable lands thereby directed to be allotted and divided as aforesaid and of
surveying qualitying exonerating from tithes and exchanging the old inclosures and
hereditaments aforesaid and of preparing and enrolling this award and of making
supporting and maintaining the fences to be made for the said George Watts and the said
Trustees of lands given by Thomas Saunders and of making maintaining and supporting
such fences gates stiles drains or other matters as the said Commissioners should think
reasonable and just to be made supported and maintained by and at the expense of the
proprietors in general or any number of them and which cannot according to the
provisions and directions therein contained concerning the fences to be made for the
several allotments thereinbefore mentioned or with justice and equity be ordered
directed to be made supported and maintained by and at the **separate expense** of any
one of the said proprietors and also of providing sowing and managing the grass seeds
which might be sowed in pursuance of the said Act and all the charges and expenses of
the said Commissioners for their own time and trouble in and about the obtaining and
executing the said Act and all other necessary expenses of the several persons to be
employed by the said Commissioners or any of them either before or after the executing
the said Awards respectively or otherwise in or about the premises and all other

*Queen's College
to appoint
replacement of
deceased
commissioner*

*expenses of the
award to fall
on landowners*

46

50

55

60

65

70

75

80

95

100

101   necessary expenses in about or concerning the same premises should be paid borne and defrayed by the several proprietors and owners and persons interested in the said lands in the said open and common fields common meadows common pastures downs and other commonable lands respectively and by the proprietors and owners of such of the

105   said cottages tenements farmhouses and old inclosures as should be exchanged or exonerated from tithes by virtue of the said Act (except the said Vicar of Uffington and the said Trustees before mentioned and except the said John Archer so far as concerns the share or proportion of the said Vicar) in such shares and proportions and at such time or times and in such manner as the said Commissioners should in and by their

110   award or by any other writing under their hands either before or at the time or after the execution of the said Award order direct and appoint. **And it was** thereby further **enacted** that the said Commissioners and their successors should and they were thereby required at the time of signing and executing their said award to deliver the said proprietors accounts in writing signed by them of all monies by them the said

115   Commissioners laid out and assessed in about or concerning the said dividing allotting or inclosing. **And it was thereby provided** and further **enacted** that if any of the proprietors or persons interested in the lands and grounds thereby directed to be divided and allotted or any other person or persons on their behalf should advance and pay any money in discharge of the fees or other expenses of obtaining the said Act the same and

120   the interest thereof after the rate of five pounds per centum per annum should be repaid and satisfied out of the monies which should be first raised to defray expenses by virtue thereof. **And it was** thereby further **enacted** that the said Commissioners should and they were thereby required to give public notice in the parish church of Uffington upon some Sunday immediately after divine service of the time and place of the **first meeting**

notice of
meetings   *125*   of the said Commissioners for executing the powers thereby vested in them at least six days before such meeting and also should give the like notice of six days of every subsequent meeting for putting in execution the powers vested in them by the said Act in the parish church aforesaid (meetings by adjournment only excepted) and that none of the meetings to be held by the said Commissioners for putting the said Act in execution

130   should be held at any greater distance from the lands and grounds intended to be divided and allotted than Wantage or Chipping Lamborne in the county of Berks as in and by the said in part scribed Act of Parliament amongst divers other clauses and provisos therein contained (reference being thereunto had) will more fully and at large appear. **And whereas** the said James King and John Brothers together with the said Francis Burton

135   (since deceased) did give public notice in the parish church of Uffington aforesaid on Sunday the twenty fifth day of May one thousand seven hundred and seventy seven that the said Commissioners did intend to hold their first meeting for executing the powers vested in them by the said Act at the Bear Inn in Wantage on Wednesday the fourth day of June then next being six days and upwards before their said first meeting and the like

140   public notice of six days hath been given by the Commissioners named

4 **And appointed** in and by virtue of the said Act of every subsequent meeting by them held in pursuance of the said Act (meetings by adjournment only excepted) **And whereas** the said James King William Fillingham John Brothers and John Watt met in pursuance of the said first mentioned notice at the Bear Inn in Wantage aforesaid on the said fourth day of June last and then and there severally took and subscribed before each other the Oath of a Commissioner directed by the said Act to be by them respectively taken and subscribed and which oaths so taken and subscribed are hereunto annexed to the intent that the same may be enrolled at the same time and place as these presents are as by the said Act directed to be enrolled **And whereas** the said Commissioners did at a public meeting by them held by adjournment at the said Bear Inn in Wantage on Saturday the seventh day of the said month of June by writing under their hands **nominate and appoint** John Hughes of Odstone in the parish of Ashbury aforesaid John Pocock of Fawley in the said county of Berks and John Stephens of Farnborough in the county of Berks aforesaid gentlemen to quality and value and the said John Hughes John Pocock and John Stephens did accordingly quality and value the said open and common fields common meadows common pastures downs commons and commonable lands within the said Township of Uffington and hamlets of Balking and Woolston otherwise Wolverstone and such of the old inclosures within the said Township and hamlets as are by the said Act directed to be discharged from tithes or to accommodate the exchanges hereinafter set forth **And whereas** the said Francis Burton departed this life on or about the fourteenth day of July last having qualified himself to act as a Commissioner for putting the said Act into execution and thereupon the **Provost and Scholars** of Queens College in Oxford and the said Philip Brown Vicar of Sparsholt aforesaid by a certain writing under the seal of the said College and under the hand of the said Vicar bearing date the second day of August now last past did in pursuance power and authority given to and vested in them in and by the said Act of Parliament hereinbefore and therein partly ...scribed elect the said John Mitchell by the name and description of John Mitchell of South Weston in the county of Oxford gentleman a Commissioner in the stead and place of the said Francis Burton deceased to put in execution and to execute the several powers and authorities in the said in part recited Act of Parliament mentioned vested given and granted and to have the same or the like powers authorities emoluments benefits and advantages as by virtue of the said Act of Parliament the said Francis Burton deceased was invested with **And whereas** the said John Mitchell did in pursuance of his said election as aforesaid at a public meeting of the Commissioners by them held by adjournment at the Bear Inn in Wantage aforesaid on the twelfth day of August last take and subscribe the oath of a Commissioner as by the said Act is directed and the oath so by him taken and subscribed is also hereunto annexed to the intent that the same may be enrolled as by the said Act is required **And whereas** the quality and value of the said open and common fields common meadows common pastures downs commons and commonable lands and of such old inclosures as aforesaid made and taken by the said John Hughes John Pocock and John Stephens the qualitymen appointed by the said Commissioners as aforesaid and also a **true and perfect survey** and admeasurement made and taken of the same by George King of Daventry aforesaid the surveyor for that purpose named and appointed in and by the said scribed Act have been laid before the said Commissioners and such survey and admeasurements hath been reduced into

appointment of qualitymen

replacement of Francis Burton deceased

appointment of surveyor

1

5

10

15

20

25

30

35

40

45

areas to be allotted

46 writing and the number of acres roods and perches belonging to each proprietor have been therein specified declared and set forth and the said survey and admeasurement hath been laid before the said Commissioners at their several meetings held subsequent to the making of the same **And whereas** it appears to the said Commissioners by the said

50 survey and admeasurement and otherwise that the several **open and common** fields and commonable lands by the said Act directed to be divided and allotted as aforesaid are known and distinguished by the several names and do consist of the respective quantities following that is to say in the Township of Uffington the common meadow called Uffington Meadow two hundred and thirteen acres and thirty four perches the common

55 pasture called Uffington Common three hundred and eighty six acres two roods and thirty nine perches the arable fields on the north or lower side of Ickleton Way seven hundred and twelve acres and twenty five perches the arable fields on the south or upper side of the said Ickleton Way four hundred and eighteen acres and ten perches the Down called Uffington Down one hundred and twenty eight acres and nine perches making

60 together in the said Township of Uffington one thousand eight hundred and fifty eight acres and thirty seven perches in the hamlet of Woolston otherwise Wolverston the common meadow called Woolston Meadow one hundred and six acres three roods and thirty seven perches the common pasture called Woolston Common one hundred and eighty nine acres three roods and eight perches the arable fields on the north or lower

65 side of Ickleton Way three hundred and seventy six acres three roods and twenty eight perches the arable fields on the south or upper side of Ickleton Way three hundred and eighty one acres two roods and sixteen perches the down called Woolston Down three hundred and ninety six acres three roods and thirty eight perches making together in the said hamlet of Woolston otherwise Wolverston one thousand four hundred and fifty two

70 acres one rood and seven perches in the hamlet of Balking the common meadow called Old Field three hundred and twenty five acres one rood and four perches and the common meadow called Bagmoor thirty seven acres one rood and thirty four perches making together in the said hamlet of Balking three hundred and sixty two acres two roods and thirty eight perches and which said common fields and commonable lands in the said

75 Township of Uffington and hamlets of Woolston otherwise Wolverston and Balking do contain and amount all together to three thousand six hundred and seventy three acres one rood and two perches **And whereas** upon due enquiry made into the premises the said Commissioners do find that the said **William Lord Craven** and his lessees

full list of owners of open fields etc

respectively hereinafter named the said Bartholomew Tipping the said Abraham Atkins

80 the said John Archer the said George Watts the Rt Honourable John Earl Spencer the said Lovelace Bigg the Revd John Hippesley clerk the said Provost and Scholars of Queens College in Oxford and the said Philip Brown their Lessee Edward Thornhill Esquire and Collier his wife John Hyde Esquire Henry Aston Esquire the Trustees of a certain society called the Presbyterian Society at Wantage the Dean and Chapter of the Collegiate

95 Church of St. Peter in Westminster and John Morest Esquire their lessee the said Robert Leaver John Williams Joseph Wirdnam Roger Spanswick the said Trustees or assignees of Robert Fettiplace Esquire both in respect of their freehold property and as lessees of the said Provost and Scholars of Queens College in Oxford the said Jeffry Church the said Joseph Mayon William Thatcher William Chamberlain the Trustees of certain lands

100 given by Thomas Saunders deceased for maintaining a schoolmaster at Uffington the said

John Stallard Joseph Cooke Lawrence Woodroffe Charles Young and Sarah his wife and *101*
Mary Allen an infant Joseph Dixon Elizabeth Hoar William Mifflin and James Mundy are
the owners and proprietors of the said open and common fields and commonable lands
in the said Township of Uffington and hamlets of Balking and Woolston otherwise
Wolverston by the said Act directed to be divided and allotted as aforesaid **And whereas** *105*
the said Commissioners have carefully viewed all and singular the said common fields
common meadows common pastures downs commons and other commonable lands
within the said Township of Uffington and hamlets of Balking and Woolston otherwise
Wolverston by the said Act directed to be divided and allotted as aforesaid and have well
and **duly considered t**he several matters in and by the said Act directed and enacted and *110*   *consideration*
in making the allotments hereinafter mentioned and set forth have had due regard to the   *of evidence*
quality situation and convenience as well as quantity both of the lands and grounds
belonging to each proprietor at the time of making such allotments and of the lands and
grounds hereinafter allotted in lieu thereof and have upon examination of witnesses upon
oath and upon other proper and sufficient evidence and enquiry heard and finally *115*
determined all disputes which have arisen between the parties interested in the said
division or allotment or any of them touching and concerning the respective shares rights
and interests which they or any of them claimed in the said lands and grounds by the said
Act directed to be divided and allotted or touching or concerning the respective shares
and proportions which they or any of them had or ought to have on or in the said division *120*
and allotments (except any differences or dispute which have arisen touching the rights
or title to lands or other rights that have been or may be claimed in the said open and
common fields for which the parties are by the said Act authorised to commence and
prosecute such suits or remedies as they shall be advised and think proper) **Now therefore**
know ye that the said Commissioners having completed and finished the said partitions *125*
and allotments of the said open and common fields common pastures common meadows
downs and other commonable lands within the said Township of Uffington and hamlets of
Balking and Woolston by the said Act directed to be divided and allotted as
aforesaid pursuance to the purport and directions of the said Act do make and publish
this their Award of and concerning the same as follows that is to say. **The Said** *130*
Commissioners in pursuance of the power vested in them in and by the said Act of
Parliament **have** set out divided ascertained and allotted and by these presents **do** award
and confirm all the said open and common fields common meadows common pastures
downs commons and other commonable lands within the said Township and

1   **5** **Hamlets** unto and amongst the several persons entitled to and interested therein in proportion to their several and respective shares rights or interests of common tithes or other properties in or over the same as hereinafter mentioned subject to such rules order and regulations as are in the said Act declared and **first** the

5   said Commissioners **have** set out allotted and ascertained and by these presents **do** award and confirm **to the said William Lord Craven** as Lord of the Manor of Uffington aforesaid **one plot** or parcel of land situate in Uffington Common containing eight acres and nine perches (exclusive of all roads and ways through and over the same) bounded on the south the west and part of the north by the town of Uffington on the remaining

LC1

10   part of the north by the twentieth allotment and on the east by the twenty first allotment to the said William Lord Craven the fences for inclosing this allotment on the south across the end of Friday Street on the west across the end of Little Lane and across the end of Broad Street and on the north against the town Green in the said Town of Uffington the said commissioners do award order and direct shall be made and forever

15   after maintained and repaired by the said William Lord Craven and the owners of this allotment for the time being. **To the said Bartholomew Tipping** as Lord of the Manor

BT1   of Woolston otherwise Wolverston aforesaid **one plot** or parcel of land situate in Woolston Fields on the north or lower side of Ickleton Way containing one acre three roods and one perch (exclusive of all roads and way through and over the same) bounded

20   on part of the north by a lane leading into the village of Woolston on the remaining part of the north and on the east by old inclosures belonging to the said Bartholomew Tipping on the south by other land allotted to the said Bartholomew Tipping and on the west by land allotted to the said Lovelace Bigg. The fences for inclosing this allotment on the north across the end of the aforesaid lane the said Commissioners do award order and

25   direct shall be made and forever after maintained and repaired by the said Bartholomew Tipping and the owners of this allotment for the time being. **To the said Abraham Atkins** as Lord of the Manor of Kingston Lisle (the hamlet of Baulking aforesaid being

AA1   part of the said Manor) **one plot** or parcel of land situate in Old Field aforesaid containing one rood and four perches (exclusive of all roads and ways through and over the same)

30   bounded on the east by land allotted to the said William Lord Craven and Robert Quarme his lessee on the south by the public road there and on the west and north by other land allotted to the said Abraham Atkins which said allotment last hereinbefore described is hereinafter exchanged by the said Abraham Atkins with the said William Lord Craven for land in the hamlet of Kingston Lisle. The fences for inclosing this

35   allotment on the east against land allotted to the said William Lord Craven and Robert Quarme his lessee and on the south against the said public road the said Commissioners do award order and direct shall be made and forever after maintained and repaired by the said Abraham Atkins or by the said William Lord Craven on his taking the same in exchange as aforesaid and the owners of this allotment for the time being which said

40   three several allotments to the said William Lord Craven Bartholomew Tipping and

Lords of Manor   Abraham Atkins respectively as Lords of the respective Manors aforesaid are in the
compensated   judgement of the said Commissioners and by them hereby adjudged and declared to be
for rights   a full equivalent satisfaction and recompense to the said William Lord Craven Bartholomew Tipping and Abraham Atkins respectively for their respective right and

45   rights of soil in and over the waste lands within the said Township of Uffington and

Hamlets of Baulking and Woolston otherwise Wolverston directed by the said Act to be allotted and divided. **And the said Commissioners** have in further pursuance of and in obedience to the directions of the said Act laid out assigned and allotted and by these presents **do** assign award and confirm unto and for the said John Archer and the said George Watts and his successors Vicars of Uffington for and in lieu of their several and respective impropriate and Vicarial tithes yearly issuing arising or renewing out of all and every the said open and common fields and common meadows common pastures downs commons and other commonable lands within the Township of Uffington and Hamlet of Balking aforesaid (other than and except a certain piece of common ground called Balking Green which is directed by the said Act not to be inclosed and other than and except the common pasture called Uffington Common and such part and parts of the Meadows called Old Field Meadow and Bagmoor in the Hamlet of Balking) as is or are tithe free and over and above the allotment hereinafter awarded to the said Vicar in respect of his glebes and for and in lieu of the tithes of all and every the messuages tenements gardens orchards and inclosed meadows and pastures and other ancient inclosures and lands held in severalty within the Township of Uffington (except a messuage and close of pasture ground belonging to John Lockey containing three roods and fourteen perches a cottage and garden belonging to Ambrose Brookes containing seventeen perches a messuage garden and part of a close called Hall Close belonging to James Nipper containing three roods and fourteen perches and a messuage and garden belonging to Thomas Thatcher containing thirty six perches which are the only two messuages gardens orchards and ancient inclosures held in severalty within the Township of Uffington of which the owners had not at the time of passing the said Act or at the time of making the allotments in pursuance thereof land or common right in the said open and common fields and other commonable lands sufficient for the purpose of discharging such messuages tenements gardens orchards and other ancient inclosures from the payment of tithes) five plots or allotments of land parcel of the said open and common fields common meadows common pastures downs commons and other commonable lands last mentioned (except as aforesaid). **One plot** or parcel whereof is situate in Uffington Fields on the north or lower side of Ickleton Way and contains one hundred and eighty nine acres two roods and thirty perches (exclusive of all roads and ways through and over the same) bounded on a small part of the north and part of the east by land allotted to the said William Lord Craven on other part of the east by an allotment to the said William Lord Craven and William Mundy his Lessee an allotment to the said William Lord Craven and Edward Warren his lessee an allotment to the Trustees of Uffington School lands and an allotment for glebe land to the Vicar on other part of the east and on part of the north by other allotments to the said Vicar on other part of the east and on the south east by land allotted to the said William Lord Craven below Ickleton Way on the south by Ickleton Way on part of the west by other land allotted to the said John Archer and George Watts in Woolston Fields and an allotment to the said John Archer for tithes of Old Inclosures in Woolston on the remaining part of the west by another allotment to the said John Archer on other part of the north by old Inclosures at Uffington on other part of the east by a lane leading to the Town of Uffington and on the remaining parts of the east and north by several inclosures and homesteads in Uffington aforesaid. One other of the said five plots or allotments of land is situate in

46

*vicar &
impropriator
compensated*

50 for tithes

55

60

65

70

GW/JA1

75

80

95

100 GW/JA2

101 Uffington Fields aforesaid on the north or lower side of Ickleton Way containing thirty one acres and eight perches (exclusive of all roads and ways through and over the same) bounded on the east and part of the south by land allotted to the said William Lord Craven on the remaining part of the south by an allotment to the Trustees for Uffington *105* School Land on the west by an allotment to the said William Lord Craven and Edward Warren his lessee and an allotment to the said William Lord Craven and William Mundy his lessee and on the north by other lands allotted to the said William Lord Craven. One

GW/JA3

other of the said five plots or allotments of land is situate in Uffington Meadow containing twenty one acres and thirty three perches (exclusive of all roads and ways through and *110* over the same) bounded on the south east by land allotted to the said William Lord Craven in Uffington Common and by several old Inclosures in Uffington on the south by a small allotment to the said William Lord Craven at the south end of the said Meadow on the north west and part of the west by an inclosed farm belonging to the said William Lord Craven in the occupation of Richard Geering and on the remaining part of the west *115* and on the north by other land allotted to the said William Lord Craven in the said

GW/JA4

Meadow. One other of the said plots or allotments of land is situate in Uffington Fields on the south or upper side of Ickleton way and contains nine acres two roods and two perches (exclusive of all roads and ways through and over the same) bounded on the east or south east by land allotted to the said William Lord Craven on the west by land allotted *120* to the said John Archer and George Watts in Woolston Fields and on the north by

GW/JA5

Ickleton Way. And the other of the said five plots or allotments of land is situate in Uffington Fields on the south or upper side of Ickleton Way and contains one hundred and fifty six acres two roods and seventeen perches (exclusive of all roads and ways through and over the same) bounded on the south east by a Several Farm belonging to *125* the said William Lord Craven now or late in the occupation or Joseph Lousley on the south by the second allotment to the said John Archer for tithes of old Inclosures at Woolston hereinafter exchanged with the said William Lord Craven on the north west by other part of the said Several Farm on the south west and west by other part of the said Several Farm hereinafter exchanged with the said John Archer and on the north by land

proportion of *130* allotted to the said William Lord Craven which said five several **plots** or allotments of
total allotted land do contain together four hundred and eight acres and ten perches and (quantity and
to GW/JA in quality considered) do contain or are equal to one fifth of all the arable land in the said
Uffington open and common fields and one ninth of the said common meadows common pastures downs commonable lands (except as in the said Act as hereinbefore is excepted) and one

6 **Sixth of the** arable lands held in Severalty and one seventh of the said gardens orchards and inclosed meadows and pastures and other ancient inclosures within the said Township of Uffington (except those which are hereinbefore particularly mentioned to belong to the said John Lockey Ambrose Brookes James Nipper and Thomas Thatcher respectively and are not by virtue of the said Act discharged or exonerated from the payment of tithes) and which said five plots or allotments have been taken and deducted as by the said Act is directed from and out of the respective shares of the said Open and Common fields and other commonable lands belonging to the several persons whose commonable or other lands are by virtue and in pursuance of the said Act exonerated from tithes and are by the said Act and hereby declared to be in full satisfaction and discharge of and for the said several and respective impropriate and vicarian tithes issuing arising or renewing from and out of the said open and common fields common meadows and pastures downs commons and other commonable lands within the township of Uffington and hamlet of Balking aforesaid (except as before excepted) and out of the said messuages tenements gardens orchards meadows pastures and ancient inclosures and lands held in severalty within the said Township of Uffington for which lands are allotted as aforesaid. **And the said Commissioners** in further pursuance of and in obedience to the said ascribed Act of Parliament **have** laid out assigned and allotted and by these presents **do** assign award and confirm unto and for the said John Archer and the said George Watts and his successors Vicars of Uffington aforesaid for and in lieu of all and every the impropriate and vicarial tithes yearly arising issuing or renewing out of all and every said open and common fields common meadows downs and other commonable lands within the said hamlet of Woolston otherwise Wolverstone two plots or allotments of land parcel of the said open and said common fields common meadows downs and other commonable lands last mentioned **one plot** or allotment whereof is situate in Woolston Fields on the north or lower side of Ickleton Way and contains seventy seven acres and twenty two perches (exclusive all roads and ways through and over the same) bounded on the east by the first allotment to the said John Archer and George Watts in Uffington on part of the south by Ickleton Way on part of the west and another part of the south by a public stonepit hereinafter set out at a place called The Wells in Woolston on other part of the west by an allotment to the said Bartholomew Tipping on part of the north and other part of the west by an allotment to Jeffry Church on other part of the west and other part of the south by an allotment to the said Lovelace Bigg exchanged with the said Jeffry Church on the remaining part of the south by an allotment to the said Bartholomew Tipping also exchanged with the said Jeffry Church on other part of the west by a lane leading into the village of Woolston and by an old inclosure called Pond Close belonging to the said Lovelace Bigg on other part of the north and remaining part of the west by an allotment to the said Lovelace Bigg and on the remaining part of the north by an allotment to the said John Archer for tithes of inclosures in Woolston and the other of the said two plots or allotments of land is situate in Woolston Fields and Down on the south or upper side of Ickleton Way and contains one hundred acres three roods and twenty three perches (exclusive of all roads and ways through and over the same) bounded on part of the east by the fourth allotment to the said John Archer and George Watts in Uffington Fields on part of the south east part of the south other part of the south east other part of the east and on part of the

1

5

10

15

20

25 *GW/JA6*

30

35

40 *GW/JA7*

45

46 north by land allotted to the said William Lord Craven on the remaining parts of the east and south east by that part of the Several Farm belonging to the said William Lord Craven which is hereinafter exchanged with the said John Archer on other part of the south by a Several Down in Woolston belonging to the said Bartholomew Tipping on

50 the remaining parts of the south on several parts of the west and north west by an allotment to the said Bartholomew Tipping and on the remaining part of the north by Ickleton Way which said two plots or allotments of land make up an amount together to one hundred and seventy eight acres and five perches and (quantity and quality considered) do contain or are equal to one fifth part of all the arable land in the said

proportion of total allotted to GW/JA in Woolstone

55 open and common fields and one ninth part of the common meadows common downs and other commonable lands in Woolston aforesaid (save and except that out of such allotments is deducted an equivalent for all Vicarial Tithes of such commonable lands for which the said George Watts as vicar as aforesaid is entitled to and is allotted an equivalent or compensation in manner directed by the said Act and which plots or

60 allotments do adjoin upon and are situate as nearly as may be to the said other plots or allotment hereinbefore assigned and allotted unto and for the said John Archer and George Watts as aforesaid and are taken and deducted from and out of the respective allotments of the said open and common fields and other commonable lands in Woolston otherwise Wolverstone aforesaid belonging to the several persons whose

65 commonable lands are exonerated from the said tithes or from or out of the land which is allotted to them respectively in lieu of such commonable lands and are by the said Act and hereby declared to be in full satisfaction and discharge of and for all and every the impropriate and Vicarial tithes issuing arising or renewing from or out of the said open and common fields common meadows downs and other commonable lands within the

70 said hamlet of Woolston otherwise Wolverston aforesaid. **And** the said Commissioners **have** as by the said Act they are required laid out assigned and allotted and **do** by these presents award confirm unto and for the said John Archer fifteen acres of meadow and pasture land in Uffington Meadow being part and parcel of the third allotment

JA1

hereinbefore awarded to the said John Archer and George Watts and lying contiguous or

75 as near as may be to the other allotments made to the said John Archer bounded on part of the south east by land allotted to the said William Lord Craven in Uffington Common on the remaining part of the south east by an old inclosure in Uffington on the south by other part of the said third allotment hereinafter assigned to the said George Watts and on the west and north by land allotted to the said William Lord Craven in the said

80 meadow and which said fifteen acres of meadow and pasture ground are hereinafter

Exchange LC/JA

exchanged by the said John Archer with the said William Lord Craven for part of an inclosed piece of meadow ground called West Ham which lies adjoining to the other allotments made to the said John Archer the fences for inclosing the said fifteen acres of meadow and pasture land hereby allotted to the said John Archer on the south against

95 land hereinafter assigned and allotted to the said George Watts the said commissioners do award order and direct shall be made and foreverafter maintained and repaired by the said John Archer or by the said William Lord Craven on his taking the same in exchange as aforesaid and the owners of this allotment for the time being. **And whereas** it is in and by the said ascribed Act of Parliament provided and enacted that after the said several

100 plots or allotments should be so made or allotted to or for the said John Archer and

George Watts and his successors Vicars of Uffington as aforesaid for and in lieu of their *101*
several impropriate and Vicarial ties respectively from and out of the said common fields
and common grounds within the said Township of Uffington and Hamlets of Balking
and Woolston otherwise Wolverston respectively (except as in the said Act and
hereinbefore is excepted) the said Commissioners were thereby required to subdivide *105*
assign and allot the said several plots or allotments last mentioned (other than and
except the said fifteen acres of meadow and pasture thereinbefore directed to be and
hereinbefore allotted to the said John Archer only) in as entire and convenient parcels
and divisions as might be and with due regard to the contiguity of each party's allotment
unto and between the said John Archer and the said George Watts and his successors *110*
Vicars as aforesaid in proportion to their respective rights and interest in the tithes in
lieu whereof the said plots or allotments are thereby before directed to be and hereby
before awarded and made and in proportion to the value of such impropriate and vicarial
tithes respectively. **Therefore** the said Commissioners in obedience to the directions of
the said Act **have** accordingly subdivided assigned and allotted and by these presents **do** *115*
subdivide assign allot award and confirm the said several plots or allotments last
mentioned (except the said fifteen acres of meadow and pasture land and aforesaid) unto
and between the said John Archer and George Watts in manner following (that is to say)
to the said John Archer four plots or allotments of land **one plot** or allotment whereof   *JA2*
(which is distinguished throughout this award as the second allotment to the said John *120*
Archer) containing one hundred and fifty seven acres one rood and thirty two perches as
the same is now staked and set out exclusive of all roads and ways through and over he
same) eighty acres one rood and ten perches whereof are situate in Uffington Fields on
the north or lower side of Ickleton Way and are part and parcel of the aforesaid first
allotment to the said John Archer and George Watts and the remaining seventy seven *125*
acres and twenty two perches thereof are situate in Woolston Fields on the north or
lower side of Ickleton Way and are the whole of the sixth allotment hereinbefore awarded
to the said John Archer and George Watts and which plot or allotment now hereby
awarded and confirmed to the said John Archer is bounded on a small part of the north
and part of the east by land allotted to the said William Lord Craven on other part of the *130*
east by an allotment to the said William Lord Craven and William Mundy his lessee and
allotment to the said William Lord Craven and Edward Warren his lessee an allotment
to the Trustees of Uffington School Lands and an allotment of Glebe land to the said
Vicar on part of the south and other part of the east by land allotted to the said Vicar on
other part of the south by Ickleton Way on part of the west an another part of the *135*

7

South by the aforesaid public stonepit at a place called the Wells on the other part of the west by an allotment to the said Bartholomew Tipping on other part of the north and other part of the west by an allotment to Jeffry Church on other part of the west and other part of the south by an allotment to the said Lovelace Bigg exchanged with the said Jeffry Church on the remaining part of the south by an allotment to the said Bartholomew Tipping also exchanged with the said Jeffry Church on other part of the west by a lane leading to the village of Woolston and by the aforesaid old Inclosure called Pond Close on other part of the north and other part of the west by an allotment to the said Lovelace Bigg on other part of the north and other part of the west by an allotment to the said John Archer for tithes of Inclosures at Woolston on the remaining part of the west by other allotments to the said John Archer on other part of the north by old inclosures at Uffington on other part of the east by a lane leading into the town of Uffington and on the remaining part of the east and north by several old inclosures and homesteads in Uffington the fences for inclosing this allotment on the north against land allotted to the said William Lord Craven being across a public road leading through the said allotment on the south and east against land allotted to the said George Watts on the south against Ickleton Way on the west and south against the said public stonepit on the south against allotments to the said Lovelace Bigg and Bartholomew Tipping respectively exchanged with the said Jeffry Church on the west across the end of the said Lane leading into Woolston and on the east across the end of the said Lane leading into Uffington the said Commissioners do award order and direct shall be made and foreverafter maintained and repaired by the said John Archer and the owners of this allotment for the time being **One Other** of the said four plots or allotments (which is distinguished through this award as the third allotment to the said John Archer) containing one hundred and ten acres one rood and twenty five perches (exclusive of all roads and ways through and over the same) as now staked and set out whereof nine acres two roods and two perches are situate in Uffington Fields on the south or upper side of Ickleton Way and are the whole of the aforesaid fourth allotment to the said John Archer and George Watts and the remaining one hundred acres three roods and twenty three perches are situate in Woolston Fields and Down on the south or upper side of Ickleton Way and are the whole of the aforesaid seventh allotment to the said John Archer and George Watts and which plot or allotment now hereby awarded and confirmed to the said John Archer is bounded on part of the east and south east by land allotted to the said William Lord Craven in Uffington on other part of the south east part of the south other part of the south east other part of the east and on part of the north by land allotted to the said William Lord Craven in Woolston on the remaining part of the east and south east by that part of the Several Farm belonging to the said William Lord Craven which is hereinafter exchanged with the said John Archer on other part of the south by the aforesaid Several Down in Woolston belonging to the said Bartholomew Tipping on the remaining parts of the south and several parts of the west and north west by an allotment to the said Bartholomew Tipping and on the remaining part of the north by Ickleton Way the boundaries for ascertaining this allotment on the east and south east against land allotted to the said William Lord Craven in Uffington and on all parts against land allotted to the said William Lord Craven in Woolston the said Commissioners do award order and direct shall be made and foreverafter maintained

JA3

and repaired by the said John Archer and owners of this allotment for the time being. *46*   *JA4*
One other of the said four plots or allotments of land (which is distinguished throughout
this award as the fourth allotment to the said John Archer) containing eighty one acres
one rood and thirty one perches (exclusive of all roads and ways through and over the
same) as now staked and set out situate in Uffington Fields on the south or upper side of *50*
Ickleton Way (being part and parcel of the fifth allotment hereinbefore awarded to the
said John Archer and George Watts) bounded on the east and south by the allotment
next hereinafter awarded to the said John Archer and hereinafter exchanged with the said
William Lord Craven on the south west and on the west by that part of the said Several
Farm belonging to the said William Lord Craven which is hereinafter exchanged with *55*
the said John Archer and on the north by land allotted to the said William Lord Craven
the boundaries for ascertaining this allotment on the east and south against the said
allotment to the said John Archer hereinafter exchanged as aforesaid the said Commission
do award order and direct shall be made and foreverafter maintained and repaired by the
said John Archer and the owners of this allotment for the time being **And the Other** of *60*   *JA5*
the said four plots or allotments of land (distinguished throughout this award as the fifth
allotment to the said John Archer) containing seventy five acres and twenty six perches
(exclusive of all roads and ways through and over the same) as staked and set out situate
in the said Uffington Fields on the south or upper side of Ickleton Way being the
remaining part of the fifth allotment hereinbefore awarded to the said John Archer and *65*
George Watts bounded on the south east by the said Several Farm belonging to the said
William Lord Craven on the south by an allotment to the said John Archer for tithes of
inclosures in Woolston and which is hereinafter exchanged with the said William Lord
Craven on the northwest by other part of the said Several Farm on part of the north and
on the west by the fourth allotment hereinbefore awarded to the said John Archer and *70*
on the remaining part of the north by land allotted to the said William Lord Craven
which said allotment is hereinafter exchanged by the said John Archer with the said
William Lord Craven. **To the said George Watts** and his successors Vicars of Uffington
aforesaid four plots or allotments of land **one plot** or allotment whereof (which is   *GW1*
distinguished throughout this award as the first allotment to the said George Watts) *75*
containing one hundred and nine acres one rood and twenty perches (exclusive or all
roads and ways through and over the same) as now staked and set out is situate in
Uffington Fields on the north or lower side of Ickleton Way and is part and parcel of the
first allotment hereinbefore awarded to the said John Archer and George Watts bounded
on a small part of the east by an allotment to the said George Watts for Glebe on other *80*
part of the east and on part of the north by another allotment to the said George Watts
on other part of the north by another allotment to the said George Watts on the
remaining part of the east and on the south east by land allotted to the said William Lord
Craven on the south by Ickleton Way and on the west and north by an allotment to the
said John Archer the fences for inclosing this allotment on the south against Ickleton *95*
Way the said commissioners do award order and direct shall be made and for the term of
seven years maintained and repaired at the expense of the other proprietors as by the
said Act is directed and after the expiration of the said term of seven years from the time
of making the same such fences shall be forever maintained and repaired by and at the
expense of the said George Watts and his successors Vicars of Uffington aforesaid. One *100*

GW2

101 other of the said four plots or allotments of land (distinguished throughout this award as the second allotment to the said George Watts) contains six acres and thirty three perches (exclusive of all roads and ways through and over the same) as now staked and set out and is situate in Uffington Meadow (being the remaining part of the allotment

105 there set out for the said John Archer and George Watts as aforesaid) bounded on the south east by several old inclosures in the town of Uffington on the south by a small allotment to the said William Lord Craven on the south end of the said Meadow on the north west and west by the aforesaid inclosed Farm in the occupation of Richard Geering and on the north by the aforesaid fifteen acres of Meadow hereinbefore awarded to the

110 said John Archer and hereinafter exchanged with the said William Lord Craven. One

GW3

other of the said four plots or allotments of land (distinguished throughout this award as the third allotment to the said George Watts) contains twelve acres two roods and four perches as the same is now staked and set out and is situate in Uffington Fields on the north or lower side of Ickleton Way (being part and parcel of the second allotment

115 hereinbefore awarded to the said John Archer and George Watts) bounded on the east by land allotted to the said William Lord Craven on the south by an allotment next hereinafter awarded to the said George Watts on the west by land allotted to the said William Lord Craven and William Mundy his lessee and on the north by other land allotted to the said William Lord Craven which said plot or allotment of land is

120 hereinafter exchanged by the said George Watts with the said William Lord Craven for old Inclosures in Uffington the fences for inclosing this allotment on the east against land allotted to the said William Lord Craven on the south against the allotment next hereinafter awarded to the said George Watts and on the west against an allotment to the said William Lord Craven and the said William Mundy his lessee the said Commissioners

125 do award order and direct shall be made and foreverafter maintained and repaired by the said William Lord Craven on his taking the same in exchange as aforesaid and the owners of this allotment for the time being. And the other of the said four plots or allotments of

GW4

land (distinguished throughout this award as the fourth allotment to the said George Watts) contains eighteen acres two roods and four perches (exclusive of all roads and

130 ways through and over the same) as now staked and set out and is situate in Uffington Field aforesaid on the north or lower side of Ickleton Way (being the remaining or other part of the aforesaid second allotment hereinbefore awarded to the said John Archer and

8 **George Watts** bounded on the east and part of the south by land allotted to the *1*
said William Lord Craven on the remaining part of the south by an allotment
to the Trustees for Uffington School Land on the west by an allotment to the
said William Lord Craven and the said Edward Warrren his lessee and on the north by
the last allotment hereinbefore awarded to the said George Watts and which said plot or *5*
allotment of land is the same plot or allotment which the said Commissioners have
hereinafter assigned and allotted to and for the said William Lord Craven in exchange
for certain old Inclosures by the said Act vested in the said George Watts and his
successors Vicars of Uffington aforesaid. The fences for inclosing this allotment on the
east against the land allotted to the said William Lord Craven so far as this allotment *10*
adjoins Uffington Common on the south against the allotment to the Trustees of
Uffington School Land and on the west against the allotment to the said William Lord
Craven and Edward Warren his lessee the said Commissioners do award order and
direct shall be made and foreverafter maintained and repaired by the said William Lord
Craven on his taking the same in exchange as aforesaid and the owners of this allotment *15*
for the time being and which said plots or allotments hereinbefore made or allotted to
and for the said John Archer and George Watts as first hereinbefore mentioned are by
the said Commissioners subdivided assigned and allotted (except as aforesaid) in as
entire and convenient parcels and divisions as may be and with due regard to the
contiguity of each parties' allotment unto and between the said John Archer and the said *20*
George Watts and his successors Vicars as aforesaid in proportion to their respective
rights and interests in the tithes in lieu whereof the said plots or allotments are so
awarded and made and in proportion to the value of such impropriate and vicarial tithes
respectively and in which allotment to the said George Watts and his successors the said
Commissioners have allotted a larger proportion of land on the north or lower side of *25*
the said Ickleton Way than his just proportion arising out of the lands commons and
meadows lying on the same side of the said road or way the said George Watts having
signified his desire and consent in writing to the said commissioners on or before the
tenth day of October now last past to accept the same on the said North or lower side of
Ickleton Way. **And the Said Commissioners** in further pursuance of and in observance *30*
for the directions of the said scribed Act of Parliament **have** set out assigned and allotted
and by those presents **do** set out assign award and confirm unto and for the said George
Watts and his successors Vicars of Uffington as aforesaid for and in lieu of and in full
satisfaction and compensation for all payments and sums of money or compositions
which the said George Watts was at the time of passing the said Act or now is entitled to *35*
for or in lieu of tithes of milk calf arising and renewing within a certain common pasture
within the Township of Uffington called Uffington Common (and which in the said Act
of Parliament ascribed to amount together on an average to the yearly sum of six pounds
and five shillings or thereabouts and in lieu whereof it is also ascribed that the owners or
proprietors of the said Meadows or Common or other persons entitled to the soil and *40*
food or produce thereof were willing to give land of the yearly value of twelve pounds
and ten shillings in manner therein mentioned). **One plot** or allotment of land   *GW5*
containing thirteen acres three roods and twenty perches (exclusive of all roads and
ways through and over the same) as now staked and set out situate in Uffington Fields
on the north or lower side of Ickleton Way bounded on the south east and east by land *45*

46   allotted to the said William Lord Craven on the south and west by other land allotted to the said George Watts and on the north by land allotted to the Trustees of Uffington School Land the fences for inclosing this allotment on the north against the allotment to the Trustees of Uffington School Land the said Commissioners do award order and

50   direct shall be made and for the term of seven years maintained and repaired at the expense of the other proprietors as by the said Act is directed and hereinafter mentioned and after the expiration of the said term of seven years from the time of making the same such fences shall belong to and be forever maintained and repaired by the said George Watts and his successors Vicars of Uffington aforesaid and which said plot or allotment

55   of land is by the said Commissioners hereby adjudged of the yearly value of twelve pounds and ten shillings. **And the said Commissioners** have also in pursuance of the directions of the said Act set out and allotted and **do** by these presents award and confirm to and for the said George Watts and his successors Vicars of Uffington aforesaid in lieu of and in full satisfaction and compensation for the Tithes of lamb and wool and

60   other small tithes arising in and from the said Common Pasture called Uffington

GW6

Common. **One plot** or parcel of land situate in Uffington Fields on the north or lower side of Ickleton Way containing three acres and two roods (exclusive of all roads and ways through and over the same) bounded on the east by the allotment last hereinbefore awarded to the said Vicar on the south and west by the first allotment hereinbefore

65   awarded to the said Vicar and on the north by an allotment hereinafter awarded to the said Vicar for Glebe Land and to and for the said John Archer as Improprietor as aforesaid in lieu of an in full satisfaction and compensation for all such tithes as the said John Archer was at the time of passing the said Act or now is or may be entitled to from

JA6

or out of the said pasture called Uffington Common. **One plot** or parcel of land

70   (distinguished throughout this award as the sixth allotment to the said John Archer) situate in Uffington Fields on the North or lower side of Ickleton Way containing one acre (exclusive of all roads and ways through and over the same) as now staked and set out bounded on the east by an allotment to the said John Archer for tithes or old inclosures at Woolston on the south west by an allotment to the said Provost and

75   Scholars of Queens College and the Trustees of Robert Fettiplace esquire as lessees of the said College on the west by an inclosure in Woolston called Wiseman's Ham and on the north by an inclosure in Uffington called West Ham which said three several plots or allotments last hereinbefore awarded to the said George Watts and John Archer as aforesaid have been taken and deducted from and out of the respective shares of the said

80   open and common fields and other commonable lands belonging to the several persons whose shares or rights in the said common pasture called Uffington Common are so exonerated from tithes or from and out of the land allotted to them respectively in lieu thereof and do adjoin and are laid to the other allotments made to the said George Watts and John Archer respectively in pursuance of the said Act and immediately after the

95   execution of this award are to be deemed and taken in full of all Great and Vicarial tithes arising or to arise from the said pasture called Uffington Common foreverafter. **And in Regard** that it is by the said Act of Parliament enacted that the said Commissioners should and are thereby required to assign and allot unto the said George Watts and his successors Vicars as aforesaid for or in lieu and satisfaction or all vicarial tithes and all

100   payments in lieu thereof from or out of certain messuages cottages gardens orchards and

inclosed meadows and pastures and other old Inclosures and certain lands in the open *101*
and common fields and other commonable places within the hamlet of Woolston
otherwise Wolverston aforesaid the property of certain persons therein named and
others (out of which it is in the said Act ascribed that the said George Watts as Vicar of
Uffington is entitled to divers moduses or ancient compositions or payments for or in *105*
lieu of all Vicarial tithes amounting annually on an average to the sum of nine pounds
and five shillings or thereabouts) and in lieu of all moduses and ancient compositions
for the said lands in the open and Common fields meadows and commonable places of
Woolston otherwise Wolverston aforesaid and as a rate tithe for the same a yearly sum of
eighteen pounds and seven shillings or an equivalent in land for the same in manner *110*
thereinafter directed and also to assign and allot unto and for the said John Archer in lieu
or satisfaction of all tithes he was or might be entitled to (if any) out of the same gardens
orchards meadows pastures and other old inclosures such sum of money by way of rate
tithe or such equivalent in land as the said Commissioners should in their judgement
deem equivalent thereto such several yearly sums or equivalents in land to be paid or *115*
made in manner therein and hereinafter mentioned (that is to say) that the said
Commissioners should direct and appoint in what shares and proportions the said
several annual payments or other equivalents should be paid or made by the said several
owners and proprietors of the said messuages tenements gardens orchards and old
inclosures and lands last mentioned according to their respective rights and interest *120*
therein **the said Commissioners** upon due enquiry made into the premises do find that
the said messuages cottages gardens orchards and enclosed meadows and pastures and
other old inclosures and also the land in the open and common fields and other
commonable places within the said hamlet of Woolston which by the said Act are
directed to be discharged and exonerated from tithes and all payments in lieu thereof in *125*
manner hereinbefore last mentioned do belong to and are the property of the said
Bartholomew Tipping Lovelace Bigg (both in respect of his estate there at the time of
passing of the said Act and of the estate purchased by him of Sir William Guise Baronet
since the passing thereof) Jeffry Church Joseph Mayon William Thatcher and the said
Provost and Scholars of Queens College and John William Willaume and Abraham *130*
Chambers Trustees of Robert Fettiplace esquire as lessee of the said College and the
said Commissioners do direct and appoint that the said annual payment or yearly sum
of eighteen pounds and seven shillings or an equivalent in land for the same shall be paid
or made by them the said Bartholomew Tipping Lovelace Bigg Jeffry Church Joseph
Mayon William Thatcher and the said Provost and Scholars of Queens College or their *135*
said lessees according to their respective rights and interests as aforesaid in the shares
and proportions following (that is to say) the sum of ten pounds and seven shillings part
thereof or an equivalent in land for the same by the said Bartholomew Tipping the sum
of four pounds seventeen shillings and six pence other part thereof or an

1   **9** **Equivalent** in land for the same by the same Lovelace Bigg the sum of one pound and one shilling other part thereof or an equivalent in land for the same by the said Jeffry Church the sum of one pound and five shillings other part thereof or an equivalent in land for the same by the said Joseph Mayon the sum of thirteen

5   shillings and six pence other part thereof or an equivalent in land for the same by the said William Thatcher and the sum of three shillings residue thereof or an equivalent in land for the same by the said Provost and Scholars their said lessees and the said Commissioners having upon enquiry also found that the yearly sum of twenty nine pounds and ten pence or an equivalent in land for the same ought to be paid or made by the said Bartholomew

10   Tipping Lovelace Bigg Jeffry Church Joseph Mayon William Thatcher and the said Provost and Scholars of Queens College or their said lessees to the said John Archer in lieu or satisfaction of all tithes he is or maybe entitled to out of the same gardens orchards meadows pastures and other old inclosures **do** hereby direct and appoint that the same shall be by them paid or made in the shares and proportions following (that is to say) the

15   sum of nineteen pounds and one half penny part thereof or an equivalent in land for the same by the said Bartholomew Tipping the sum of five pounds eighteen shillings and nine pence other part thereof or an equivalent in land for the same by the said Lovelace Bigg the sum of eighteen shillings and five pence other part thereof or an equivalent in land for the same by the said Jeffry Church the sum of two pounds eight shillings and five

20   pence other part thereof or an equivalent in land for the same by the said Joseph Mayon the sum of eleven shillings and five pence other part thereof or an equivalent in land for the same by the said William Thatcher and the sum of three shillings and nine pence halfpenny residue thereof or an equivalent in land for the same by the said Provost and Scholars or their lessees and it being by the said Act of Parliament enacted that such of

25   the proprietors of the said messuages tenements gardens orchards and old inclosures and lands last mentioned who are also proprietors of or interested in any lands or commonable grounds by the said Act directed to be allotted or inclosed should make such satisfaction in land out of their respective shares in the said open fields and commonable grounds unto the said George Watts and his successors Vicars as aforesaid and the said John

30   Archer as in the judgement of the said Commissioners should be deemed equal or equivalent to the share or proportion of the said several annual sums which such proprietors should be so liable to pay or give in equivalent for as aforesaid and the said Bartholomew Tipping Lovelace Bigg Jeffry Church Joseph Mayon William Thatcher and the said Provost and Scholars of Queens College and their said lessees being respectively

35   proprietors of an interest in divers parts of the said lands and commonable grounds by the said Act directed to be allotted or inclosed the said Commissioners have accordingly proceeded to deduct an equivalent or satisfaction in land to the said George Watts and John Archer respectively to the said respective annual sums of eighteen pounds and seven shillings and twenty nine pounds and ten pence from and out of the respective

40   shares of the said Bartholomew Tipping Lovelace Bigg Jeffrey Church Joseph Mayon William Thatcher and the said Provost and Scholars and their said lessees respectively in the said open fields or commonable grounds and have so deducted the same according to their said several and respective proportions of the same annual sums respectively hereinbefore mentioned and after such deductions so made as aforesaid the said

45   Commissioners have thought proper in compliance with directions of the said Act to assign and allot and do hereby assign allot award and confirm such equivalent in land to *46* the said George Watts and John Archer respectively as follows (that is to say) **To the said George Watts** and his successors Vicars of Uffington aforesaid for and in lieu and satisfaction of all Vicarial tithes and all payments of in lieu thereof from or out of the said gardens orchards and inclosures meadows and pastures and other old inclosures and in *50* lieu of all moduses and ancient compositions for the said lands in the open and common fields meadows and commonable places of Woolston otherwise Wolverston aforesaid. **One plot** or parcel of land (distinguished throughout this award as the seventh allotment   *GW7* to the said George Watts) situate in Woolston Common containing seventy acres three roods and eighteen perches (exclusive of all roads and ways through and over the same) *55* as now staked and set out bounded on part of the east and part of the north by an old inclosure called Middle Several on the remaining part of the east by land allotted to the said Lovelace Bigg on the south the west and part of the north west by an allotment to the said Jeffry Church and on the remaining part of the north west by an allotment to the said Lovelace Bigg. **To the said John Archer** for an in lieu and satisfaction of all tithes he *60* is or may be entitled to out of the same gardens orchards meadows pastures and other old inclosures in Woolston otherwise Wolverston aforesaid two plots or parcels of land and **one plot** or parcel whereof (distinguished throughout this award as the seventh   *JA7* allotment to the said John Archer) this situate in Woolston fields on the north or lower side of Ickleton way containing twenty five acres three roods and twenty eight perches as *65* now staked and set out bounded on the west by an allotment to the said Lovelace Bigg and an allotment to the said Provost and Scholars of Queens College and the said Trustees of Robert Fettiplace on the north by an allotment to the said John Archer in Uffington Fields and on the east and south by another allotment to the said John Archer and the other **plot** or parcel of land (distinguished through this award as the eighth *70* *JA8* allotment to the said John Archer) is situate in Uffington Fields on the south or upper side of Ickleton Way containing seventeen acres and twenty nine perches (exclusive of all roads and ways through and over the same) as now staked and set out bounded on the east by part of the said Several Farm belonging to the said William Lord Craven on the south by land allotted to the said William Lord Craven on the south west north west and *75* north east by other part of the said Several Farm and on the north by another allotment hereinbefore awarded to the said John Archer and which is hereinafter exchanged with the said William Lord Craven which said plot or parcel of land hereinbefore last described is also hereinafter exchanged by the said John Archer with the said William Lord Craven the boundaries for ascertaining this allotment on the south against land allotted to the *80* said William Lord Craven the said Commissioners do award and direct shall be made and foreverafter maintained and repaired by the said William Lord Craven on his taking the said allotment in exchange as aforesaid and the owners of the same allotment for the time being. **Which** allotments so made to the said George Watts and John Archer respectively as last hereinbefore mentioned are in the judgement of the said *95* Commissioners deemed to be **equivalent** to the said respective annual payments or   *equivalence of* yearly sums of eighteen pounds and seven shillings and twenty nine pounds and ten   *GW/JA* pence hereinbefore mentioned and the said Bartholomew Tipping Lovelace Bigg Jeffry   *allotments to* Church Joseph Mayon William Thatcher and the said Provost and Scholars and their said   *tithes previously* lessees have made such satisfaction in the said respective allotments out of their respective *100* *payable*

101 shares in the said open fields and commonable grounds to the said George Watts and his successors Vicars as aforesaid and the said John Archer as in the judgment of the said Commissioners is hereby deemed to be equal or equivalent to the share or proportion of the said several annual sums which each of them was liable to pay or give an equivalent

105 for as aforesaid and the same allotments to the said George Watts and John Archer respectively are added to their other allotments in the same fields and grounds in such manner as hereinbefore is mentioned and all which said several allotments hereinbefore awarded to the said John Archer and George Watts respectively as aforesaid do make up and amount together to six hundred and sixty five acres one rood and thirty perches **and**

110 **with** respect to the owners and proprietors of all such messuages tenements gardens orchards and old inclosures in Woolston otherwise Woolverston who have no land or common right in the said open fields and commonable grounds by the said Act directed to be divided and allotted or not sufficient for the purposes aforesaid namely Thomas Bowles Charles Young the elder Charles Young the younger Joseph Aiers Timothy

115 Willoughby Thomas Clark Christopher Savory Sarah Deane Thomas Lewis Edward Golding Job Corfe Thomas Woodroff Thomas Withs Thomas Thatcher John Nelson Thomas Lewis the younger Ralph Collier Cripps Willis Charles Wilkins and Joshua Bolsher **the said Commissioners do** in further pursuance of the directions of the said Act of Parliament in and by this their award made in the manner directed by the said Act

tithe compensation payments by those who own no land or have no rights in open fields

120 **award and appoint** that they the said Thomas Bowles Charles Young the Elder Charles Young the younger Joseph Aiers Timothy Willoughby Thomas Clark Christopher Savory Sarah Deane Thomas Lewis Edward Golding Job Corfe Thomas Woodroff Thomas Withs Thomas Thatcher John Nelson Thomas Lewis the younger Ralph Collier Cripps Willis Charles Wilkins and Joshua Bolsher shall respectively annually pay the said George

125 Watts and his successors Vicars as aforesaid in satisfaction of his and their right to tithes therein and all payments in lieu thereof the several and respective sums of money following that is to say the said Thomas Bowles for an in respect of his Close of Meadow Ground called the Moor the sum of ten shillings the said Charles Young the elder for and in respect of his messuages garden and orchard the sum of two shillings the said Charles

130 Young the younger for and in respect of his cottage and garden the sum of four pence the said Joseph Aiers for an in respect of his cottage and garden the sum of two pence the said Timothy Willoughby Thomas Clark Christopher Savory Sarah Deane Thomas Lewis Edward Golding Job Corke for and in respect of their several and respective cottages and gardens held by leases determinable on lives under the said Bartholomew Tipping the

135 sum of one penny each the said Thomas Woodroff for and in respect of his cottage garden and orchard held by lease under the said Barthomew Tipping for the remainder of a long term of years the sum of one shilling and six pence the said Thomas Wicks Thomas Thatcher John Nelson and Thomas Lewis the younger for and in respect of their several cottages and gardens likewise held by leases for long terms of years under the said

140 Bartholomew Tipping the sum of one penny each the said Ralph Collier Cripps Willis Charles Wilkins and Joshua Bolsher for and in respect of the several cottages and gardens

10

In Their respective occupations and commonly called Town or Parish houses the sum of one penny each which said respective rents and sums of money are by the said Act declared to be from henceforth charged upon and issuing out of the said premises respectively out of which the same are appointed to be paid as aforesaid and are to be paid to the said George Watts and his successors Vicars as aforesaid at Michelmas in every year forever the first payment whereof is by the said Act directed to be made on the Michelmas Day next after the date of this award and the said Vicar and his Successors will by virtue of the said Act at all times after the execution of this Award have and exercise such and the same remedies and powers by distress and entry for recovering the said respective yearly rents so ascertained and appointed to be paid as aforesaid when the same shall be in arrear as by the laws now in force are prescribed for and given to the Landlords for recovering of rack rents in arrear and the said Commissioners do hereby declare that the several allotments hereinbefore set out to and for the said John Archer and George Watts respectively as aforesaid in lieu of their tithes arising from the said downs do in the judgement of them the said Commissioners (all circumstances considered) improve from their respective rents or values at the time of passing the said Act in the same proportion as the lands and grounds (out of which such tithes arose) improve after the said allotting and dividing from the rents or values thereof at the time of passing the said Act. **And the said Commissioners** in further pursuance and according to the directions of the said Act **have** set out allotted and appointed and by these presents **do** set out allot and appoint **as and for a public pit** of stone gravel chalk or rubble within the township of Uffington. **One Plot** of land or ground situate in Uffington Fields on the south or upper side of Ickleton Way and near a place called White Shoot containing three acres (exclusive of all roads and ways) bounded on all sides by the thirty fifth allotment to the said William Lord Craven **and as and for public pits** of stone gravel chalk or rubble within the hamlet of Woolston otherwise Wolverston two plots or parcels of land or ground (containing together three acres) **one plot** or parcel whereof is situate in Woolston Fields on the north or lower side of Ickleton Way and contains three roods and twenty four perches as now staked and set out bounded on part of the north and on the east by land allotted to the said John Archer on the south and west by Ickleton Way and on the remaining part of the north by an allotment to the said Bartholomew Tipping and the other plot or parcel thereof is situate in Woolston Field on the south or upper side of the said way called Ickleton Way and contains two acres and sixteen perches as now staked and set out (exclusive of all roads and ways awarded over the same) bounded on the east and south by land allotted to the said Bartholomew Tipping and on the west and north west by land allotted to the said Lovelace Bigg which said pits are to be used in common by the owners and proprietors of lands and estates within the said township and hamlet respectively and their respective tenants as well for their own necessary use within the said township and hamlet as for the repairs of the public and private roads within the said township or hamlet and all which said public pits or the value thereof as also the value of all the land and ground set out and allotted for public roads through and over the new allotments are taken from and out of the value of the lands and grounds by the said Act directed to be divided and allotted before any of the new allotments were made to any of the persons entitled thereto in proportion to the rights and interests of the

1

5

10

15

20

25

30

35

40

45

Uffington stone pit

Woolstone stone pits

46   proprietors of the said lands and grounds and other persons interested therein respectively as by the said Act is directed **and as to all the residue** and remainder of the said open and common fields common meadows common pastures downs and other commonable lands lying within the township of Uffington and Hamlets of Baulking and

50   Woolston otherwise Wolverston directed by the said Act to be divided and allotted (except as therein excepted) after making the allotments before mentioned and described and after deducting a sufficient quantity of the said lands and grounds for the roads and highways hereinafter mentioned the said Commissioners **have** set out divided assigned and allotted and by these presents **do** assign award and confirm the same unto

55   and amongst the said William Lord Craven the said Earl Spencer Bartholomew Tipping Lovelace Bigg (both for his own original estate and the estate by him purchased of the said Sir William Guise since the passing of the said Act) John Hippesley John Archer and to the said other person entitle to and interested in the same in such quantities shares and proportions as are hereinafter particularly mentioned and set forth that is to say **To**

60   **and for the said William Lord Craven** in lieu of and as a just and full recompense satisfaction and equivalent for all such of his lands and grounds rights of common and other properties in and over the said fields and commonable lands by the said act directed to be divided and allotted as were heretofore demised by the late Right Honourable Fulwar Lord Craven deceased by Indenture of Lease dated the twenty

65   eighth day of March one thousand seven hundred and forty nine to Charles Garrard also deceased at the yearly reserved rent of one pound five shillings and eight pence. **One plot** or parcel of land being the second allotment to the said William Lord Craven situate in Uffington Meadow aforesaid containing forty acres one rood and six perches (exclusive of all roads and ways through and over the same) bounded on the south east

70   by the thirteenth and twelfth allotments to the said William Lord Craven on part of the south by an allotment to the said John Archer exchanged by him with the said William Lord Craven as hereinafter mentioned on part of the west and remaining part of the south by the thirty third allotment to the said William Lord Craven on the remaining part of the west by the said inclosed Farm belonging to the said William Lord Craven

75   and on the north by the sixth fifth fourth and third allotments to the said William Lord Craven the fences for inclosing this allotment on the south against the said allotment to the said John Archer exchanged as aforesaid and on the south against the thirty third allotment to the said William Lord Craven the said Commissioners do award order and direct shall be made and forever after maintained and repaired by the said William Lord

80   Craven and the owners of this allotment for the time being. **To and for the said William Lord Craven** in lieu of and as a just and full recompense satisfaction and equivalent for all such of his lands and grounds rights of common and other properties in and over the said fields and commonable lands by the said act directed to be divided and allotted as were heretofor demised by the said Fulwar Lord Craven deceased to Jane Brooks Widow

95   by lease dated the first day of May one thousand seven hundred and fifty two at the yearly reserved rent of six shillings and nine pence. **One plot** or parcel of land (being the third allotment to the said William Lord Craven) likewise situate in Uffington Meadow aforesaid containing seven acres and two roods bounded on the north east by the fourteenth and thirteenth allotments to the said William Lord Craven on the south by

100   the second on the west by the fourth and on the north by the ninth allotments to the

LC2

LC3

said William Lord Craven. The fences for inclosing this allotment on the south and west *101* against the second and fourth allotments to the said William Lord Craven the said Commissioners do award order and direct shall be made and foreverafter maintained and repaired by the said William Lord Craven and the owners of this allotment for the time being. **To and for the said William Lord Craven** in lieu of and as a just and full *105* recompense satisfaction and equivalent for all such of his lands and grounds rights of common and other properties in and over the said fields and commonable lands by the said act directed to be divided and allotted as were heretofore demised by the said Fulwar Lord Craven deceased to John Alder by Lease dated the fourteenth day of March one thousand seven hundred and forty four at the yearly reserved rent of two shillings and *110* ten pence. **One plot** or parcel of land or ground (being the fourth allotment to the said *LC4* William Lord Craven) likewise situate in Uffington Meadow aforesaid containing two acres and eleven perches bounded on the east by the third on the south by the second on the west by the fifth and on the north by the ninth allotment to the said William Lord Craven. The fences for inclosing this allotment on the south and west against the said *115* second and fifth allotments the said Commissioners do award order and direct shall be made and foreverafter maintained by the said William Lord Craven and the owners of this allotment for the time being **To and for the said William Lord Craven** in lieu of and as a just and full recompense satisfaction and equivalent for all such of his lands and grounds rights of common and other properties in and over the said fields and *120* commonable lands by the said act directed to be divided and allotted as were heretofore demised by the said Fulwar Lord Craven deceased to Joseph Brooks by lease dated the twenty ninth day of September one thousand seven hundred and forty two at the yearly reserved rent of fourteen shillings. **One plot** or parcel of land or ground being the fifth *LC5* allotment to the said William Lord Craven likewise situate in Uffington Meadow *125* aforesaid containing sixteen acres and seven perches (exclusive of all roads and ways through and over the same) bounded on part of the east and part of the north by the ninth on the remaining part of the east by the fourth on the south by the second on the west by the sixth and seventh and on the remaining part of the north by the eighth allotments to the said William Lord Craven the fences for inclosing this allotment on the *130* south against the said second and on the west against the said sixth and seventh

1

11

Allotments to the said William Lord Craven the said Commissioners do award order and direct shall be made and foreverafter maintained and repaired by the said William Lord Craven and the owners of this allotment for the time being. **To and for the said William Lord Craven** in lieu of and as a just and

5 full recompense satisfaction and equivalent for all such of his lands and grounds rights of common and other properties in and over the said fields and commonable lands by the said act directed to be divided and allotted as were heretofore demised by the late Right Honourable William Lord Craven deceased by lease to John Clarke dated the twentieth day of March one thousand seven hundred and twenty six at the yearly reserved rent of

LC6   *10* ten shillings. **One plot** or parcel of land (being the sixth allotment to the said William Lord Craven) situate likewise in Uffington Meadow aforesaid containing eight acres (exclusive of all roads and ways through and over the same) bounded on the east by the fifth and on the south by the second allotment to the said William Lord Craven on the south west and west by the said inclosed farm belonging to the said William Lord Craven

15 in the occupation of Richard Geering and on the north by the seventh allotment to the said William Lord Craven the fences for inclosing this allotment on the south against the said second allotment to the said William Lord Craven the said Commissioners do award order and direct shall be made and foreverafter maintained and repaired by the said William Lord Craven and the owners of this allotment for the time being. **To and for the**

20 **said William Lord Craven** in lieu of and as a just and full recompense satisfaction and equivalent for all such of his lands and grounds rights of common and other properties in and over the said fields and commonable lands by the said act directed to be divided and allotted as were heretofor demised by the said William Lord Craven deceased to William Chamberlain by lease dated the twentieth day of July one thousand seven hundred and

LC7   *25* thirty three at the yearly reserved rent of thirteen shillings and four pence. **One plot** or parcel of land (being the seventh allotment to the said William Lord Craven) situate in Uffington Meadow aforesaid containing seventeen acres and sixteen perches (exclusive of all roads and ways through and over the same) bounded on the east by the said fifth and on the south by the said sixth allotment to the said William Lord Craven on parts of

30 the west and south west by the said inclosed farm in the occupation of Richard Geering on the remaining part of the west by certain inclosures in the hamlet of Woolston called The Moors and on the north by the eighth allotment to the said William Lord Craven the fences for inclosing this allotment on the south against the said sixth allotment the said Commissioners do award order and direct shall be made and forever after maintained

35 and repaired by the said William Lord Craven and the owners of this allotment for the time being. **To and for the said William Lord Craven** in lieu of and as a just and full recompense satisfaction and equivalent for all such of his lands and grounds rights of common and other properties in and over the said fields and commonable lands by the said act directed to be divided and allotted as were heretofore demised by the said William

40 Lord Craven deceased to Charles Garrard by lease dated the fifteenth day of November one thousand seven hundred and twenty two at the yearly reserved rent of one pound

LC8   and ten shillings. **One plot** or parcel of land (being the eighth allotment to the said William Lord Craven) situate in Uffington Meadow aforesaid containing thirty three acres two roods and nineteen perches (exclusive of all roads and ways through and over

45 the same) bounded on the east by the ninth allotment and on the south by the fifth and

seventh allotments to the said William Lord Craven on the west by the said old Inclosures *46*
in Woolston called the Moors and by a lane leading towards Longcot called Moor Lane
and on the north by the Lordship of Fernham the fences for inclosing this allotment on
the south against the fifth and seventh allotments and against the said Moor Lane the said
Commissioners do award order and direct shall be made and forever after maintained *50*
and repaired by the said William Lord Craven and the owners of this allotment for the
time being. **To and for the said William Lord Craven** in lieu of and as a just and full
recompense satisfaction and equivalent for all such of his lands and grounds rights of
common and other properties in and over the said fields and commonable lands by the
said act directed to be divided and allotted as were heretofore demised by the said Fulwar *55*
Lord Craven deceased to Joseph Green senior by lease dated the twentieth day of April
one thousand seven hundred and fifty four at the yearly reserved rent of one pound
fourteen shillings and eight pence. **One plot** or parcel of land (being the ninth allotment   *LC9*
to the said William Lord Craven) situate in Uffington Meadow aforesaid containing
thirty acres one rood and thirty eight perches (exclusive of all roads and ways through *60*
and over the same) bounded on the south east by certain inclosures in Uffington aforesaid
called Moor Mill Closes and by the fourteenth allotment to the said William Lord Craven
on part of the south by the third and fourth allotments on the remaining part of the south
and part of the west by the fifth and on the remaining part of the west by the eighth
allotment to the said William Lord Craven on the north by the said Lordship of Fernham *65*
on the west [east?] by the tenth allotment to the said William Lord Craven and on the
north west [north east?] by an allotment to the said William Lord Craven and Angel
Lockey his lessee the fences for inclosing this allotment on the south against the said
third and fourth allotments on the south and west against the said fifth allotment on the
west against the said eighth allotment to the said William Lord Craven and on the north *70*
west [east?] against the allotment to the said William Lord Craven and the said Angel
Lockey his lessee the said Commissioners do award order and direct shall be made and
foreverafter maintained and repaired by the said William Lord Craven and the owners of
this allotment for the time being. **To and for the said William Lord Craven** in lieu of
and as a just and full recompense satisfaction and equivalent for all such of his lands and *75*
grounds rights of common and other properties in and over the said fields and
commonable lands by the said act directed to be divided and allotted as were heretofore
demised by the said Fulwar Lord Craven deceased to Angel Lockey by lease bearing date
the first day of May one thousand seven hundred and fifty five at the yearly reserved rent
of six shillings and eight pence. **One plot** or parcel of land (being the tenth allotment to *80* *LC10*
the said William Lord Craven) situate in Uffington Meadow aforesaid containing seven
acres two roods and eight perches (exclusive of all roads and ways through and over the
same) bounded on the east by the seventh [eleventh?] allotment to the said William Lord
Craven on the south and south east by the said allotment to the said William Lord Craven
and Angel Lockey his lessee on the west by the ninth allotment to the said William Lord *95*
Craven and on the north by the said Lordship of Fernham the fences for inclosing this
allotment on the west against the said ninth allotment the said Commissioners do award
order and direct shall be made and forever after maintained and repaired by the said
William Lord Craven and the owners of this allotment for the time being **To and for the**
said William Lord Craven in lieu of and as a just and full recompense satisfaction and *100*

101 equivalent for all such of his lands and grounds rights of common and other properties in and over the said fields and commonable lands by the said act directed to be divided and allotted as were heretofor demised by the said William Lord Craven deceased to Anthony Shilton by lease bearing date the twenty fifth day of May one thousand seven hundred

LC11

105 and thirty seven at the yearly reserved rent of six shillings and ten pence. **One plot** or parcel of land being the eleventh allotment to the said William Lord Craven situate in Uffington Meadow aforesaid containing three acres two roods and sixteen perches (exclusive of all roads and ways through and over the same) bounded on part of the east by certain old inclosures at Uffington aforesaid now or lately in the occupation of John

110 Lockey on part of the south and the remaining part of the east by a Lane called Moor Mill lane on the remaining part of the south by the said allotment to the said William Lord Craven and Angel Lockey his lessee on the west by the said tenth allotment to the said William Lord Craven and on the north by the said lordship of Fernham the fences for inclosing this allotment on the south and east against the said Moor Mill Lane and on the

115 west against the said tenth allotment to the said William Lord Craven the said Commissioners do award order and direct shall be made and foreverafter maintained and repaired by the said William Lord Craven and the owners of this allotment for the time being. **To and for the said William Lord Craven** in lieu of and as a just and full recompense satisfaction and equivalent for all such of his lands and grounds rights of

120 common and other properties in and over the said fields and commonable lands by the said act directed to be divided and allotted as were heretofore demised by the said Fulwar Lord Craven deceased to George Watts clerk since deceased by lease bearing date the first day of June one thousand seven hundred and forty two at the yearly reserved rent of two pounds one shilling and six pence. **One Plot** or parcel of land (being the twelfth allotment

LC12

125 to the said William Lord Craven) situate in Uffington Common at a place there called Old Lands containing twenty nine acres three roods and thirty three perches (exclusive of all roads and ways through and over the same) bounded on part of the east by the fourteenth allotment to the said William Lord Craven on the remaining part of the east and on the south by several old inclosures at the town of Uffington on the north west by

130 an allotment to the said John Archer exchanged as aforesaid by the second allotment to the said William Lord Craven and on the north east by the thirteenth allotment to the said William Lord Craven the fences for inclosing this allotment on the north west against

12

The Said allotment to the said John Archer exchanged as aforesaid and *1* against the said second allotment to the said William Lord Craven the said Commissioners do award order and direct shall be made and forever after maintained and repaired by the said William Lord Craven and the owners of this allotment for the time being. To and for the said William Lord Craven in lieu of and as a *5* just and full recompense satisfaction and equivalent for all such of his lands and grounds rights of common and other properties in and over the said fields and commonable lands by the said act directed to be divided and allotted as were heretofore demised by the said William Lord Craven deceased to Oliver Lockey by lease bearing date the seventeenth day of June one thousand seven hundred and thirty one at the yearly *10* reserved rent of one pound nineteen shillings and two pence. **One plot** or parcel of land *LC13* (being the thirteenth allotment to the said William Lord Craven) situate in Uffington Common at a place there called the Old Lands as a aforesaid containing sixteen acres (exclusive of all roads and ways through and over the same) bounded on the north east and east by the fourteenth allotment on the south west by the twelfth allotment and on *15* the north west by the second and third allotments to the said William Lord Craven the fences for inclosing this allotment on the south west against the twelfth allotment and on the north west against the said second and third allotments to the said William Lord Craven the Commissioners do award order and direct shall be made and foreverafter maintained and repaired by the said William Lord Craven and the owners of this *20* allotment for the time being. To and for the said William Lord Craven in lieu of and as a just and full recompense satisfaction and equivalent for all such of his lands and grounds rights of common and other properties in and over the said fields and commonable lands by the said act directed to be divided and allotted as were heretofore demised by the said William Lord Craven deceased to John Green by lease bearing date the *25* twentieth day of October one thousand seven hundred and twenty four at the yearly *LC14* reserved rent of twelve pounds. **One plot** or parcel of land (being the fourteenth allotment to the said William Lord Craven) situate on Uffington Common aforesaid containing one hundred and six acres three roods and thirty seven perches (exclusive of all roads and ways through and over the same) bounded on part of the north east, part *30* of the north west other part of the north east and other part of the north west by several old inclosures called Moor Mill Closes and Green Stirt on other part of the north west by the said lane called Moor Mill Lane on the remaining part of the north east by the hamlet of Baulking on the south east by the fifteenth eighteenth and nineteenth allotments to the said William Lord Craven on part of the south west by the twentieth *35* allotment to the said William Lord Craven on other part of the north west on part of the south on the east and the remaining part of the south by several old Inclosures at the town of Uffington on part of the west by the twelfth allotment on other part of the west and the remaining part of the west and south west by the thirteenth allotment and on the remaining part of the north west by the third and ninth allotments to the said *40* William Lord Craven the fences for inclosing this allotment on such parts of the north east and north west against the said Moor Mill Closes as have usually been or of right ought to have been made and maintained by the owners and occupiers of lands and commons in Uffington aforesaid on the north west across the said Moor Mill Lane on the south west against the said twentieth allotment on the west against the said twelfth *45*

46   allotment on the west and south west against the said thirteenth allotment and on the north west against the said third and ninth allotments to the said William Lord Craven the said Commissioners do award order and direct shall be made and foreverafter maintained and repaired by the said William Lord Craven and the owners of this *50* allotment for the time being. To and for the said William Lord Craven in lieu of and as a just and full recompense satisfaction and equivalent for all such of his lands and grounds rights of common and other properties in and over the said fields and commonable lands by the said act directed to be divided and allotted as were heretofore demised by the said Fulwar Lord Craven deceased to Lawrence Woodroff by lease bearing date the *55* first day of May one thousand seven hundred and forty six at the yearly reserved rent of six shillings and six pence. **One plot** or parcel of land (being the fifteenth allotment to the said William Lord Craven) situate in Uffington Common containing ten acres three roods and fifteen perches bounded on the north east by inclosures in the hamlet of Baulking on the south east by the sixteenth on the south west on the eighteenth and on *60* the north west by the fourteenth allotment to the said William Lord Craven the fences for inclosing this allotment on such parts of the north east against the hamlet of Baulking as have usually been or of right ought to have been made and maintained by the owners and occupiers of lands and commons in Uffington aforesaid on the south west against the said eighteenth allotment and on the north west against the said *65* fourteenth allotment to the said William Lord Craven the said Commissioners do award order and direct shall be made and foreverafter maintained and repaired by the said William Lord Craven and the owners of this allotment for the time being. To and for the said William Lord Craven in lieu of and as a just and full recompense satisfaction and equivalent for all such of his lands and grounds rights of common and other properties *70* in and over the said fields and commonable lands by the said act directed to be divided and allotted as were heretofore demised by the said Fulwar Lord Craven deceased to Henry Cook by indenture of lease bearing date the fourteenth day of March one thousand seven hundred and forty four at the yearly reserved rent of one pound twelve shillings and ten pence halfpenny and commonly called by the name of Stamps (other *75* than and except such of the said lands and common rights called Stamps as are now held and enjoyed under or by virtue of the said lease by Edmund Cook son of the said Henry Cook and in lieu whereof an allotment is hereinafter awarded to the said William Lord Craven and the said Edmund Cook). **One plot** or parcel of land (being the sixteenth allotment to the said William Lord Craven) situate in Uffington Common containing *80* twenty one acres one rood and ten perches bounded on the north east by inclosures in the hamlet of Baulking aforesaid on the south east by the twenty sixth allotment on the south west by the seventeenth and eighteenth allotments and on the north west by the fifteenth allotment to the said William Lord Craven the fences for inclosing this allotment on the north east against the hamlet of Balking on the south east against the *95* said seventeenth and eighteenth allotments and on the north east against the said fifteenth allotments to the said William Lord Craven the said Commissioners do award order and direct shall be made and foreverafter maintained and repaired by the said William Lord Craven and the owners of this allotment for the time being. To and for the said William Lord Craven in lieu of and as a just and full recompense satisfaction and *100* equivalent for all such of his lands and grounds rights of common and other properties

LC15

LC16

in and over the said fields and commonable lands by the said act directed to be divided   *101*
and allotted as were heretofore demised by the said Fulwar Lord Craven deceased to
Elizabeth Puzey by lease bearing date the thirtieth day of July one thousand seven   **LC17**
hundred and fifty three at the yearly reserved rent of twenty shillings. **One plot** or parcel
of land (being the seventeenth allotment to the said William Lord Craven) situate in   *105*
Uffington Common containing seventeen acres and thirty two perches bounded on the
east by the said twenty sixth and part of the south west by the twenty fifth allotment to
the said William Lord Craven on the remaining part of the south west by an allotment
to the said William Lord Craven and John Stallard his lessee on the north west by the
nineteenth and eighteenth allotments and on the north east by the sixteenth allotment   *110*
to the said William Lord Craven the fences for inclosing this allotment on the south
west against the said twenty fifth allotment and the said allotment to the said William
Lord Craven and John Stallard his lessee and on the north west against the said
nineteenth and eighteenth allotments to the said William Lord Craven the said
Commissioners do award order and direct shall be made and foreverafter maintained   *115*
and repaired by the said William Lord Craven and the owners of this allotment for the
time being. To and for the said William Lord Craven in lieu of and as a just and full
recompense satisfaction and equivalent for all such of his lands and grounds rights of
common and other properties in and over the said fields and commonable lands by the
said act directed to be divided and allotted as were heretofore demised by the said   *120*
William Lord Craven deceased to William Moss by lease bearing date the thirtieth day   **LC18**
of May one thousand seven hundred and twenty three at the yearly reserved rent of four
shillings and six pence. **One Plot** or parcel of land (being the eighteenth allotment to
the said William Lord Craven) situate in Uffington Common containing seven acres
one rood and twenty perches bounded on the north east by the fifteenth   *125*
and sixteenth allotments to the said William Lord Craven on the south east by the said
seventeenth allotment on the south west by the said nineteenth allotment and on the
north west by the said fourteenth allotment to the said William Lord Craven the fences
for inclosing this allotment on the south west against the said nineteenth allotment and
on the north west against the said fourteenth allotment the said Commissioners to   *130*
award order and direct shall be made and foreverafter maintained and repaired by the
said William Lord Craven and the owners of this allotment for the time being. To and
for the said William Lord Craven in lieu of and as a just and full recompense satisfaction
and equivalent for all such of his lands and grounds rights of common and other
properties in and over the said fields and commonable lands by the said act directed to   *135*
be divided and allotted as were heretofore demised by the said William Lord Craven
deceased to Thomas Taylor by lease bearing date the nineteenth day of

LC19

1   **13** **August** one thousand seven hundred and thirty one at the yearly reserved rent of three shillings. **One plot** or parcel of land (being the nineteenth allotment to the said William Lord Craven) situate in Uffington Common aforesaid containing four acres and two roods bounded on the north east by the said *5* eighteenth allotment and on the south east by the said seventeenth allotment to the said William Lord Craven on the south west by an allotment to the said William Lord Craven and John Stallard his lessee and on the north west by the twentieth and fourteenth allotments to the said William Lord Craven the fences for inclosing this allotment on the south west against the said allotment to the said William Lord Craven and John *10* Stallard his lessee and on the north west against the said twentieth and fourteenth allotments to the said William Lord Craven the said commissioners do award order and direct shall be made and foreverafter maintained and repaired by the said William Lord Craven and owners of this allotment for the time being. **To and For the said William Lord Craven** in lieu of and as a just recompense satisfaction and equivalent for all such *15* of his lands grounds rights of common and other properties in and over the said fields and commonable lands by the said act directed to be divided and allotted as were heretofore demised by the said Fulwar Lord Craven deceased to the said Henry Cook by lease bearing date the thirtieth day of March one thousand seven hundred and fifty six at the yearly reserved rent of one pound and seventeen shillings commonly called by the *20* name of Saunders other than and except such of the said lands and common rights called Saunders as are now held and enjoyed under or by virtue of the said lease by the said Edmund Cook son of the said Henry Cook and in lieu whereof an allotment of land is

LC20

hereinafter awarded to the said William Lord Craven and Edmund Cook. **One plot** or parcel of land (being the twentieth allotment to the said William Lord Craven) situate *25* on Uffington Common aforesaid containing twenty two acres three roods and twenty nine perches (exclusive of all roads and ways through and over the same) bounded on the north east by the said fourteenth allotment to the said William Lord Craven on the south east by the said nineteenth allotment to the said William Lord Craven and the allotments to the said William Lord Craven and John Stallard Richard Hinchman Joseph *30* Dixon and Charles Young and Sarah his wife and Mary Allen respectively as his (the said William Lord Craven) lessees on the south west by the twenty first allotment to the said William Lord Craven by the first allotment to the said William Lord Craven (as Lord of the Manor) and by the Town Green of Uffington aforesaid and on the north west by several houses homesteads and inclosures at the town of Uffington aforesaid the fences *35* for inclosing this allotment on the south west against the said twenty first allotment against the said allotment to the said William Lord Craven (as Lord of the Manor) and against the said Town Green the said Commissioners do award order and direct shall be made and foreverafter maintained and repaired by the said William Lord Craven and the owners of this allotment for the time being. **To and For the said William Lord Craven** *40* in lieu of and as a just and full recompense satisfaction and equivalent for all such of his lands grounds and rights of common and other properties in and over the said fields and commonable lands by the said Act directed to be divided and allotted as were heretofore demised by the said William Lord Craven deceased to William Smith by lease bearing date the thirtieth day of March one thousand seven hundred and twenty three at the

LC21

45 yearly reserved rent of seven shillings and six pence. **One plot** or parcel of land (being

the twenty first allotment to the said William Lord Craven) situate in Uffington *46*
Common aforesaid containing three acres two roods and twelve perches (exclusive of all
roads and ways through and over the same) bounded on the north east by the said
twentieth allotment to the said William Lord Craven and by an allotment to the said
William Lord Craven and Charles and Sarah his wife and Mary Allen his lessees on the *50*
south east by a public road hereinafter awarded from Uffington towards Fawler on the
south by the twenty second allotment to the said William Lord Craven and by several
houses homesteads and inclosures at the town of Uffington aforesaid and on the west by
the said first allotment to the said William Lord Craven (as Lord of the Manor) the
fences for inclosing this allotment on the south east across the said public road and on *55*
the west against the allotment to the said William Lord Craven (as Lord of the Manor as
aforesaid) the said Commissioners do award order and direct shall be made and
foreverafter maintained and repaired by the said William Lord Craven and the owners of
this allotment for the time being. **To and For the said William Lord Craven** in lieu of
and as a just and full recompense satisfaction and equivalent for all such of his lands and *60*
grounds rights of common and other properties in and over the said fields and
commonable lands by the said Act directed to be divided and allotted as were heretofore
demised by the said William Lord Craven deceased to Richard Dean by lease bearing
date the twenty first day of August one thousand seven hundred and twenty six at the
yearly reserved rent of ten shillings. **One Plot** or parcel of land (being the twenty second *65* *LC22*
allotment to the said William Lord Craven) situate in Uffington Common aforesaid
containing two acres and twenty five perches (exclusive of all roads and ways through
and over the same) bounded on the north east by a public road hereinafter described
from Uffington toward Fawler aforesaid on the south by allotments to William Miflin
and Elizabeth Hoar respectively on a small part of the west by an allotment to James *70*
Mundy on the remaining part of the west by an old inclosure and homestead at Uffington
aforesaid and on the north by the twenty first allotment to the said William Lord Craven
the fences for inclosing this allotment on the north east against the said public road on
the south against the said allotments to the said William Miflin and Elizabeth Hoar
respectively and on the north against the said twenty first allotment to the said William *75*
Lord Craven the said Commissioners do award order and direct shall be made and
foreverafter maintained and repaired by the said William Lord Craven and the owners of
this allotment for the time being. **To and For the said William Lord Craven** in lieu of
and as a just and full recompense satisfaction and equivalent for all such of his lands and
grounds rights of common and other properties in and over the said fields and *80*
commonable lands by the said Act directed to be divided and allotted as were heretofore
demised by the said William Lord Craven deceased to John and Oliver Lockey by lease
bearing date the seventeenth day of June one thousand seven hundred and thirty one at
the yearly reserved rent of three pounds and eleven shillings. **One plot** or parcel of land   *LC23*
(being the twenty third allotment to the said William Lord Craven) situate on Uffington *95*
Common aforesaid containing twenty seven acres two roods and seven perches
(exclusive of all roads and ways through and over the same) bounded on a small part of
the north east by the twenty fifth allotment to the said William Lord Craven on the other
part of the north east by an allotment to William Chamberlain on the east and part of
the south by the twenty seventh allotment to the said William Lord Craven on the *100*

101   remaining part of the south by the thirty fourth allotment to the said William Lord Craven on the west or south west by land allotted to the said Vicar of Uffington exchanged by him with the said William Lord Craven and by the twenty ninth allotment to the said William Lord Craven and on the north west by an allotment to the said

105   Joseph Cook and by a public road hereinafter awarded from Uffington to Fawler. The fences for inclosing this allotment across the said public road the said Commissioners do award order and direct shall be made and forever after maintained and repaired by the said William Lord Craven and the owners of this allotment for the time being. **To and For the said William Lord Craven** in lieu of and as a just and full recompense

110   satisfaction and equivalent for all such of his lands and grounds rights of common and other properties in and over the said fields and commonable lands by the said Act directed to be divided and allotted as were heretofore demised by the said Fulwar Lord Craven deceased to William Stallard by lease bearing date the fourteenth day of March one thousand seven hundred and forty four at the yearly reserved rent of five shillings

LC24   115   and six pence. **One plot** or parcel of land (being the twenty fourth allotment to the said William Lord Craven) situate in Uffington Common aforesaid containing five acres and seventeen perches (exclusive of all roads and ways through and over the same) bounded on the north east and south east by the twenty fifth allotment to the said William Lord Craven on the south west by a public road hereinafter described from Uffington towards

120   Fawler and on the north west by an allotment to the said William Lord Craven and Edmund Cook his lessee the fences for inclosing this allotment on the south west against the said public road and on the north west against the said allotment to the said William Lord Craven and Edmund Cook the said Commissioners do award order and direct shall be made and foreverafter maintained and repaired by the said William Lord Craven

125   and the owners of this allotment for the time being. **To and for the said William Lord Craven** in lieu of and as a just and full recompense satisfaction and equivalent for all such of his lands and grounds rights of common and other properties in and over the said fields and commonable lands by the said act directed to be divided and allotted as were heretofore demised by the said William Lord Craven deceased to

130   William Stallard by lease bearing date the twentieth day of July one thousand seven hundred and thirty seven at the yearly reserved rent of nine shillings and seven pence.

LC25   **One plot** or parcel of land (being the twenty fifth allotment to the said William Lord Craven) situate in Uffington Common aforesaid containing twelve acres and twenty four perches (exclusive of all roads and ways through and over the same) bounded

14

On the east by the twenty sixth allotment to the said William Lord Craven on the south and south east by the allotment to William Chamberlain on part of the south west by the twenty third allotment to the said William Lord Craven and by a public road hereinafter described from Uffington towards Fawler on part of the north west and the remaining part of the south west by the twenty fourth allotment to the said William Lord Craven on the remaining part of the north west by an allotment to the said William Lord Craven and John Stallard his lessee and on the north east by the seventeenth allotment to the said William Lord Craven the fences for inclosing this allotment on the south against the allotment to the said William Chamberlain on the south west against the said twenty third allotment to the said William Lord Craven and the said public road on the north west and south west against the said twenty fourth allotment to the said William Lord Craven and on the north west against the allotment to William Lord Craven and John Stallard the said Commissioners do award order and direct shall be made and forever after maintained and repaired by the said William Lord Craven and the owners of this allotment for the time being. **To and For the said William Lord Craven** in lieu of and as a just and full recompense satisfaction and equivalent for all such of his lands and grounds rights of common and other properties in and over the said fields and commonable lands by the said Act directed to be divided and allotted as were heretofore demised by the said Fulwar Lord Craven deceased to Charles Garrard by lease bearing date the fifteenth day of April one thousand seven hundred and forty two at the yearly reserved rent of fourteen shillings and five pence. **One plot** or parcel of land (being the twenty sixth allotment to the said William Lord Craven) situate in Uffington Field on the north or lower side of Ickleton Way in a certain place there called the Hitchin containing nineteen acres and eighteen perches bounded on the north east by inclosures in the hamlet of Balking on the south east and east by the hamlet of Fawler on the south by the allotment to the said William Chamberlain on the west by the twenty fifth and seventeenth allotments to the said William Lord Craven and on the north west by the sixteenth allotment to the said William Lord Craven the fences for inclosing this allotment on the north east against the hamlet of Balking on the south against the said allotment to the said William Chamberlain on the east against the said twenty fifth and seventeenth allotments and on the north west against the said sixteenth allotment to the said William Lord Craven the said commissioners do award order and direct shall be made and forever after maintained repaired by the William Lord Craven and the owners of this allotment for the time being. **To and For the said William Lord Craven** in lieu of and as a just and full recompense satisfaction and equivalent for all such of his lands and grounds rights of common and other properties in and over the said fields and commonable lands by the said Act directed to be divided and allotted as were heretofore demised by the said Fulwar Lord Craven deceased to John Garrard by lease bearing date the twenty sixth day of August one thousand seven hundred and fifty four at the yearly reserved rent of one pound and eight pence. **One plot** or parcel of land being the twenty seventh allotment to the said William Lord Craven situate in Uffington Fields on the north or lower side of Ickleton Way containing thirty seven acres and twenty three perches (exclusive of all roads and ways through and over the same) bounded on the east and north east by the hamlet of Fawler on the south east by

1

5

10

15

20

LC26

25

30

35

40

LC27

45

46 the twenty eighth allotment to the said William Lord Craven on part of the west by the thirty fourth allotment to the said William Lord Craven on part of the north and on the remaining part of the west by the twenty third allotment to the said William Lord Craven and on the remaining part of the north by an allotment to the said William

50 Chamberlain the fences for inclosing this allotment on the south east against the said twenty eighth allotment on the west against the said thirty fourth allotment and on the north and west against the said twenty third allotment to the said William Lord Craven the said Commissioners do award order and direct shall be made and forever after maintained and repaired by the said William Lord Craven and the owners of this

55 allotment for the time being. **To and for the said William Lord Craven** in lieu of and as a just and full recompense satisfaction and equivalent for all such of his lands and grounds rights of common and other properties in and over the said fields and commonable lands by the said Act directed to be divided and allotted as were heretofore demised by the said Fulwar Lord Craven deceased to John Isles by lease

60 bearing date the first day of June one thousand seven hundred and forty two at the yearly reserved rent of one pound and seventeen shillings. **One plot** or parcel of land (being the twenty eight allotment to the said William Lord Craven) situate in Uffington Fields on the north or lower side of the said Ickleton Way containing fifty seven acres two roods and seven perches (exclusive of all roads and ways through and over the

65 same) bounded on the north east by the hamlet of Fawler on part of the east part of the south other part of the east other part of the south and on the west by the thirty fourth allotment to the said William Lord Craven and on the north west by the twenty seventh allotment to the said William Lord Craven the fences for inclosing this allotment on the east south and west against the said thirty fourth allotment the said Commissioners do

70 award order and direct shall be made and foreverafter maintained and repaired by the said William Lord Craven and the owners of this allotment for the time being. **To and for the said William Lord Craven** in lieu of and as a just and full recompense satisfaction and equivalent for all such of his lands and grounds rights of common and other properties in and over the said fields and commonable lands by the said Act

75 directed to be divided and allotted as were heretofore demised by the said Fulwar Lord Craven deceased to Mary Saunders by lease bearing date the ninth day of July one thousand seven hundred and fifty three at the yearly reserved rent of thirteen shillings and four pence. **One plot** or parcel of land (being the twenty ninth allotment to the said William Lord Craven) situate in Uffington Fields on the north or lower side of the said

80 Ickleton Way containing nine acres and three roods bounded on the north east by an allotment to the said Joseph Cook and the twenty third allotment to the said William Lord Craven on the south by an allotment to the said Vicar of Uffington exchanged with the said William Lord Craven as hereinafter mentioned on the west by the thirtieth allotment to the said William Lord Craven and on the north by an allotment to the said

95 William Lord Craven and James Mundy his lessee the fences for inclosing this allotment on the north east against the allotment to the said Joseph Cook and the said twenty third allotment to the said William Lord Craven on the south against the allotment to the said Vicar exchanged as aforesaid the said Commissioners do award order and direct shall be made and foreverafter maintained and repaired by the said William Lord

100 Craven and the owners of this allotment for the time being. **To and For the said**

LC28

LC29

William Lord Craven in lieu of and as a just and full recompense satisfaction and *101*
equivalent for all such of his lands and grounds rights of common and other properties
in and over the said fields and commonable lands by the said Act directed to be divided
and allotted as were heretofor demised by the said Fulwar Lord Craven deceased to
John Garrard by lease bearing date the tenth day of August one thousand seven hundred *105*
and fifty at the yearly reserved rent of fifteen shillings and eight pence. **One plot** or
parcel of land (being the thirtieth allotment to the said William Lord Craven) situate in
Uffington Fields on the north or lower side of Ickleton Way containing seventeen acres
one rood and twenty four perches (exclusive of all roads and ways through and over the
same) bounded on part of the east and part of the north by an allotment to the said *110*
William Lord Craven and James Mundy his lessee on the remaining part of the east by
the twenty ninth allotment to the said William Lord Craven on part of the south by an
allotment to the said Vicar of Uffington exchanged with the said William Lord Craven
and by an allotment to the said William Lord Craven and William Mundy his lessee on
part of the west and on the remaining part of the south by an allotment to the said John *115*
Archer on the remaining part of the west by several old inclosures at the town of
Uffington aforesaid and on the remaining part of the north by an allotment to the said
John Stallard and an allotment to the said William Lord Craven and Edward Warren his
lessee exchanged with the said William Lord Craven as hereinafter mentioned the
fences for inclosing this allotment on the east against the allotment to the said William *120*
Lord Craven and James Mundy his lessee on the east against the said twenty ninth
allotment to the said William Lord Craven on the south against the allotment to the
said Vicar of Uffington exchanged as aforesaid and against the allotment to the said
William Lord Craven and William Mundy and on the west against the allotment to the
said John Archer the said Commissioners do award order and direct shall be made and *125*
foreverafter maintained and repaired by the said William Lord Craven and the owners
of this allotment for the time being. **To and for the said William Lord Craven** over
and besides the said thirty several allotments hereinbefore described in lieu of and as a
just and full recompense satisfaction and equivalent for all such of his lands and grounds
rights of common and other properties in and over the said fields and commonable land *130*
within the said township of Uffington and hamlets of Balking and Woolston otherwise
Wolverston by the said Act directed to be divided and allotted as are not comprised in
any of the leases hereinbefore or hereinafter mentioned but which with the said several
lands grounds rights of common and other rights in lieu or in respect whereof the last
twenty nine of the said thirty allotments are hereinbefore awarded to the said William *135*
Lord Craven as aforesaid are now in the possession holding or occupation of the said
William Lord Craven his respective lessees or tenants rack rent. Nine several plots or
parcels of land **one plot** or parcel whereof (being the thirty first allotment to the said
William Lord Craven) situate in Uffington Fields on the north or lower side of
Ickleton Way containing five acres and eighteen perches (exclusive of all roads and ways *140*
through and over the same) bounded on the east by an allotment to

LC30

LC31

15 *1* **The said** William Lord Craven and James Mundy his lessee on the south by an allotment by the said William Lord Craven and Edward Warren his lessee exchanged as hereinafter mentioned on the north west by the Town Street of Uffington aforesaid and on the north by an old Inclosure belonging to *5* John Lockey. The fences for inclosing this allotment on the east against the allotment to the said William Lord Craven and James Mundy his lessee on the south against the allotment to the said William Lord Craven and Edward Warren exchanged as aforesaid and on the north west against the said Town Street the said Commissioners do award order and direct shall be made and foreverafter maintained and repaired by the said

LC32 *10* William Lord Craven and the owners of this allotment for the time being. **One other** of the said nine plots or parcels of land (being the thirty second allotment to the said William Lord Craven) is situate at a certain place called the Meadow Gate and being part of Uffington Common aforesaid containing one rood and twenty seven perches (exclusive of all roads and ways through and over the same) bounded on the east by a

15 close called Farm Close exchanged by the said William Lord Craven with the Vicar of Uffington and a public road or lane leading into the Town of Uffington aforesaid on the south south east and west by several old inclosures belonging to the said William Lord Craven and on the north by an allotment to the said Vicar of Uffington the fences for inclosing this allotment on the east across the said public road or lane and on the north

20 against the allotment to the said Vicar the said Commissioners do award order and direct and foreverafter maintained and repaired by the said William Lord Craven and

LC33 the owners of this allotment for the time being. **One other** of the said nine plots or parcels of land (being the thirty third allotment to the said William Lord Craven) is situate in Uffington Meadow aforesaid and contains twelve acres two roods and twenty

25 eight perches (exclusive of all roads and ways through and over the same) bounded on part of the north and on part of the east by the second allotment to the said William Lord Craven and on the remaining part of the east by an allotment to the said John Archer exchanged with the said William Lord Craven on the south the west and the remaining part of the north by the said old inclosed Farm belonging to the said William

30 Lord Craven in the occupation of Richard Geering the fences for inclosing this allotment the east against the said second allotment to the said William Lord Craven and against the said allotment to the said John Archer exchanged as aforesaid the said commissioners do award order and direct shall be made and foreverafter maintained and repaired by the said William Lord Craven and the owners of this allotment for the

LC34 *35* time being. **One other** of the said nine plots or parcels of land (being the thirty fourth allotment to the said William Lord Craven) is situate in Uffington Fields on the north or lower side of the said Ickleton Way and contains two hundred and fifteen acres two roods and thirty five perches (exclusive of all roads and ways through and over the same) bounded on the north east part of the east and on the south east by the hamlet of

40 Fawler on the south by Ickleton Way on part of the west and north west by land allotted to the said Vicar of Uffington on other part of the west by land allotted to the Trustees of Uffington School land on part of the north and other part of the west by other land allotted to the said Vicar of Uffington and exchanged by him with the said William Lord Craven on other part of the north by the twenty third allotment to the said William

45 Lord Craven on other part of the east by the twenty seventh allotment to the said

William Lord Craven on other part of the east other part of the north other part of the *46* west and the remaining part of the north and west by the twenty eighth allotment to the said William Lord Craven. The fences for inclosing this allotment on all parts against Fawler Fields and Ickleton Way on the west and north west against land allotted to the said Vicar of Uffington on the west against the allotment to the said Trustees of *50* Uffington School land on the north and west against land allotted to the said Vicar of Uffington exchanged as aforesaid and on the north against the said twenty third allotment to the said William Lord Craven the Commissioners do award order and direct shall be made and foreverafter maintained and repaired by the said William Lord Craven and the owners of this allotment for the time being. **One other** of the said nine *55* **LC35** plots or parcels of land (being the thirty fifth allotment to the said William Lord Craven) is situate in Uffington Fields on the south or upper side of the said Ickleton Way containing one hundred and eighty one acres three roods and twenty perches (exclusive of all roads and ways through and over the same) bounded on part of the east by fields in the hamlet of Fawler aforesaid on part of the south other part of the east part of the *60* north and part of the east by part of the said Several Farm belonging to the said William Lord Craven on other part of the south by land allotted to the said John Archer on several parts of the west north and south by other part of the said Several Farm on part of the north west by other land allotted to the said John Archer on other part of the north by Ickleton Way on the remaining several parts of the east on the south east other *65* parts of the north on the north west and remaining part of the west by other part of the said Several Farm and on the remaining part of the north by Ickleton Way which allotment lastly described surrounded and totally circumscribes the said public stone pit in Uffington. The boundaries for ascertaining this allotment on the east against Fawler Fields and on the south against the several allotment to the said John Archer and on all *70* parts against the said public stone pit the said Commissioners do award order and direct shall be made and foreverafter maintained and repaired by the said William Lord Craven and the owners of this allotment for the time being. One **other** of the said nine plots or **LC36** parcels of land (being the thirty sixth allotment to the said William Lord Craven) situate in Uffington Fields and Downs on the south or upper side of Ickleton way containing *75* one hundred and sixty one acres one rood and twenty two perches (exclusive of all roads and ways through and over the same) bounded on the north east and part of the north by part of the said Several Farm in the occupation of Joseph Lousley on the east by Kingston Warren Farm on a small part of a south by Lambourn Fields on the south West and west by other part of the said Several Farm and on the north by land allotted to the *80* said John Archer exchanged with the said William Lord Craven. **One other** of the said **LC37** nine plots or parcels of land (being the thirty seventh allotment to the said William Lord Craven) and on which are marked out the figure and form or representation of a horse, commonly called The White Horse and of a castle near to the same is situate in Woolston Down and contains twenty four acres two roods and thirty five perches *95* (exclusive of all roads and ways through and over the same) bounded on the east and south east by part of the said Several Farm in the occupation of Joseph Lousley and on the south the west the north west and north by the second [third?] allotment to the said John Archer which said allotment lastly described is by the said Act declared to be forever hereafter deemed and considered as within and part of the Manor of Uffington *100*

LC38

101 and in lieu whereof the said Commissioners have hereinafter described so much of the land belonging to the said William Lord Craven within the Manor and township of Uffington now in the occupation of Joseph Lousley as in the judgement of the said Commissioners is equivalent thereto and which by the said Act is declared to be forever

105 hereafter deemed and considered as lying within and part of the Manor of Woolston otherwise Wolverstone aforesaid. **One other** of the said nine plots or parcels of land (being the thirty eighth allotment to the William Lord Craven) is situate in Old Field in the hamlet of Balking aforesaid and contains eighty three acres three roods and eleven perches (exclusive of all roads and ways through and over the same) bounded on the

110 east by an allotment to the said Abraham Atkins hereinafter exchanged with the said William Lord Craven on part of the south by an allotment to the said Robert Leaver exchanged with the said William Lord Craven and an allotment to the said Provost and Scholars of Queens College and the said Philip Brown their lessee on part of the west and other part of the south by an allotment to the said Provost and Scholars of Queens

115 College and the said Trustees of Robert Fettiplace their lessees on other part of the south by the next allotment hereinafter awarded to the said William Lord Craven exchanged with the said Trustees of Robert Fettiplace as hereinafter mentioned on other part of the west and the remaining part of the south by several old inclosures within the hamlet of Baulking on the remaining part of the west by an allotment to the said Edward

120 Thornhill and Collier his wife and on the north by the Lordship of Standford the fences for inclosing this allotment on the east against the allotment to the said Abraham Atkins exchanged as aforesaid on the south against the allotment to the said Robert Leaver and the allotment to the said Provost and Scholars of the said Trustees of Robert Fettiplace and against the said allotment to the said William Lord Craven exchanged with the said

125 Trustees and on the north against the Lordship of Standford in such parts and places as have usually been or of right ought to have been maintained and repaired by the owners and occupiers of lands and commons in Old Field aforesaid the said Commissioners do award order and direct shall be made and foreverafter maintained and repaired by the said William Lord Craven and owners of this allotment for the time being. And the

LC39

130 **other** of the said nine plots or parcels of land (being the thirty ninth allotment to the said William Lord Craven) is situate in Old Field containing one rood and twenty three perches bounded on the east by an allotment to the said Provost and Scholars of Queens College and the Trustees of the said Robert Fettiplace their lessee on the south by an allotment to the said Trustees of Robert Fettiplace on the west by old inclosures in the

135 hamlet of Balking aforesaid and on the north by the thirty eighth allotment to the said William Lord Craven which allotment last hereinbefore described is exchanged with the said Trustees of Robert Fettiplace for land in the hamlet of Kingstone Lisle as hereinafter mentioned. **To and for the said William Lord Craven and George Reade** his lessee according to their respective estates and interests in the premises comprised in a certain

140 Indenture of lease being date the twenty ninth day of September one thousand seven hundred and sixty eight and made between the late Right Honourable William Lord Craven deceased of the one part and the said George Reade of the other part purporting to be a lease for ninety nine years determinable on three lives and as a just and full recompense satisfaction and equivalent for all the lands grounds rights of

16

Common and other properties in the said fields and commonable lands which are comprised in the same Lease. **One plot** or parcel of land situate in Old Field aforesaid containing two acres one rood and seven perches bounded on the east by an allotment to the Dean and Chapter of Westminster and John Morest their lessee on the south and west by old inclosures in the hamlet of Balking and on the north and north east by an allotment to the said Edward Thornhill and Collier his wife the fences for inclosing this allotment on the east against the allotment to the said Dean and Chapter and their said Lessee and on the north and north east against the allotment to the said Edward Thornhill and Collier his wife the said Commissioners do award order and direct shall be made and during the continuance of the said lease maintained and repaired by the said George Reade and after the determination of such Lease the said fences shall belong to and be forever maintained and repaired by the said William Lord Craven and the owners of this allotment for the time being **To and for the said William Lord Craven and Robert Quarme Esquire** his lessee according to their respective estates and interests in the premises comprised in a certain Indenture of Lease bearing date the twenty ninth day of September one thousand seven hundred and sixty eight and made between the said late Right Honourable William Lord Craven deceased of the one part and the said Robert Quarme of the other part purporting to be a lease for ninety nine years determinable on three lives and as a just and full recompense satisfaction and equivalent for all the lands grounds rights of common and other properties in the said fields and commonable lands which are comprised in the same Lease. **One Plot** or parcel of land situate in Old Field aforesaid containing eleven acres three roods and eighteen perches (exclusive of all roads and ways through and over the same) bounded on the east by the second allotment to the said John Hippesley on the south by a public road and on the west and north by land allotted to the said Abraham Atkins and hereinafter exchanged with the said William Lord Craven the fences for inclosing this allotment on the east against the said allotment to the said John Hippesley and on the south against the said public road the said Commissioners do award order and direct shall be made and during the continuance of the said Lease maintained and repaired by the said Robert Quarme and after the determination of the said lease the said fences shall belong to and be maintained and repaired by the said William Lord Craven and the owners of this allotment for the time being. **To and for the said William Lord Craven and Angel Lockey** his lessee according to their respective estates and interests in the premises comprised in a certain Indenture of Lease bearing date the twentieth day of June one thousand seven hundred and fifty four and made between the said Fulwar Lord Craven deceased of the one part and John Lockey since deceased of the other part purporting to be a lease for ninety nine years (determinable on lives) and as a just and full recompense satisfaction and equivalent for all the lands and grounds rights of common and other properties in the said fields and commonable lands which are comprised in the same lease. **One plot** or parcel of land situate in Uffington Meadow aforesaid containing four acres two roods and two perches bounded on a small part of the east by a lane called Moor Mill Lane on part of the south east and remaining part of the east by old inclosures called Moor Mill Closes belonging to the said William Lord Craven and the said Angel Lockey his lessee on the south west by the ninth allotment to the said William Lord Craven on the north west and part of the north by the tenth allotment to the said William Lord Craven and on the

1

LC/GR

5

10

15

20

LC/RQ

25

30

35

LC/AL

40

45

46 remaining part of the north by the eleventh allotment to the said William Lord Craven the fences inclosing this allotment on the east against the said Moor Mill Lane on the north west and north against the said tenth allotment and on the north against the said eleventh allotment to the said William Lord Craven the said Commissioners do award order and

50 direct shall be made and during the continuance of the said lease maintained and repaired by the said Angel Lockey and after the determination of the said lease such fences shall belong to and be maintained and repaired by the said William Lord Craven and owners of this allotment for the time being. **To and for the said William Lord Craven and Richard Hinchman** his Lessee according to their respective estates and interests in the premises

55 comprised in a certain Indenture of Lease bearing date the ninth day of June one thousand seven hundred and fifty three and made between the said Fulwar Lord Craven deceased of the one part and the said Richard Hinchman of the other part purporting to be a lease for ninety nine years (determinable on lives) and as a just and full recompense satisfaction and equivalent for all the lands and grounds rights or common and other properties in the

LC/RH   *60* said fields and commonable lands which are comprised in the same lease. **One Plot** or parcel of land situate in Uffington Common aforesaid containing three acres and twelve perches bounded on the north east by an allotment to the said William Lord Craven and John Stallard his lessee on the south east by an allotment to the said William Lord Craven and Edmund Cook his lessee on the south west by an allotment to the said William Lord

65 Craven and Joseph Dickson his lessee and on the north west by the said twentieth allotment to the said William Lord Craven the fences for inclosing this allotment on the south west against the allotment to the said William Lord Craven and Joseph Dickson and on the north west against the said twentieth allotment to the said William Lord Craven the said Commissioners do award order and direct shall be made and during the continuance of

70 the said lease maintained and repaired by the said Richard Hinchman and after the determination of the said lease such fences shall belong to and be forever maintained and repaired by the said William Lord Craven and the owners of this allotment for the time being. **To and for the said William Lord Craven and Joseph Dickson** his lessee according to their respective estates and interests in the premises comprised in a certain

75 indenture of lease bearing date the thirtieth day of April one thousand seven hundred and forty eight and made between the said Fulwar Lord Craven deceased of the one part and William Stallard of the other part purporting to be a lease for ninety nine years (determinable on lives) and as a just and full recompense satisfaction and equivalent for all the lands grounds rights of common and other properties in and over the said fields and commonable

LC/JD   *80* lands which are comprised in the same lease. **One Plot** or parcel of land situate in Uffington Common aforesaid containing one acre three roods and twenty eight perches bounded on the north east by an allotment to the said William Lord Craven and the said Richard Hinchman his lessee on the south east by an allotment to the said William Lord Craven and Edmund Cook his lessee on the south west by an allotment to the said William Lord

95 Craven and Charles Young and Sarah his wife and Mary Allen his lessees and on the north west by the said twentieth allotment to the said William Lord Craven the fences for inclosing this allotment on the south west against the allotment to the said William Lord Craven and the said Charles Young and Sarah his wife and Mary Allen his lessee and on the north west against the said twentieth allotment to the said William Lord Craven the

100 said commissioners do award and direct shall be made and during the continuance of the

said lease maintained and repaired by the said Joseph Dickson and after the determination *101*
of the said lease such fences shall belong to and be forever maintained and repaired by the
said William Lord Craven and the owners of this allotment fot the time being. **To and for**
the said William Lord Craven and Charles Young and Sarah his Wife and Mary Allen
his lessees according to their respective estates and interests in the premises comprised in *105*
a certain Indenture of lease bearing date the fourteenth day of March one thousand seven
hundred and forty four and made between the said Fulwar Lord Craven deceased of the
one part and the said Joseph Cook of the other part purporting to be a lease for ninety nine
years (determinable on lives) and as a just and full recompense satisfaction and equivalent
for all the lands grounds rights of common and other properties in the said fields and *110*
commonable lands which are comprised in the same lease. **One plot** or parcel of land   *LC/CY*
situate in Uffington Common aforesaid containing two acres three roods and twenty five
perches (exclusive of all roads and ways through and over the same) bounded on the north
east by an allotment to the said William Lord Craven and the said Joseph Dickson his
lessee on the south east by an allotment to the said William Lord Craven and Edmund *115*
Cook his lessee on the south west by a public road from Uffingon to Fawler and by the
twenty first allotment to the said William Lord Craven and on the north west by the
twentieth allotment to the said William Lord Craven the fences for inclosing this allotment
on the south west against the said public road and the said twenty first allotment and on
the north west against the said twentieth allotment to the said William Lord Craven the *120*
said Commissioners do award order and direct shall be made and during the continuance
of the said lease maintained and repaired by the said Charles Young and Sarah his wife and
Mary Allen and after the determination of the said lease such fences shall belong to and be
forever maintained and repaired by the said William Lord Craven and the owners of this
allotment for the time being. **To and for the said William Lord Craven and John Stallard** *125*
his lessee according to their respective estates and interests in the premises comprised in
a certain Indenture of lease bearing date the fourteenth day of March one thousand seven
hundred and forty four and made between the said Fulwar Lord Craven deceased of the
one part and Jonathan Stallard since deceased of the other part purporting to be a lease for
ninety nine years (determinable on lives) as a just and full recompense satisfaction and *130*
equivalent for all the lands grounds rights of common and other properties in the said
fields and commonable lands which are comprised in the same lease. **One Plot**   *LC/JS*
or parcel of land situate in Uffington Common aforesaid containing ten acres three roods
and thirty perches bounded on the north east by the nineteenth and seventeenth allotments
to the said William Lord Craven and on the south east by the twenty fifth allotment to the *135*
said William Lord Craven on the south west by an allotment to the said William Lord
Craven and Edmund Cook his lessee and an allotment to the said William Lord Craven
and Richard Hinchman his lessee and on the north west by the said twentieth
allotment to the said William Lord Craven. The fences for inclosing this allotment on the
south west against the allotments to the said William Lord Craven and Edmund Cook and *140*
the allotment to the said William Lord Craven and Richard Hinchman and on the north
west against the said twentieth allotment to the said William Lord Craven
the said Commissioners do award order and direct shall be made and during the
continuance of the said lease maintained and repaired by the said John Stallard and after
the determination thereof such fences shall belong and be forever maintained and *145*

17

1 **Repaired** by the said William Lord Craven and the owners of this allotment for the time being. **To and for the said William Lord Craven and Edmund Cook** his lessee according to their respective estates and interests in certain parts of the premises comprised in one indenture of lease bearing
5 date of the fourteenth day of March one thousand seven hundred and forty four and made between the said Fulwar Lord Craven deceased of the one part and Henry Cook also deceased of the other part purporting to be a lease of another estate called Stamps for ninety nine years (determinable on lives) and as a just and full recompense satisfaction and equivalent for such of the lands and grounds rights of common and other properties
10 in and over the said fields and commonable lands by the said Act directed to be divided and allotted as belong to and are now or at the time of passing of the said Act were vested in the said Edmund Cook by virtue of or under the said Lease. **One plot** or parcel of land situate in Uffington Common aforesaid containing four acres one rood and twenty three perches (exclusive of all roads and ways through and over the same) bounded on the
15 north east by an allotment to the said William Lord Craven and John Stallard his lessee on the south east by an allotment to the said William Lord Craven and Edmund Cook for an estate known by the name of Sanders on the South west by a public road and on the north west by an allotment to the said William Lord Craven and the said Charles Young and Sarah his wife and Mary Allen an allotment to the said William Lord Craven
20 and Joseph Dickson and an allotment to the said William Lord Craven and Richard Hinchman the fences for inclosing this allotment on the south west against the said public road and on the north west against the allotment to the said William Lord Craven and the said Charles Young and Sarah his wife and Mary Allen and the said Joseph Dixon and Richard Hinchman respectively the said Commissioners do award order and direct
25 shall be made and during the continuance of the said Lease maintained and repaired by the said Edmund Cook and after the determination of the said Lease such fences shall belong to and be forever maintained and repaired by the said William Lord Craven and the owners of this allotment for the time being. **To and for the said William Lord Craven** and the said **Edmund Cook** his lessee according to their respective estates and
30 interests in certain parts of the premises comprised in one Indenture of lease bearing date the thirtieth day of March one thousand seven hundred and fifty six and made between the said Fulwar Lord Craven deceased of the one part and the said Henry Cook also deceased of the other part purporting to be a lease of an estate called Sanders for ninety nine years (determinable on lives) and as a just and full recompense satisfaction
35 and equivalent for the said lands and grounds rights of common and other properties in and over the said fields and commonable lands by the said Act directed to be divided and allotted as belong to and are now or at the time of passing the said Act were vested in the said Edmund Cook by virtue or under the said lease. **One plot** or parcel of land situate in Uffington Common aforesaid containing eight acres one rood and five perches (exclusive
40 of all roads and ways through and over the same) bounded on the north east by an allotment to the said William Lord Craven and John Stallard his lessee on the south east by the twenty fourth allotment to the said William Lord Craven on the south west by a public road and on the north west by an allotment last hereinbefore awarded to the said William Lord Craven and the said Edmund Cook the fences for inclosing this allotment
45 on the south west against the said public road and on the north west against the said

LC/EC1

LC/EC2

allotment to the said William Lord Craven and Edmund Cook the said Commissioners *46*
do award order and direct shall be made and during the continuance of the said lease
maintained and repaired by Edmund Cook and after the determination of the said lease
such fences shall belong to and be forever maintained and repaired by the said William
Lord Craven and the owners of this allotment for the time being **To and For the said** *50*
William Lord Craven and James Mundy his lessee according to their respective estates
and interests in the premises comprised in a certain Indenture of lease bearing date the
twenty first day of May one thousand seven hundred and forty eight and made between
the said William Lord Craven deceased of the one part and William Mundy since
deceased of the other part purporting to be a lease for ninety nine years (determinable *55*
on lives) and as a just and full recompense satisfaction and equivalent for all the lands
grounds rights of common and other properties in the said fields and commonable lands
which are comprised in the same lease. **One plot** or parcel of land situate in Uffington   *LC/JMY*
Fields on the north or lower side of Ickleton Way containing twelve acres one rood and
six perches (exclusive of all roads and ways through and over the same) bounded on the *60*
east to allotments to the said Elizabeth Hoar the said Charles Young and Sarah his wife
and Mary Allen the said Lawrence Woodroffe and the said Joseph Cook respectively on
part of the south by the twenty ninth allotment to the said William Lord Craven on the
remaining part of the south and on part of the west by the thirtieth allotment to the said
William Lord Craven and on the remaining part of the west by an allotment to the said *65*
William Lord Craven and Edward Warren his Lessee exchanged with the said William
Lord Craven by the thirty first allotment to the said William Lord Craven and by several
homesteads and inclosures at the town of Uffington aforesaid and on the north by an
allotment to the said James Mundy the fences for inclosing this allotment on the east
against the several allotments to the said Elizabeth Hoar Charles Young and Sarah his *70*
wife and Mary Allen Lawrence Woodroffe and Joseph Cook respectively and on the
south against the said twenty ninth and thirtieth allotments to the said William Lord
Craven the said Commissioners do award order and direct shall be made and during the
continuance of the said Lease maintained and repaired by the said James Mundy and
after the determination of the said Lease such fences shall belong to and be forever *75*
maintained and repaired by the said William Lord Craven and the owners of this
allotment for the time being. **To and For the said William Lord Craven and William**
Mundy his Lessee according to their respective estates and interests in the premises
comprised in a certain Indenture of Lease bearing date the fourteenth day of March one
thousand seven hundred and thirty eight and made between the said William Lord *80*
Craven deceased of the one part and the said William Mundy deceased of the other part
purporting to be a lease for ninety nine years (determinable on lives) and as a just and
full recompense satisfaction and equivalent for all the lands grounds rights of common
and other properties in the said fields and commonable lands which are comprised in the
same lease. **One plot** or parcel of land situate in Uffington Fields on the north or lower *95*   *LC/WM*
side of Ickleton Way containing nine acres one rood and thirty nine perches (exclusive of
all roads and ways through and over the same) bounded on the east by an allotment to
the said Vicar of Uffington exchanged with the said William Lord Craven on the south by
an allotment to the said William Lord Craven and Edward Warren his Lessee on the west
by land allotted to the said John Archer and on the north by the thirtieth allotment to the *100*

101 said William Lord Craven the fences for inclosing this allotment on the south against the allotment to the said William Lord Craven and Edward Warren and on the west against land allotted to the said John Archer the said Commissioners do award order and direct shall be made and during the continuance of the said lease maintained and repaired by *105* the said William Mundy and after the determination of the said lease such fences shall belong to and be forever maintained and repaired by the said William Lord Craven and the owners of this allotment for the time being **To and for the said William Lord Craven and Edward Warren** his Lessee according to their respective estates and interests in the premises comprised in a certain Indenture of lease bearing date the first day of *110* February one thousand seven hundred and fifty three and made between the said Fulwar Lord Craven deceased of the one part and the said Edward Warren of the other part purporting to be a lease for ninety nine years (determinable on lives) and as a just and full recompense satisfaction and equivalent for all the lands grounds rights of common and other properties in the said fields and commonable lands which are comprised in the

LC/EW1 *115* same lease. Two plots or parcels of land **one plot** or parcel whereof is situate in Uffington Fields on the north or lower side of Ickleton Way aforesaid and contains sixteen acres two roods and ten perches (exclusive of all roads and ways through and over the same) bounded on the east by land allotted to the said Vicar of Uffington exchanged by him with the said William Lord Craven on the south by the allotment to the Trustees for *120* Uffington School Land on the west by land allotted to the said John Archer and on the north by an allottment to the said William Lord Craven and the said William Mundy his lessee. The fences for inclosing this allotment on the south against the allotment to the Trustees of Uffington School Land and on the west against land allotted to the said John Archer the said Commissioners do award order and direct shall be made and during the *125* continuance of the said lease maintained and repaired by the said Edward Warren and after the determination of the said lease such fences shall belong to and be for ever maintained and repaired by the said William Lord Craven and the owners of the allotment

LC/EW2 for the time being. And the other of the said **two plots** or parcels of land is also situate in Uffington fields on the north or lower side of Ickleton Way aforesaid contained four acres *130* one rood and one perch (exclusive of all roads and ways through and over the same) bounded on the east by an allotment to the said William Lord Craven and the said James Mundy his lessee on part of the south by the thirtieth allotment to the said William Lord Craven on the remaining part of the west and the remaining part of the south by an allotment to John Stallard exchanged with the said William Lord Craven as hereinafter *135* mentioned on the remaining part of the west by the Town street of Uffington aforesaid and on the north by the thirty first allotment to the said William Lord Craven which allotment last hereinbefore described is exchanged by the said Edward Warren with the said William Lord Craven as hereinafter mentioned. The fences for inclosing this allotment on the east against the allotment to the said William Lord Craven and the said *140* James Mundy his lessee on the south against the said thirtieth allotment to the said William Lord Craven and on the west and south against the said allotment to the said John Stallard and on the west against the said Town street of Uffington the said Commissioners do award order and direct shall be made and for ever after

18

Maintained and repaired by the said William Lord Craven on his taking the same in exchange and the owners of this allotment for the time being. **To and for the said Earl Spencer** in lieu of and as a just and full recompense satisfaction and equivalent for all his lands grounds rights of common and other properties in and upon the said fields and commonable lands by the said Act directed to be divided and allotted. **One plot** or parcel of land situate in a certain meadow called Bagmoor within the hamlet of Baulking aforesaid containing seven acres three roods and twenty seven perches bounded on part of the north by the Lordship of Shillingford on the east and another part of the north by land allotted to the Presbyterian Society of Wantage and on the south by old inclosures in the hamlet of Baulking. The fences for inclosing this allotment against the said land allotted to the said Presbyterian Society the said commissioners do award order and direct shall be made and forever after maintained and repaired by the said Earl Spencer and the owners of this allotment for the time being. **To and for the said Bartholomew Tipping** in lieu of and as a just and full recompense satisfaction for all the lands and grounds rights of common and other properties over and upon the said fields and commonable lands by the said act directed to be divided and allotted over and besides the allotment herein before awarded to the said Bartholomew Tipping as Lord of the Manor of Woolston. (A deduction being first made and added to and comprised in the allotment to the said provost and scholars of Queens College and the said John Williams Willaume and Abraham Chambers trustees of the estate of the said Robert Fettiplace as lessees of the said college for their rights to the feeding and pasturing of one oxon from Whitsun to the feast of Saint Michael the Archangel yearly in a certain pasture ground called the Oxlease in Woolston otherwise Woolverston now in the occupation of James Mattingly as lessee of the said Bartholomew Tipping according to the direction of the said Act). **Six Plots** or parcels of land. **One plot** of parcel whereof (being the second allotment to the said Bartholomew Tipping) is situate in Woolston meadow containing thirteen acres two roods and one perch bounded on the east and south by an inclosed farm belonging to the said Bartholomew Tipping now in the occupation of James Mattingly on the west by land allotted to the said Lovelace Bigg and on the north by an allotment to the said Lovelace Bigg exchanged with the said Bartholomew Tipping as herein after mentioned. The fences for inclosing this allotment on the west against land allotted to the said Lovelace Bigg the said commissioners do award order and direct shall be made and for ever after maintained and repaired by the said Bartholomew Tipping and the owners of this allotment for the time being. **One other** of the said six plots or parcels of land (being the third allotment to the said Bartholomew Tipping is situate in Woolston fields on the north or lower side of Ickleton Way and contains twenty one acres and fourteen perches (exclusive of all roads and ways through and over the same) bounded on the east by land allotted to the said Jeffry Church and John Archer respectively on part of the south by a public stone pit on the south west and remaining part of the south by Ickleton Way on the west by an allotment to the said Lovelace Bigg on the north by the first allotment to the said Bartholomew Tipping as Lord of the Manor of Woolston and by an inclosure belonging to the said Bartholomew Tipping. The fences for inclosing this allotment on the east against land allotted to the said Jeffry Church and the said John Archer respectively on the south against the said public stone pit and on the south west and south against Ickleton Way the said

1

5   *SPEN*

10

15

20

25   *BT2*

30

BT3

35

40

45

46 commissioners do award order and direct shall be made and for ever after maintained and repaired by the said Bartholomew Tipping and the owners of this allotment for the time

BT4 being. One **other** of the said six plots or parcels of land (being the fourth allotment to the said Bartholomew Tipping) is situate in Woolston fields on the south or upper side of the

50 said Ickleton Way and contains one hundred and forty six acres one rood and thirty four perches (exclusive of all roads and ways through and over the same) bounded on part of the east on the south east on other part of the east part of the north other part of the east and on other part of the north by land allotted to the said John Archer on the remaining several parts of the east on several parts of the south and on the remaining part of the

55 south east by a Several Down belonging to the said Bartholomew Tipping on part of the west and on the remaining part of the south by an allotment to the said William Thatcher on other part of the west by an allotment to the said Lovelace Bigg on other part of the north and on the remaining part of the west by a public stone pit on the north west by other land allotted to the said Lovelace Bigg and on the remaining part of the north and

60 on the north east by Ickleton Way. The boundaries for ascertaining this allotment against the allotment to the said John Archer and against the said public stone pit the said commissioners do award order and direct shall be made and for ever after maintained and repaired by the said Bartholomew Tipping and the owners of this allotment for the time

BT5 being. One **other** of the said six plots or parcels of land (being the fifth allotment to the

65 said Bartholomew Tipping) is situate in Woolston Downs and contains twenty eight acres two roods and ten perches (exclusive of all roads and ways through and over the same) bounded on the north east by the said Several Downs belonging to the said Bartholomew Tipping on the south east and south west by Lamborne fields and downs and on the north west by land allotted to the said Lovelace Bigg. The boundaries for

70 ascertaining this allotment on the south east and south west against the said common fields and downs the said commissioners do award order and direct shall be made and for ever after maintained and repaired by the said Bartholomew Tipping and the owners of

BT6 this allotment for the time being. **One other** of the said six plots or parcels of land (being the sixth allotment to the said Bartholomew Tipping) is situate in Woolston fields on the

75 north or lower side of Ickleton Way and contains three acres two roods and thirteen perches bounded on the east by an allotment to the said Lovelace Bigg exchanged with the said Jeffry Church on the south by land allotted to the said Jeffry Church on the west by an old inclosure belonging to the said Lovelace Bigg also exchanged with the said Jeffry Church and on the north by land allotted to the said Jeffry Church which said plot

80 or parcel of land last therein before described is herein after exchanged by the said

BT7 Bartholomew Tipping with the said Jeffry Church. And the **other** of the said six plots or parcels of land (being the seventh allotment to the said Bartholomew Tipping) is situate in Woolston fields on the north or lower side of the said Ickleton Way and containing two roods and six perches (exclusive of all roads and ways through and over the same)

95 bounded on the east by an allotment to the said William Thatcher on the south and west by an allotment to the said Joseph Mayon and on the north by an allotment to the said Jeffry Church exchanged with the said Joseph Mayon (which said allotment last herein before described is herein after exchanged by the said Bartholomew Tipping with the said Joseph Mayon.) **To and for the said Lovelace Bigg** in lieu of and as a just and full

100 recompense satisfaction and equivalent for all his lands and grounds rights of common

and other properties in over and upon the said fields and commonable lands by the said *101*
act directed to be divided and allotted (as well as those which he had in his own right at
the time of passing the said act as those which he hath since purchased of Sir William
Guise Baronet). **Seven Plots** or parcels of land **one plot** or parcel whereof is situate in   *LB1*
Woolston Meadow Woolston Common and Woolston Fields below Ickleton Way and   *105*
contains one hundred and ninety six acres and twenty perches (exclusive of all roads and
ways through and over the same) bounded on part of the east by an inclosed farm
belonging to the said Bartholomew Tipping on part of the south and on other part of the
east by another allotment to the said Lovelace Bigg exchanged with the said Bartholomew
Tipping as herein after mentioned on other part of the east by the second allotment to the   *110*
said Bartholomew Tipping by other part of the said inclosed farm belonging to the said
Bartholomew Tipping and by a certain lane called Claypit Lane leading towards the town
of Uffington on other part of the east and part of the north by old inclosures in Woolston
on other part of the east other part of the south other part of the east and on other part of
the north by an allotment to the provost and scholars of Queens College and the said   *115*
trustees of the estate of the said Robert Fettiplace on the remaining part of the east by old
inclosures and the homestead belonging to the said Lovelace Bigg and by a lane in the
village of Woolston on other part of the south by an allotment to William Thatcher on
other part of the south and on part of the west by an allotment to the said Joseph Mayon
on the other part of the west by an allotment to the said Jeffry Church and by an allotment   *120*
to the said Vicar of Uffington on other part of the north other part of the west and part of
the south east by an old inclosure called Middle Several on the remaining small part of the
south east by other part of the said allotment to the said vicar of Uffington on other part
of the west and on the remaining part of the south by other part of the said allotment to
the said Jeffry Church on other part of the west by the Lordship of Knighton and on the   *125*
remaining parts of the west and north by the common fields of Longcot which said last
described allotment surrounds and totally circumscribes three small old inclosures lying
together known by the name of Three pence a Week and the Sheep House Bartons (which
are exchanged by the former owners thereof with the said Lovelace Bigg). The fences for
inclosing the same allotment on such parts of the east against the inclosed farm belonging   *130*
to the said Bartholomew Tipping as have usually been or of right ought to have been
maintained and repaired by the owners and occupiers of land and common rights in the
common fields of Woolston aforesaid in that part of the east against the allotment to the
said provost and scholars of Queens College and the Trustees of the estate of Robert
Fettiplace which extends across a certain piece of ground called the Drove on the south   *135*
against the said allotment to the said provost and scholars of Queens College and the said
Trustees of Robert Fettiplace their lessees on the east across the said lane in the village of
Woolstone on the south against the allotment to the said William Thatcher

1

19 **On the South** and west against the allotment to the said Joseph Mayon so far as this allotment extends northward on the said Woolston Fields on the west and south east against the allotment to the said Vicar of Uffington on the west and south against the allotment to the said Jeffrey Church on the west against

5 the said Lordship of Knighton and on the west and north against the said common fields of Longcot aforesaid the said commissioners do award order and direct shall be made and foreverafter maintained and repaired by the said Lovelace Bigg and the owners of this allotment for the time being. **One other** of the said seven plots or parcels of land being the second allotment to the said Lovelace Bigg is situate in Woolston fields on the

10 north or lower side of Ickleton Way and contains seventeen acres two roods and two perches (exclusive of all roads and ways through and over the same) bounded on the east and south by land allotted to the said John Archer on the west by several old inclosures and by lane leading into the village of Woolston and on the north by an allotment to the said provost and scholars of Queens College and the said Trustees of the Estate of Robert

15 Fettiplace the fences for inclosing this allotment on the east and south against land allotted to the said John Archer and on the west across the said lane the said Commissioners do award order and direct shall be made and foreverafter maintained and repaired by the said Lovelace Bigg and the owners of the allotment for the time being. **One other** of the said seven plots or parcels of land being the third allotment to the said Lovelace Bigg is

20 likewise situate in the fields of Woolston on the north or lower side of the said Ickleton Way and contains forty one acres two roods and thirty two perches (exclusive of all roads and ways through and over the same) bounded on several parts of the east part of the south and part of the north by several old inclosures belonging to the said Lovelace Bigg on the remaining part of the east by land allotted to the said Bartholomew Tipping on the

25 south by Ickleton Way on the west by a farm called Hardwell Farm in the township of Uffington and on the north by an allotment to the said Joseph Mayon the fences for inclosing this allotment on the east against land allotted to the said Bartholomew Tipping on the south against Ickleton Way and on a small part of the north against the allotment to Joseph Mayon across a private road hereinafter described the said Commissioners do

30 award order and direct shall be made and foreverafter maintained and repaired by the said Lovelace Bigg and the owners of this allotment for the time being. **One other** of the said seven plots or parcels of land (being the fourth allotment to the said Lovelace Bigg) is situate in Woolston Fields and Downs on the south or upper side of the said Ickleton Way and contains three hundred and eighty four acres and twenty perches (exclusive of

35 all roads and ways through and over the same) bounded on part of the south east by an allotment to the said Bartholomew Tipping and by other part of the south east and east by a public stonepit in Woolston on other part of the east by other part of said allotment to the said Bartholomew Tipping on other part of the east by an allotment to the said William Thatcher on part of the south other part of the east other part of the south other

40 part of the east and on part of the north by an old Inclosure called Botty Barn belonging to the said Bartholomew Tipping and exchanged by him by the said Lovelace Bigg as hereinafter mentioned on other part of the east and on other part of the north by other part of the said allotment to the said William Thatcher on the remaining part of the east and on small parts of the south and north by the said Several Down belonging to the said

45 Bartholomew Tipping on other part of the south by the fifth allotment to the said

LB2

LB3

LB4

Bartholomew Tipping on a small part of the west by Lambourne Downs on other part of   *46*
the west other part of the south on the south west and on other part of the west by the
Lordship of Knighton on the remaining several parts of the west and south and on several
parts of the north by Hardwell Farm aforesaid and on the remaining part of the north by
Ickleton Way the boundaries for ascertaining this allotment on the south east against the   *50*
said allotment to the said Bartholomew Tipping on the south east and east against the
public stonepit on the east against the allotment to the said Bartholomew Tipping on the
east and north against the said allotment to the said William Thatcher on the south
against the said fifth allotment to the said Bartholomew Tipping and on such parts against
the said Lambourne Downs and on the said Lordship of Knighton and Hardwell Farm as   *55*
have usually been or of right ought to have been made and maintained by the owners and
occupiers of lands and commons in the hamlet of Woolston the said commissioners do
award order and direct shall be made and foreverafter maintained and repaired by the
said Lovelace Bigg and the owners of this allotment for the time being. **One other** of the   *LB5*
said seven plots or parcels of land (being the fifth allotment to the said Lovelace Bigg) is   *60*
situate in Woolston Fields on the north or lower side of the said Ickleton Way and
contains two acres and thirty five perches bounded on the south by land allotted to the
said Jeffrey Church on the west by an allotment to the said Bartholomew Tipping
exchanged by him with the said Jeffrey Church and on the north and east by an allotment
to the said John Archer which said allotment last hereinbefore awarded to the said   *65*
Lovelace Bigg is hereinafter exchanged by him with the said Jeffrrey Church. The fences
for inclosing the same allotment on the east against the said John Archer's allotment the
said Commissioners do award order and direct shall be made and foreverafter maintained
and repaired by the said Jeffrey Church on his taking the same in exchange and the
owners of the same allotment for the time being. **One other** of the said seven plots or   *70* *LB6*
parcels of land (being the sixth allotment to the said Lovelace Bigg) is situate in Woolston
fields aforesaid on the north or lower side of the said Ickleton Way and contains three
roods and twenty eight perches (exclusive of all roads and ways through and over the
same) bounded on the north and east by an allotment to the said William Thatcher on
the south by an allotment to the said Jeffrey Church exchanged with the said Joseph   *75*
Mayon and on the west by an allotment to the said Joseph Mayon which said allotment
last hereinbefore described is hereinafter exchanged by the said Lovelace Bigg with the
said Joseph Mayon and **the other** of the said seven plots or parcels of land (being the   *LB7*
seventh allotment to the said Lovelace Bigg) is situate in Woolston Meadow aforesaid
containing four acres three roods and twenty seven perches bounded on the east by the   *80*
said inclosed farm called Oxlease belonging to the said Bartholomew Tipping on the
south by the second allotment to the said Bartholomew Tipping and on the west and
north by the first allotment to the said Lovelace Bigg which said allotment last
hereinbefore described is hereinafter exchanged by the said Lovelace Bigg with the said
Bartholomew Tipping the fences for inclosing the same allotment on the west and north   *95*
against the said allotment to the said Lovelace Bigg the said Commissioners do award
order and direct shall be made and foreverafter maintained and repaired by the said
Bartholomew Tipping on his taking the same in exchange and the owners of the same
allotment for the timing being. To and For the said John Hippesley in lieu of and as a just
and full recompense satisfaction and equivalent for all his lands and grounds rights of   *100*

JH1

101   common and other properties in over and upon the same fields and commonable lands by the said Act directed to be divided and allotted. Two Plots or parcels of land **one plot** or parcel whereof is situate in Old Field aforesaid and contains twenty six acres three roods and twelve perches (exclusive of all roads and ways through and over the same)

105   bounded on part of the east by an allotment to the said John Williams on a small part of the south and on parts of the east and north east by old inclosures within the hamlet of Balking on part of the south east and the remaining part of the south by Sparsholt Meadow and old inclosures by part of the south west and the remaining part of the south east by other old inclosures within the hamlet of Balking on the north west and west by

110   an allotment to Joseph Wirdnam and on the north by a public road hereinafter set out across the said Old Field the fences for inclosing this allotment on the east against the allotment to the said John Williams on the north west and west against the allotment to Joseph Wirdnam and on the north against the said public road the said Commissioners do award order and direct shall be made and foreverafter maintained and repaired by the

JH2   115   said John Hippesley and the owners of the same allotment for the time being.. And **the other** of the said two plots or parcels of land is likewise situate in Old Field aforesaid and contains eighteen acres three roods and thirty eight perches (exclusive of all roads and ways through and over the same) bounded on the east by the Lordship of Standford on the south by the said public road in Old Field on the west by an allotment to the said

120   William Lord Craven and Robert Quarme his lessee and on the north by land allotted to the said Abraham Atkins hereinafter exchanged with the said William Lord Craven the fences for inclosing this allotment on the east against the said Lordship of Standford and on the north against the said public road the said commissioners do award order and direct shall be made and foreverafter maintained and repaired by the said John Hippesley

125   and the owners of the allotment for the time being. To and For the said John Archer in lieu of and as a just and full recompense satisfaction and equivalent for all his lands and grounds rights of common and other rights and properties in over and upon the said fields and commonable lands by the said Act directed to be divided and allotted (except Tithes as aforesaid) and the land by him lately purchased of the said George Watts for

JA9   130   which an allotment is hereinafter awarded. **One Plot** or parcel of land (being the ninth allotment to the said John Archer) situate in Uffington Fields on the north or lower side of the said Ickleton Way containing nineteen acres one rood and twenty three perches (exclusive of all roads and ways through and over the same) bounded on the east the south and the west by land allotted to the said John Archer on the north west by an old

135   inclosure called Westham belonging to the said William Lord Craven and exchanged by him with the said John Archer and on the north by the next allotment hereinafter awarded to the said John Archer the fences for inclosing this allotment on the north west against the said inclosure called Westham exchanged as aforesaid and on the north against the said allotment next hereinafter awarded to the said John Archer the said Commissioners

140   do award order and direct shall be made and forever after maintained and repaired by the said John Archer and the owners of this allotment for the time being. Also to and for the said John Archer in lieu of and as a just and full recompense satisfaction and equivalent for all such of his lands and grounds rights of common and other properties in over and upon the said fields and commonable lands by the said Act directed to be divided and

145   allotted as he hath purchased of and from the said George Watts since the

20 **Passing** of the said Act. **One Plot** or parcel of land or ground (being the tenth allotment to the said John Archer) situate in a place called the Drove in Uffington aforesaid being part and parcel of Uffington Common containing three acres two roods and twenty perches (exclusive of all roads and ways through and over the same) bounded on the north and the north east by the said old Inclosed Farm belonging to the said William Lord Craven in the occupation of Richard Gearing on a small part of the east and south by land allotted to the said John Archer on the south west and south east by the said inclosure called West Ham and on the west by the said farm in Woolston belonging to the said Barthlomew Tipping called the Oxlease. To and for the said Provost and Scholars of Queens College and the said Philip Brown their lessee in lieu of and as a just and full recompense satisfaction and equivalent for all such of their lands and grounds rights of common and other rights in and over the said meadow called Old Field part of the commonable lands by the aid Act directed to be divided and allotted as are comprised in the lease now subsisting between the said Provost and Scholars and the said Philip Brown. **One Plot** or parcel of land or ground situate in the Old Field aforesaid containing two acres and sixteen perches (exclusive of all roads and ways through and over the same) bounded on the east by an allotment to the said Robert Leaver exchanged by him with the said William Lord Craven on the south by a public road on the west by an allotment to the said Provost and Scholars of Queens College and the said Trustees of the estate of the said Robert Fettiplace their lessees and on the north by land allotted to the said William Lord Craven the fences for inclosing this allotment on the east against the allotment to the said Robert Leaver and on the south against the said public road the said commissioners do award order and direct shall be made and during the continuance of the said lease maintained and repaired by the said Philip Brown and after the determination thereof such fences shall belong to and be forever maintained and repaired by the said Provost and Scholars of Queens College and the owners of the same allotment for the time being. To and for the said Abraham Atkins in lieu of and as a just and full recompense satisfaction and equivalent for all his lands and grounds rights of common and other rights and properties in over and upon the said common meadows called Old Field and Bagmoor and all other the said fields and commonable lands by the said Act directed to be divided and allotted which are situate within the said hamlet of Balking and over and besides the allotment hereinbefore awarded to the said Abraham Atkins as Lord of the Manor of Kingston Lisle which comprises the said hamlet of Balking. **One Plot** or parcel of land or ground situate in Old Field aforesaid containing ninety three acres two roods and twenty perches (exclusive of all roads and ways through and over the same) bounded on part of the east by Old Inclosures in the Lordship of Standford on part of the south by the second allotment to the said John Hippersly on other part of the south and other part of the East an allotment to the said William Lord Craven and the said Robert Quarme his lessee on other parts of the south and the remaining part of the east by the allotment to the said Abraham Atkins as Lord of the Manor on the remaining part of the south by a public road on the west by an allotment to the said Robert Leaver exchanged with the said William Lord Craven and by land allotted to the said William Lord Craven and on the north by the Lordship of Standford. Which said Allotment is hereinafter exchanged by the said Abraham Atkins with the said Lord Craven for land in the hamlet of Kingston Lisle the fences for inclosing

1   *JA10*

5

10

15   *QC/PB*

20

25

30

AA2

35

40

45

46   this allotment on the east against the said Old Inclosures within the parish of Standford on the south against the said allotment to the said John Hippersly on the south and east against the said Allotment to the said William Lord Craven and Robert Quarme his lessee on the south against the said public road and against such parts of the said Open and

50   Common fields of Standford as have usually been or of right ought to have been made and maintained by the owners and occupiers or lands or common rights in Old Fields aforesaid the said Commissioners do award order and direct shall be made and forever after maintained and repaired by the said Abraham Atkins or the said William Lord Craven on his taking the same in exchange the owners of the same allotment for the time

55   being. To and for the said Edward Thornhill and Collier his wife and the owners of this lot for the time being in lieu of and as a just and full recompense satisfaction and equivalent for all their lands and grounds rights of common and other properties in over and upon the said fields and commonable lands by the said Act directed to be divided and allotted which are situate within the hamlet of Balking. **One Plot** or parcel of land or ground

ET

60   situate in the said meadow called Old Field containing fifteen acres two roods and thirty perches (exclusive of all roads and ways through and over the same) bounded on the east by land allotted to the said William Lord Craven on part of the south by inclosures within the hamlet of Balking on part of the south west by an allotment to the said Dean and Chapter of Westminster and the said John Morest their lessee on the remaining parts of

65   the south west and south by an allotment to the said William Lord Craven and George Reade his lessee on the west by other inclosures in the hamlet of Balking and by an allotment to the said John Hyde and on the north by the lordships of Shillingford and Standford aforesaid. The fences for inclosing this allotment on the east against land allotted to the said William Lord Craven and on the north against the said Lordships of

70   Shillingford and Standford in such shares and proportions and in such parts and places as shall usually been or as of right ought to have been made and maintained by the owners and occupiers of lands and commons within the said meadow called Old Field the said commissioners do award order and direct shall be made and forever after maintained and repaired by the said Edward Thornhill and Collier his wife and the owners of this

75   allotment for the time being. To and For the said John Hyde in lieu of and as a just and full recompense satisfaction and equivalent for all his lands and grounds rights or common and other properties in over and upon the said fields and commonable lands by

JHYD1

the said Act directed to be divided and allotted. Two Plots or parcels of land **one plot** or parcel whereof is situate in Old Field within the hamlet of Baulking aforesaid and contains

80   twenty six acres one rood and thirty five perches (exclusive of all roads and ways through and over the same) bounded on the east by an allotment to the said Edward Thornhill and Collier his wife on part of the south on the west and on the remaining part of the south and on the north west by old inclosures within the hamlet of Baulking aforesaid belonging to the said John Hyde and on the north by the Lordship of Shillingford

95   aforesaid the fences for inclosing this allotment on the east against the allotment to the said Edward Thornhill and Collier his wife and on such parts of the north west against the said inclosures in the hamlet of Baulking aforesaid and against the said Lordship of Shillingford as have usually been or of right ought to have been made and maintained by the owners and occupiers of lands and commons within the said meadow called Old

100 Field the said Commissioners do award order and direct shall be made and foreverafter

maintained and repaired by the said John Hyde and the owners of this allotment for the *101*

time being. And **the other** of the said two plots or parcels of land is situate in the said meadow called Bagmoor and contains ten acres two roods and ten perches bounded on the south by inclosures in the hamlet of Baulking belonging to the said John Hyde on the west by an allotment to the said Henry Aston and on the north east by the Lordship of *105* Shillingford aforesaid the fences for inclosing this allotment on the west against the allotment to the said Henry Aston the said Commissioners do award order and direct shall be made and forever after maintained and repaired by the said John Hyde and the owners of this allotment for the time being. To and for the said Henry Aston in lieu of and as a just and full recompense and equivalent for all his lands and grounds rights or *110* common and other properties in over and upon the said fields and commonable lands by the said Act directed to be divided and allotted **One Plot** or parcel of land situate in

Bagmoor aforesaid containing nine acres two roods and seventeen perches bounded on the east by an allotment to the said John Hyde on the south by inclosures in the hamlet of Balking aforesaid on the west by an allotment to the Trustees of the Presbyterian *115* Society of Wantage and on the north by the lordship of Shillingford aforesaid the fences for inclosing this allotment on the west against the said allotment to the said Trustees of the said Presbyterian Society the said Commissioners do award order and direct shall be made and forever after maintained and repaired by the said Henry Aston and owners of this allotment for the time being. To and for the said William Hazell and John Tooley *120* William Tripp and William Hazell the younger Trustees of a certain Presbyterian Society at Wantage in the County of Berks in lieu of and as a just and full recompense satisfaction and equivalent for all the lands and grounds rights of common and other properties belonging to the said Society or their said Trustees in over and upon the said fields and commonable lands by the said Act directed to be divided and allotted. **One Plot** or parcel *125*
of land also situate in Bagmoor aforesaid containing five acres and thirty three perches (exclusive of all roads and ways through and over the same) bounded on the east by an allotment to the said Henry Aston on part of the south by inclosures in the Hamlet of Balking aforesaid on part of the west remaining parts of the south and west by land allotted to the said Earl Spencer and on the north by the lordship of Shillingford aforesaid. *130* To and for the said Dean and Chapter of the Collegiate church of St. Peter in Westminster and John Merest their lessee and according to their respective estates and interests in the premises comprised in the lease now subsisting between them in lieu of an as a just and full recompense satisfaction and equivalent for all the lands and grounds rights of common and other properties in over and upon the said fields and commonable lands by *135* the said Act directed to be divided and allotted which are comprised in the said lease **One Plot** or parcel of land situate in Old Field aforesaid containing one acres

21 *1* **Three** roods and fourteen perches bounded on the east and south by old inclosures within the hamlet of Balking aforesaid on the west by an allotment to the said William Lord Craven and George Read his lessee and on the north east by an allotment to the said Edward Thornhill and Collier his wife *5* the fences for inclosing this allotment on the north east against the said allotment to the said Edward Thornhill and Collier his Wife the said Commissioners do award order and direct shall be made and during the continuance of the said lease maintained and repaired by the said John Morest and after the determination thereof such fences shall belong to and be forever maintained and repaired by the said Dean and Chapter and the owners of *10* this allotment for the time being. **To and For the said Robert Leaver** in lieu of and as a just and full recompense satisfaction and equivalent for all his lands and grounds rights of common and other properties in over and upon the said fields and commonable lands *RL* by the said Act directed to be divided and allotted. **One Plot** or Parcel of land situate in the said meadow called Old Field containing four acres one rood and twenty eight *15* perches bounded on the east by an allotment to the said Abraham Atkins exchanged with the said William Lord Craven on the south by a public road on the west by an allotment to the said Provost and Scholars of Queens College and the said Philip Brown their lessee and on the north side by land allotted to the said William Lord Craven which allotment last hereinbefore described is exchanged by the said Robert Leaver with the said William *20* Lord Craven as hereinafter mentioned the fences for inclosing this allotment on the east against the land allotted to the said Abraham Atkins exchanged as aforesaid and on the south against the said public road the said Commissioners do award order and direct shall be made and forever after maintained and repaired by the said William Lord Craven on his taking the same in exchange and the owners of the same allotment for the time *25* being. **To and For the said John Williams** in lieu of and as a just and full recompense satisfaction and equivalent for all his lands and grounds rights of common and other properties in over and upon the said fields and commonable lands by the said Act directed *JWLL* to be divided and allotted. **One Plot** or parcel of land situate in Old Field aforesaid containing three roods and twenty perches bounded on several parts of the east and *30* south by old inclosures in the hamlet of Balking aforesaid on the west by the first allotment to the said John Hippesley and on the north by a public road the fences for inclosing this allotment on the north against the said public road the said Commissioners do award order and direct shall be made and forever after maintained and repaired by the said John Williams and the owners of this allotment for the time being. **To and for the said Joseph** *35* **Wirdnam** in lieu of and as a just and full recompense satisfaction and equivalent for all his lands and grounds rights of common and other properties in over and upon the said fields and commonable lands within the said township of Uffington and hamlets of Baulking and Woolston otherwise Wolverston aforesaid by the said Act directed to be *JWIR* divided and allotted. **One Plot** or parcel of land situate in the said Old Field containing *40* three acres one rood and five perches bounded on the east and south east by the first allotment to the said John Hippesley on the south west by inclosures in the hamlet of Balking on the west by an allotment to the said Roger Spanswick and on the north by a public road the fences for inclosing this allotment on the west against the allotment to the said Roger Spanswick and on the north against the said public road the said Commissioners *45* do award order and direct shall be made and forever after maintained and repaired by the

said Joseph Wirdnam and the owners of this allotment for the time being. **To and For the** *46*
said Roger Spanswick in lieu of and as a just and fair recompense satisfaction and
equivalent for all his lands and grounds rights of common and other properties in over
and upon the said fields and commonable lands by the said Act directed to be divided
and allotted. **One Plot** or parcel of land situate in Old Field aforesaid containing three *50*   *RS*
roods and thirty six perches bounded on the east by an allotment to the said Joseph
Wirdnam on the south east by old inclosures in the same hamlet of Balking on the west
by an allotment to the said Trustees of the Estate of the said Robert Fettiplace and on the
north by the said public road the fences for inclosing this allotment on the west against
the said allotment to the said Trustees of Robert Fettiplace and on the north against the *55*
said public road the said Commissioners do award and direct shall be made and forever
after maintained and repaired by the said Roger Spanswick and the owners of this
allotment for the time being **To and For the said John William Willaume and Abraham**
Chambers Trustees or Assignees of the estate and effects of the said Robert Fettiplace in
lieu of and as a just and full recompense satisfaction and equivalent for all their freehold *60*
lands grounds rights of common and all other their freehold properties in over and upon
the said fields and commonable lands in the hamlet of Balking by the said Act directed to
be divided and allotted **One Plot** or parcel of land situate in Old Field aforesaid containing   *RF*
eleven acres one rood and thirty three perches (exclusive of all roads and ways through
and over the same) bounded on the east by an allotment to the said Provost and Scholars *65*
of Queens College and the said Trustees of Robert Fettiplace as their lessees by a public
road and by an allotment to the said Roger Spanswick on the south west and west by old
inclosures within the hamlet of Balking and by a lane leading towards the village of
Balking and on the north by an allotment to the said William Lord Craven exchanged
with the said Trustees as hereinafter mentioned the fences for inclosing this allotment on *70*
the east against the allotment to the said Provost and Scholars and the said Trustees and
lessees and across the said public road and on the west across the end of the said lane
leading towards Balking aforesaid the said Commissioners do award order and direct
shall be made and foreverafter maintained and repaired by the said John Williams
Willaume and Abraham Chambers trustees or assignees as aforesaid and the owners of *75*
this allotment for the time being **To and For the said Provost and Scholars of Queens**
College in Oxford and the said **John Williams Willaume and Abraham Chambers** as
Trustees or Assignees of the estate and effects of the said Robert Fettiplace as aforesaid
and as Lessees of the said College (according to their respective estates and interests in
the premises comprised in the lease now subsisting between the said Provost and Scholars *80*
and the said trustees) in lieu of and as a just and full recompense satisfaction and
equivalent for all their lands and grounds rights of common and other properties in and
over the said fields and commonable lands within the hamlet of Balking aforesaid by the
said Act directed to be divided and allotted which are comprised in the said lease. **One**   *QC/RF1*
Plot or parcel of lane situate in Old Field aforesaid containing twelve acres three roods *95*
and twenty five perches (exclusive of all roads and ways through and over the same)
bounded on part of the east by an allotment to the said Provost and Scholars and Phillip
Brown their lessee on the south by a public road on the west by an allotment to the said
Trustees of Robert Fettiplace in lieu of freehold lands and by an allotment to the said
William Lord Craven exchanged with the said Trustees as hereinafter mentioned and on *100*

101   the north and the remaining part of the east by an allotment to the said William Lord Craven the fences for inclosing this allotment on the south against the said public road and on the east against the allotments to the said William Lord Craven and the said Provost and Scholars and Philip Brown their lessee the said commissioners do award

105   order and direct shall be made and during the continuance of the said lease maintained and repaired by the said John Williams Willaume and Abraham Chambers as lessees of the said College and after determination of the said lease such fences shall belong to and be forever maintained and repaired by the said Provost and Scholars and the owners of this allotment for the time being **To and for the Said Provost and Scholars of Queens**

110   **College** in Oxford and the said **John Williams Willaume and Abraham Chambers** trustees or assignees of the said Robert Fettiplace and lessees of the said College according to their respective estates and interests in the premises comprised in the aforesaid lease now subsisting between them in lieu of and as a just and full recompense satisfaction and equivalent for all such of their lands and grounds rights of common and other properties

115   in over and upon the said fields and commonable lands within the said hamlet of Woolston otherwise Wolverston by the said Act directed to be divided and allotted which are comprised in the said lease and also as an adequate satisfaction for the right of the said Provost and Scholars and the said Trustees as their lessees to the feeding and pasturing of one ox from Whitsun eve until the feast of St. Swithin the Archangel yearly in a certain

120   pasture ground called the Oxlease in Woolston otherwise Wolverston aforesaid now in the occupation of James Mattingly as Lessee of the said Bartholomew Tipping which satisfaction for such right of feeding or pasturing of the said ox the said commissioners have according to the directions of the said Act allotted and appointed to the said Provost and Scholars and the said Trustees as their lessees as aforesaid from and out of the

QC/RF2   *125*   allotment or property of the said Bartholomew Tipping **Two Plots** or parcels of land **one plot** or parcel whereof (being the second allotment to the said Provost and Scholars and their said lessees) is situate in Uffington and Woolston fields on the north or lower side of Ickleton Way and contains thirteen acres two roods and thirty four perches (exclusive of all roads and ways through and over the same) whereof two roods and six perches are

130   in the fields of Uffington and thirteen acres and twenty eight perches are in the fields of Woolston bounded on the north east and the east by land allotted to the said John Archer on part of the south by an allotment to the said Lovelace Bigg on part of the west and remaining part of the south by an old inclosure belonging to the said Lovelace Bigg on the remaining part of the west by several cottages and gardens at Woolston aforesaid

135   called the Lower Town and on the north by an inclosed meadow belonging to the said Bartholomew Tipping the fences for inclosing this allotment on the north east and east against land allotted to the said John Archer and on the south against the allotment to the said Lovelace Bigg the said Commissioners do award order and direct shall be made and during the continuance of the said lease maintained and repaired by the said Trustees as

140   lessees of the said College and after the determination thereof such fences shall

22

Belong to and be forever maintained and repaired by the said Provost and Scholars and the owners of this allotment. And **the other** of the said two plots or parcels of land is situated in Woolston Fields aforesaid on the north or lower side of the said Ickleton Way and in that part of the Common at Woolston which is called the Drove Way containing nineteen acres three roods and nine perches (exclusive of all roads and ways through and over the same) bounded on the north west and north east by the said inclosed farm called the Oxlease Farm and by a cottage and garden on part of the east by several cottages and gardens at Woolston aforesaid called the Lower Town on part of the south and the remaining part of the east by the Home Close and Homestead belonging to the said Provost and Scholars and the said Trustees their Lessees and on the remaining part of the south on part of the west and on the north and on the remaining part of the west by land allotted to the said Lovelace Bigg the fences for inclosing this allotment on the south against the land allotted to the said Lovelace Bigg on the west against land allotted to the said Lovelace Bigg so far as this allotment extends against a certain road called Marsh Way Road the said Commissioners do award order and direct shall be made and during the continuance of the said lease maintained and repaired by the said Trustees as lessees of the said College and after the determination thereof such fences shall belong to and be forever maintained and repaired by the said Provost and Scholars and the owners of this allotment for the time being. **To and For the said Jeffry Church** in lieu of and as a just and full recompense satisfaction and equivalent for all his lands grounds rights of common and other properties in over and upon the said fields and commonable lands by the said Act directed to be divided and allotted. **Three Plots** or parcels of land **one plot** or parcel thereof is situate in Woolston Fields on the North or Lower side of the said Ickleton Way and contains thirty four acres two roods and thirty six perches bounded on the east and south by land allotted to the said John Archer on part of the west by an allotment to the said Bartholomew Tipping on the other part of the west part of the north and the remaining part of the west by Old Inclosures at the town of Woolston and on the remaining part of the north by allotments to the said Lovelace Bigg and Bartholomew Tipping respectively exchanged by them with the said Jeffry Church the fences for inclosing this allotment on the east and south against land allotted to the said John Archer the said commissioners do award order and direct shall be made and forever after maintained and repaired by the said Jeffry Church and the owners of this allotment for the time being. **One Other** of the said three plots or parcels of land (being the second allotment to the said Jeffry Church) is situated in Woolston Common and Woolston Meadow and contains sixty acres three roods and twenty seven perches (exclusive of all roads and ways through and over the same) bounded on part of the north and on part of the east by an allotment to the said Lovelace Bigg on the south east other part of the east and other part of the north by an allotment to the said Vicar of Uffington on the remaining part of the east by the said allotment to the said Lovelace Bigg on the south by an allotment to the said Joseph Mayon on part of the west and on part of the south west by the said farm called Hardwell Farm and on every other part thereof by the Lordship of Knighton. The fences for inclosing this allotment on the south east and north against the said allotment to the said Vicar of Uffington on the east against the allotment to the said Lovelace Bigg on Woolston Common and on such parts

QC/RF3

JC1

JC2

1
5
10
15
20
25
30
35
40
45

46   against the said Lordship of Knighton as have usually been or of right ought to have been maintained and repaired by the owners and occupiers of lands and common rights within the said Hamlet of Woolston the said Commissioners do award order and direct shall be made and forever after maintained and repaired by the said Jeffry Church and

JC3

50   owners of this allotment for the time being. And **the other** of the said three plots or parcels of land (being the third allotment to the said Jeffry Church) is situated in Woolston fields aforesaid on the North or Lower side of the said Ickleton Way and contains two roods and thirty nine perches (exclusive of all roads and ways through and over the same) bounded on the east by an allotment to the said William Thatcher on the

55   south by an allotment to the said Bartholomew Tipping exchanged with the said Joseph Mayon on the west by an allotment to the said Joseph Mayon and on the north by an allotment to the said Lovelace Bigg exchanged with the said Joseph Mayon and which said last described allotment is hereinafter exchanged by the said Jeffry Church with the said Joseph Mayon **To and for the said Joseph Mayon** in lieu of and as a just and full

60   recompense satisfaction and equivalent for all his lands and grounds rights of common and other properties in over and upon the said fields and commonable lands by the said

JM

Act directed to be divided and allotted. **One Plot** or parcel of land or ground situated in Woolston Common and Woolston fields on the north or lower side of the said Ickleton Way containing ninety two acres two roods and twelve perches (exclusive of all roads

65   and ways through and over the same) bounded on part of the east and part of the north by the first allotment to the said Lovelace Bigg on part of the east and other part of the north by an allotment to the said William Thatcher on the other part of the east by allotments to the said Lovelace Bigg and Jeffry Church exchanged with the said Joseph Mayon as aforesaid on other parts of the east and north by an allotment to the said

70   Bartholomew Tipping exchanged with the said Joseph Mayon as aforesaid on other small part of the east by the said allotment to William Thatcher on part of the south and the remaining part of the east by old inclosures belonging to the said Lovelace Bigg and on the remaining part of the south by the third allotment to the said Lovelace Bigg on the west by the said Farm called Hardwell Farm and on the north by the second

75   allotment to the said Jeffry Church which said last described allotment to the said Joseph Mayon surrounds and totally circumscribes three small pieces of ancient inclosures called the Sheephouse Bartons two of which three parcels belong to and are the property of Joseph Mayon and the other of them is the property of the said Lovelace Bigg and is exchanged by the said Lovelace Bigg with the said Joseph Mayon as

80   hereinafter mentioned. The fences for inclosing this allotment to the said Joseph Mayon on the east against the said first allotment to the said Lovelace Bigg so far as this allotment adjoins and abuts upon the land of the said Lovelace Bigg on the Common on the south against the said third allotment to the said Lovelace Bigg (except across the private road) and on the west against the said Hardwell Farm in such parts and such

95   places as have usually been or of right ought to have been maintained and repaired by the owners and occupiers of lands and common rights within the Hamlet of Woolston aforesaid and on the north against the said allotment to the said Jeffry Church the said Commissioners do award order and direct shall be made and forever after maintained and repaired by the said Joseph Mayon and the owners of this allotment for the time

100   being. **To and For the said William Thatcher** in lieu of and as a just and full recompense

satisfaction and equivalent for all his lands and grounds rights of common and other *101*
properties in over and upon the said fields and commonable lands by the said Act
directed to be divided and allotted **Two Plots** or parcels of land **one plot** or parcel   *WT1*
whereof is situated in Woolston Fields on the north or lower side of the said Ickleton
Way and contains fifteen acres one rood and twenty seven perches (exclusive of all roads *105*
and ways through and over the same) bounded on part of the east by the Home Close
and homestead of the said William Thatcher and on a small part of the south and on
other part of the east by an inclosure belonging to the said Joseph Mayon on the
remaining part of the east by a public road or lane leading into the town of Woolston
aforesaid on other part of the south by old inclosures belonging to the said Joseph *110*
Mayon and the said Lovelace Bigg on a small part of the west (across a public road) by
an allotment to the said Joseph Mayon on other part of the west by allotments to the
said Bartholomew Tipping and Jeffry Church exchanged with the said Joseph Mayon on
other parts of the west and south by an allotment to the said Lovelace Bigg also
exchanged with the said Joseph Mayon on the remaining parts of the south and west by *115*
the allotment to the said Joseph Mayon and on the north by land allotted to the said
Lovelace Bigg the fences for inclosing this allotment on the east across the said lane or
road leading into Woolston on the west across the said public road against the allotment
to the said Joseph Mayon on the west against the said allotments to the said Bartholomew
Tipping and Jeffry Church exchanged as aforesaid on the west and south against the said *120*
allotment to the said Lovelace Bigg also exchanged as aforesaid and on the south and
west against the allotment to the said Joseph Mayon the said Commissioners do Award
Order and Direct shall be made and forever after maintained and repaired by the said
William Thatcher and the owners of this allotment for the time being. And **the other** of   *WT2*
the said two plots or parcels of land is situate in Woolston fields and downs on the south *125*
or upper side of Ickleton Way and contains seventy acres two roods and two perches
(exclusive of all public roads and ways through and over the same) bounded on the
north and east by an allotment to the said Bartholomew Tipping on the south east by
the said several down belonging to the said Bartholomew Tipping on the south and part
of the west by an allotment to the said Lovelace Bigg on other part of the west by an old *130*
Inclosure called Botty Barn belonging to the said Bartholomew Tipping and exchanged
with the said Lovelace Bigg as hereinafter mentioned and on the remaining part of the
west by other part of the said allotment to the said Lovelace Bigg. The boundaries for
ascertaining this allotment on the north and east against the said allotment to the said
Bartholomew Tipping the said Commissioners do award and direct shall be made and *135*
foreverafter maintained and repaired by the said William Thatcher and the owners of
this allotment for the time being. **To and for the said William Chamberlain** in lieu of
and as a just and full recompense satisfaction and equivalent for all his lands and grounds
rights of common and other properties in over and upon the said fields and commonable
lands by the said Act directed to be divided and allotted. **One Plot** or parcel of land *140* *WC*
situate in Uffington Common and Uffington fields on the north or lower side of the said
Ickleton Way at a place there called the Hitchin containing thirty two acres two
roods and six perches (exclusive of all roads and ways through and over the same)
bounded on the east and south east by the hamlet of Fawler on the south by the
twenty seventh on the south west by the twenty third on the north west *145*

1

23

And on part of the North by the twenty fifth and on the remaining part of the north by the twenty sixth allotment to the said William Lord Craven. The fences for inclosing of this allotment against the Hamlet of Fawler in such parts and places as have usually born as of right ought to have been

5 maintained and repaired by the owners and occupiers of lands and commons within the township of Uffington on the south against the said twenty seventh allotment on the south west against the said twenty third allotment and on the north west against the said twenty fifth allotment to the said William Lord Craven. The said Commissioners do award order direct shall be made and forever after maintained and repaired by the

10 said William Chamberlain and the owners of this allotment for the time being. **To and For** the said George Watts and his successor Vicars of Uffington as aforesaid in hereof and as a just and full recompense satisfaction and equivalent for all lands and grounds right of common and other properties belonging to the vicarage of Uffington in over and upon the said fields and commonable lands by the said act directed to be divided

15 and allotted (except tithes and moduses or compositions for tithes for which several

GW8

allotments are hereinbefore awarded to him). **One Plot or** part of Land situated in Uffington Fields on the north or lower side of the said Ickleton Way containing four acres and twenty two perches bounded on the east the south and small part of the west by other land allotted to the said Vicar on the remaining part of the west by land allotted

20 to the said John Archer and on the north by land allotted to the Trustees of Uffington School and the fences for inclosing this allotment on the west against land allotted to the said John Archer and on the north against land allotted to the said Trustees of Uffington School Land. The said Commissioners do award order and direct and be made and for the term of seven years maintained and repaired at the expense of the

25 other proprietors as by the said Act is directed and after the expiration of the term of seven years of making the same such fences shall belong to and be forever maintained and repaired by and at the expense of the said George Watts and his successor vicars of Uffington as aforesaid . **To and for the said Trustees** of certain commonable lands given by Thomas Saunders deceased for maintaining a schoolmaster at Uffington in lieu

30 of and as a just and full recompense satisfaction and equivalent for all their lands and grounds rights of common and other properties in and over the said fields and

TUS

commonable lands by the said Act directed to be divided and allotted. **One plot** or parcel of land situated in Uffington Fields on the north or lower side of Ickelton Way (the said Trustees herein signify their consent to accept the same thereof as by the said

35 Act is required) containing seventeen acres and one rood and thirty three perches (exclusive of all roads and ways through and over the same) bounded on the east by the thirty fourth allotment to the said William Lord Craven on the south by land allotted to the said Vicar of Uffington and his successor on the west by land allotted to the said John Archer and on the north by an allotment to the said William Lord Craven and

40 Edward Warren his Lessee and an allotment to the said Vicar of Uffington exchanged with the said William Lord Craven as hereinafter mentioned. The fences for inclosing this allotment on the west against land allotted to the said John Archer the said Commissioners do award order and direct shall be made and for the term of seven years maintained and repaired at the expense of the other proprietors as by the said Act is

45 directed and from and after the expiration of the said term of seven years from the time

of making the same fences shall belong to and be forever maintained and repaired by *46*
and at the expense of the said Trustees of Uffington School lands and their successors
forever. **To and For the said John Stallard** in lieu of and as a just and full recompense
satisfaction and equivalent for his fields lands and grounds rights of common and other
properties in over and upon the said fields and commonable lands by the said Act *50*
directed to be divided and allotted. **One Plot** or parcel of land containing twelve *JS*
perches bounded on the south by the thirtieth allotment to the said William Lord
Craven on the West by the Town street of Uffington aforesaid and on the north and east
by an allotment to the said William Lord Craven and Edward Warren his lessee
exchanged with the said William Lord Craven which allotment last herein before *55*
described is exchanged by the said John Stallard with the said William Lord Craven as
hereinafter mentioned. The fences for inclosing the same allotment on the south against
the said thirtieth allotment and on the west against the said Town Street of Uffington
the said Commissioners do award order and direct shall be made and forever after
maintained and repaired by the said William Lord Craven on his taking the same in *60*
exchange and the owners of this allotment for the time being. **To and for the said**
Joseph Cook in lieu of and as a just and full recompense satisfaction and equivalent for
all his lands and grounds rights of common and other properties in over and upon the
said fields and commonable lands by the said Act directed to be divided and allotted.
One Plot or parcel of land situated in Uffington Common containing nine acres and *65* *JC*
thirty eight perches bounded on the north east by a public road from Uffington to
Fawler on the south east by the twenty third allotment to the said William Lord Craven
on the south west by the twenty ninth allotment to the said William Lord Craven and
an allotment to the said William Lord Craven and James Mundy his lessee and on the
north west by an allotment to the said Lawrence Woodroffe the fences for inclosing this *70*
allotment on the north east against the said public road and on the south east against
the said twenty third allotment to the said William Lord Craven the said
Commissioners do award order and direct shall be made and forever after maintained
and repaired by the said Joseph Cook and the owners of this allotment for the time
being. **To and For the said Lawrence Woodroffe** in lieu of and as a full and just *75*
recompense satisfaction and equivalent for all his lands and grounds rights of common
and other properties in over and upon the said fields and commonable lands by the said
Act directed to be divided and allotted. **One Plot** or parcel of land situated in Uffington *LW*
Common aforesaid containing four acres three roods and fourteen perches bounded on
the north east by a public road from Uffington to Fawler on the south east by an *80*
allotment to the said Joseph Cook on the south west by an allotment to the said
William Lord Craven and James Mundy his Lessee and on the north west by an
allotment to the said Charles Young and Sarah his wife and Mary Allen. The fences for
inclosing this allotment on the north east against the said public road and on the south
east against the allotment to the said Joseph Cook the said Commissioners do award *95*
order and direct shall be made and forever after maintained and repaired by the said
Lawrence Woodroffe and the owners of this allotment for the time being. **To and For**
the said Charles Young and Sarah his Wife and Mary Allen an infant in lieu of and as
a just and full recompense satisfaction and equivalent for all their freehold lands and
grounds rights of common and other properties in over and upon the said fields and *100*

CY

101 commonable lands by the said Act directed to be divided and allotted. **One Plot** or parcel of land situated in Uffington Common aforesaid containing four acres and twenty one perches bounded on the north east by the said public road on the south east by an allotment to the said Lawrence Woodroffe on the west by an allotment to the said
105 William Lord Craven and James Mundy his lessee on part of the north west by an allotment to the said Elizabeth Hoar and on the east and the remaining part of the north west by an allotment to the said Joseph Dickson . The fences for inclosing this allotment on the north east against the said public road on the south east against the allotment to the said Lawrence Woodroffe and on the east against the allotment to the
110 said Joseph Dickson the said Commissioners do award order and direct shall be made and forever after maintained and repaired by the said Charles Young and Sarah his Wife and Mary Allen and the owners of this allotment for the time being. **To and For the said Joseph Dickson** in lieu of and as a just and full recompense satisfaction and equivalent for all his grounds lands and rights of common and other properties in over
115 and upon the said fields and commonable lands by the said Act directed to be divided

JD

and allotted. **One Plot** or parcel of land situated in Uffington Common aforesaid containing three roods and twenty two perches bounded on the north east by the said public road from Uffington to Fawler on the south east and the west by an allotment to the said Charles Young and Sarah his Wife and Mary Allen and the north west by an
120 allotment to the said Elizabeth Hoar the fences for inclosing this allotment on the north east against the said public road and on the south east against the allotment to the said Charles Young and Sarah his wife and Mary Allen the said Commissioners do award order and direct shall be made and forever after maintained and repaired by the said Joseph Dickson and the owners of this allotment for the time being. **To the for the**
125 **Said Elizabeth Hoar** in lieu of and as a just and full recompense satisfaction and equivalent for all her lands and grounds rights of common and other rights and properties in over and upon the said fields and commonable lands by the said Act

EH

directed to be divided and allotted **One Plot** or parcel of land situated in Uffington Common aforesaid containing two acres three roods and twelve perches (exclusive of
130 all roads and ways through and over the same)bounded on the south east by an allotment to the said Joseph Dickson and an allotment to the said Charles Young and Sarah his Wife and Mary Allen on the west by an allotment to the said William Lord Craven and James Mundy his Lessee and an allotment to the said James Mundy on part of the north by the twenty second allotment to the said William Lord Craven on part of
135 the east and remaining part of the north by an allotment to William Mifflin and on the north east by the said public road from Uffington towards Fawler the fences for inclosing this allotment on the south east against the said allotment to the said Joseph Dickson and the allotment to the said Charles Young and Sarah his wife and Mary Allen on the east against the said Allotment to the said William Mifflin and

24

On the north east side against the said public road the said commissioners do award order and direct shall be made and forever after maintained and repaired by the said Elizabeth Hoar and the owners of this allotment for the time being. To and for the said William Mifflin in lieu of and as a just and full recompense satisfaction and equivalent for all his lands and grounds rights of common and other properties in over and upon the said fields and commonable lands by the said Act directed to be divided and allotted **one plot** parcel of land situate in Uffington Common aforesaid containing two roods and twelve perches bounded on the north east by the said public road from Uffington to Fawler on the south and west by an allotment to the said Elizabeth Hoar and on the north by the twenty second allotment to the said William Lord Craven the fences for inclosing this allotment on the north east against the said public road and on the south against the allotment to the said Elizabeth Hoar the said commissioners do award order and direct shall be made and forever after maintained and repaired by the said William Mifflin and the owners of this allotment for the time being. And to and for the said James Mundy in lieu of and as a just and full recompense satisfaction and equivalent for all the lands and grounds rights of common and other properties in over and upon the said fields and commonable lands by the said Act directed to be divided and allotted. **One plot** or parcel of land situate in Uffington Fields on the north or lower side of Ickleton Way containing two acres one rood and thirty seven perches (exclusive of all roads and ways through and over the same) bounded on the east by the twenty second allotment to the said William Lord Craven and an allotment to the said Elizabeth Hoar on the south side by an allotment to the said William Lord Craven and the said James Mundy his lessee and on the west and north by several old inclosures and homesteads at the town of Uffington aforesaid. The fences for inclosing this allotment on the east against the said twenty second allotment and the allotment to the said Elizabeth Hoar and the south against the allotment to the said William Lord Craven and the said James Mundy his lessee the said Commissioners do award order and direct shall be made and forever after maintained and repaired by the said James Mundy and the owners of this allotment for the time being. All which said several allotments hereinbefore awarded to the several persons entitled to and interested in the said residue and remainder of the said open and common fields common meadows common pastures downs and other commonable lands lying within the township of Uffington and the hamlets of Baulking and Woolstone otherwise Wolverstone in and by the said Act directed to be divided and allotted after making the said several allotments for the manorial rights and for the tithes and public stone pits as before mentioned and after deducting a sufficient quantity of the said lands and grounds for the roads and highways as by the said Act is directed are in the several and respective quantities shares and proportions hereinbefore mentioned adjudged and determined by the said commissioners to be a just recompense and satisfaction for an equal to their several and respective lands and grounds rights of common and other properties therein except tithes and the same allotments do contain and **amount together** to two thousand nine hundred and two acres one rood and thirty perches which together with the said three allotments for manorial rights amounting to ten acres and fourteen perches the said allotments for tithes amounting to six hundred and sixty two acres one rood and thirty perches the said two allotments for public stone pits amounting to six acres and the public roads and ways hereinafter described containing

1

WM

5

10

15

JMY

20

25

30

35

40

summary of areas

45

46 eighty nine acres one rood and eight perches do make up and amount altogether to three thousand six hundred and seventy three acres one rood and two perches being the total or gross quantity of all the said fields and commonable lands within the said Township of Uffington and hamlets of Balking and Woolstone otherwise Wolverstone by the said Act

50 directed to be divided and allotted as hereinbefore described. And the said Commissioners in further pursuance of the directions of the said Act save ascertain set out and appointed by these presents do ascertain set out and appoint the several and respective Private Roads through and over the said new allotments with the sizes and breadths thereof as hereinafter particularly mentioned and described (that is to say): In the Township of

private roads *55* Uffington one **private** carriage and drift road as now staked out in the breadth of thirty
in Uffington feet from and out of the public road from Uffington to Fawler hereinafter described through and over the twentieth and fourteenth allotments to the said William Lord Craven by the side of the houses and inclosures called Uffington Row into the public road hereinafter described from Balking towards Moor Mill Lane which said road the said

60 commissioners do award order and direct shall be used and enjoyed by the said William Lord Craven and owners and occupiers for the time being of the said twentieth and fourteenth allotments and by the owners and occupiers for the time being of the said houses and old inclosures adjoining the said road. One other private carriage and drift road as now staked out of the like breadth of thirty feet from and out of the public road

65 from Broad Street to Friday Street hereinafter described by the side of several cottages and old inclosures through and over the first and twenty first allotments to the said William Lord Craven into the aforesaid public road from Uffington to Fawler which said private road the said commissioners do award order and direct shall be used and enjoyed by the said William Lord Craven and the owners and occupiers for the time being of the

70 said first and twenty first allotments and by the owners and occupiers for the time being
private roads of the said cottages and old inclosures adjoining to the said road. In the hamlet of **Balking**
in Baulking one private carriage and drift road as now staked out of the like breadth of thirty feet from and out of the public road called Portway from Balking toward Stanford through and over the allotment to the said William Lord Craven and Robert Quarm his lessee and allotment

75 to the said Abraham Atkins exchanged with the said William Lord Craven the thirty eighth allotment to the said William Lord Craven to the north east corner of the old inclosures in Balking and from thence by the north side of the said old inclosures through and over other part of the said thirty eighth allotment to the said William Lord Craven into through and over the allotment to the said Edward Thornhill and Collier his wife and

80 the first allotment to the said John Hyde to a gate leading into old inclosures in Balking belonging to the said John Lloyd which said described road the said commissioners do award order and direct shall be used and enjoyed by all the owners and occupiers for the time being of the several allotments in Old Field. One private carriage road as now staked and set out of the breadth of fifteen feet across Bagmoor through and over an allotment

95 to the trustees of land belonging to Presbyterian Society at Wantage which said road the said Commissioners do award order and direct shall be forever used and enjoyed by the said Earl Spencer and the owners and occupiers of his allotment in Bagmoor and by the said trustees of the said Presbyterian Society in Wantage and the owners and occupiers for the time being for their said allotment in Bagmoor and the said Earl Spencer and the

100 owners and occupiers for the time being of the estate in Shillingford and his farm in

Balking occupied by William Robert Prior for the purpose of a communication between *101* the said estate and farm. In the hamlet of Woolstone otherwise **Wolverston** one private road of the breadth of thirty feet as now staked out from and out of the public road herein set out from Woolstone towards Lamborne at or about the middle of Botty Barn Close across the second allotment to William Thatcher into the fourth allotment to the said *105* Bartholomew Tipping which said last described road the said commissioners do award order and direct shall be used and enjoyed as a private carriage and drift road by the said William Thatcher in respect of his said second allotment and the future owners thereof for the time being and as a carriage road (but not as a drift way) by the said Bartholomew Tipping in respect of his said fourth and fifth allotments and the owners of the said fourth *110* and fifth allotments for the time being. One other private carriage road of the breadth of twelve feet from and out of the public road herein described from Woolston to the Clay Pit gate at and by the north end and part of the west side of the home close of the said Lovelace Bigg by him lately purchased of Sir William **Enis** through allotment to Joseph Mayon into the third allotment to the said Lovelace Bigg which said last mentioned road *115* the said commissioners do award order and direct shall be used and enjoyed by the said Joseph Mayon in respect of his said allotment and the owners and occupiers thereof for the time being and by the said Lovelace Bigg in respect of his said third allotment and the owners and occupiers thereof for the time being. One other private road as now staked out of the breadth of fifteen feet from a lane on the east side of the village of Woolston *120* through and over an allotment to the said John Archer the second allotment to the said Lovelace Bigg and part of an allotment to the provost and scholars of Queens College and the Trustees of Robert Fettiplace their lessees by the east side of several old inclosures at the town of Woolston to the north east corner of an old inclosure belonging to the said Lovelace Bigg called Long Close and from there in a straight direction through and over *125* other part of the said allotment to the Provost and Scholars of Queens College the Trustees of Robert Fettiplace their lessees by the east side of certain cottages and houses in Woolston called the Lower Town to an inclosure and meadow belonging to the said Bartholomew Tipping called the Farm Ham which said last described road the said commissioners do award order and direct shall be forever used and enjoyed as a private *130* carriage and drift road by the owners and occupiers for the time being of the said allotments through which the same roads by these owners and occupiers for the time being of three cottages now belonging to Thomas Brooks Charles Young and the Overseers of Woolston and the owners and occupiers for the time being of the said inclosures and cottage houses adjoining to the said road and as a private carriage road only by the said *135* Bartholomew Tipping and by the owners and occupiers for the time being of the said meadow called Farm Ham. One other private carriage and drift road of the like breadth of fifteen feet branching out of the last described road at the said north east corner of the said Long Close through and over the allotment to the Provost and Scholars of Queens College and the Trustees of Robert Fettiplace their lessees by the north end of the said *140* Long Close to a cottage house belonging to Thomas Brooks which said last described road the said Commissioners do award and direct shall be used and enjoyed by the said Thomas Brooks and the owners and occupiers for the time being of the said cottage and by the said Provost and Scholars of Queens College and their said lessees and the owners and occupiers for the time being of their said allotment. One other private carriage and *145*

private roads in Woolstone

25 **Drift Road** as now staked out of the like breadth of fifteen feet also branching out of the said private road leading to Farm Ham nearly opposite to a cottage house belonging to the said Charles Young through the allotment to the said Provost and Scholars of Queens College and the Trustees of Robert Fettiplace their lessees to the same cottage house. Which said private road the said commissioners do award order and direct shall be used and enjoyed by the owners and occupiers for the time being of the said allotment and cottage house respectively. One other private carriage and drift road as now staked out of the breadth of fifteen feet from and out of the said private road leading to Farm Ham at the end of Woolstone Lower Town through and over a place called The Drove lying on the west side of the said Lower Town and into through and over another allotment to the said Provost and Scholars of Queens College and the Trustees of Robert Fettiplace their lessees to the said cottage house belonging to the overseers of Woolstone which said road the said commissioners do award order and direct shall be used and enjoyed by the owners and occupiers for the time being of the said two allotments through which the same leads and by the owners and occupiers for the time being of the said cottage house. **And as for and concerning the public roads** and ways through and over the said new allotments the said commissioners did as by the said Act they were **required** before any allotment was made to any proprietor or other person cause ten days notice to be given to by Richard Townsend gentleman their clerk to the right honourable William Lord Viscount Barrington of the Kingdom of Ireland and the Rev'd John Craven clerk two of His Majesty's Justice of the Peace for the Hundred of Shrivenham wherein the township of Uffington and the hamlets of Baulking and Woolstone otherwise Wolverstone respectively are situate of the time and place that they intended to visit for the purpose of ascertaining setting out and appointing such public roads and ways with the sizes and breadths thereof to the intent that the said justices might have attended if they thought proper. But the said justices or either of them not having attended pursuant to the said notice the said commissioners provided to ascertain set out and appoint and did accordingly ascertain set out and appoint and do now hereby award and confirm the several public roads and ways through and over the two allotments with the sizes and breadths thereof and hereinafter particularly mentioned (that is to say): **In the township of Uffington one public road** as now staked out of the breadth of forty feet from Fawler foredown field on the north side of part of the thirty fifth allotment to the said William Lord Craven the north side of the several farms in the occupation of Joseph Lousley the north side of other part of the thirty fifth allotment and of land allotted to the said John Archer by the south side of the thirty fourth allotment to the said William Lord Craven and of an allotment to the said Vicar of Uffington into Woolstone Fields (being part of an ancient road or way called Ickleton Way). **One other public road** as now staked and set out of the like breadth of forty feet from the several farm on the east side of Uffington fields through and over the fifth allotment to the said John Archer exchanged with the said William Lord Craven and the fourth allotment to the said John Archer by the side of the said thirty fifth allotment to the said William Lord Craven into the said several farms (being part of an ancient road or way called Ridgeway). **One other public road** as now staked and set out of the breadth of forty feet from a gate at the south part of the town of Uffington called Green Bridge Gate through and over part of the thirtieth allotment to

notice to JPs re public roads

public roads in Uffington

the said William Lord Craven by the side of an inclosure called East Coppice Close into   *46*
through and over the second allotment to the said John Archer by the west side of other
part of the said thirtieth allotment to the said William Lord Craven by the west side of an
allotment to the said William Lord Craven and William Mundy by the west side of an
allotment to the said William Lord Craven and Edward Warren by the west side of an   *50*
allotment to the Trustees of Uffington School land and by the west side of the last
allotment to the said Vicar of Uffington into through and over the first allotment to the
said Vicar of Uffington to the said public road called Ickleton Way and from there across
the said public road into through and over other part of the said thirty fifth allotment to
the said William Lord Craven by the east side of land allotted to the said John Archer into   *55*
Woolstone Fields being part of the road from Uffington towards Ashdown Park and
Baydon. **One other public road** as now staked and set out on the breadth of forty feet
from and out of a public road hereinbefore described called Ickleton Way at or near a
guide post now standing by the said road through and over the thirty fifth allotment to
the said William Lord Craven up a certain way called White Shoot to a public road herein   *60*
before described called Ridgeway and from there across the said road into through and
over the fifth allotment to the said John Archer exchanged by him with the said William
Lord Craven by the east side of the fourth allotment to the said John Archer into through
and over the eighth allotment to the said John Archer exchanged with the said William
Lord Craven into through and over the thirty sixth allotment to the said William Lord   *65*
Craven into Kingston Warren Farm (being part of the road towards Lamborne). **One
other public road** as now staked and set out of the breadth of forty feet from the end of
Broad Street in the town of Uffington through and over the first and twenty first allotments
to the said William Lord Craven to the west corner of an allotment to the said William
Lord Craven to the said Charles Young and Sarah his wife and Mary Allen his lessees and   *70*
by the south west side of the same through and over other part of the said twenty first
allotment to the said William Lord Craven to the north east corner of the twenty second
allotment to the said William Lord Craven and from thence between the south west part
of the said allotment to the said William Lord Craven and Charles Young and Sarah his
wife and Mary Allen his lessees allotments to the said William Lord Craven and Edmund   *75*
Cook his lessee and the twenty fourth and twenty fifth allotments to the said William
Lord Craven which be on the north east side thereof and the north east parts of the
twenty second allotment to the said William Lord Craven and allotments to the said
William Mifflin Elizabeth Hoar Joseph Dixon Charles Young and Sarah his wife and
Mary Allen Laurence Woodroffe and Joseph Cook respectively which lie on the south   *80*
west side of the said road into through and over the twenty third and twenty seventh
allotments to the said William Lord Craven by the side of William Chamberlain's
allotment to a gate in a lane called White Foot Lane (being part of the road from Uffington
towards Fawler.) **One other public road** as now staked and set out of the breadth of
forty feet from and out of the road last hereinbefore described through and over the first   *95*
allotment to the said William Lord Craven as Lord of the Manor of Uffington by the side
of several houses and homesteads in Uffington to the said Friday Street in the said town
of Uffington (being the road from Broad Street in the town of Uffington to Friday Street
aforesaid). **One other public road** as now staked and set out of the breadth of forty feet
from and out of the road hereinbefore described from Uffington towards Fawler through   *100*

101 and over the twentieth and fourteenth allotments to the said William Lord Craven by the north west part of an allotment to the said William Lord Craven and Charles Young and Sarah his wife and Mary Allen his lessees an allotment to the said William Lord Craven and Joseph Dickson his lessee an allotment to the said William Lord Craven and Richard

105 Hinchman his lessee an allotment to the said William Lord Craven and John Stallard his lessee and the nineteenth eighteenth and fifteenth allotments to the said William Lord Craven to a gate called Balking Gate (being part of the road from Uffington towards Balking).**One other public road** as now staked and set out of the breadth of forty feet from and out of the road last hereinbefore described through and over the fourteenth

110 allotment to the said William Lord Craven by the side of an old inclosures in the hamlet of Balking to the south east side of a lane called Moor Mill Lane (being part of the road from Balking to Moor Mill). **One other public road** as now staked and set out of the breadth of forty feet from the north west end of the said Moor Mill Lane through and over the eleventh tenth ninth and eighth allotments to the said William Lord Craven to

115 the east end of a lane called Moor Lane (being part of the road from Balking and Moor Mill to Longcott). **One other public road** as now staked and set out of the breadth of forty feet from a lane on the west side of the town of Uffington through and over the thirty second allotment to the said William Lord Craven and the second allotment to the said Vicar of Uffington by the side of the several farm belonging to the said William Lord

120 Craven in the occupation of Richard Geering into through and over the first allotment to the said John Archer exchanged with the said William Lord Craven and into through and over the second sixth seventh and the eight allotments to the said William Lord Craven to the public road hereinbefore described from Moor Mill to Moor Lane at or near a guidepost now standing in the same road (being part of the road from Uffington towards

125 Faringdon). **One other public road** as now staked and set out of the breadth of forty feet from and out of the road hereinbefore last described from Uffington towards Faringdon opposite a gate in the inclosed farm belonging to the said William Lord Craven called Morrell Leaze Gate through and over part of the sixth allotment to the said William Lord Craven to the said Morrell Leaze Gate (being part of the road from Fernham towards

130 Woolstone). **One other public road** as now staked and set out of the breadth of forty feet from another lane on the west side of the town of Uffington through and over the second allotment to the said John Archer and a piece of ground called the Drove likewise allotted to the said John Archer to a gate leading into the Oxlease Farm in the hamlet of

26

Woolston being part of the road from Uffington towards Shrivenham. *1* **One Public Bridle Road** as now staked and set out of the breadth of thirty feet from and out of a public road from Uffington to Fawler along the tract of a private road therein before described through and over the twentieth and fourteenth allotments to the said William Lord Craven by the side of several houses and *5* enclosures called the Row into the public road hereintofore described from Balking towards Moor Mill being a bridle road from Uffington towards Moor Mill. **One other Public Bridle Road** as now staked and set out the breadth of thirty feet and out of the Public Road from Broad Street to Friday Street along the tract of a private road hereinbefore described by the side of several cottages and old inclosures through and *10* over the first and twenty first allotments to the said William Lord Craven into the said public road from Uffington to Fawler. **One Other Public Bridle Road** as now staked and set out of the breadth of fifteen feet from and out of a public road herein and before described from Uffington towards Shrivenham through and over land allotted to the said John Archer by the side of Westham meadow and Wiseman's ham to a Bridle Road *15* hereinafter described in the hamlet of Woolston (being part of the bridle road from Uffington towards Woolston.) **One other Public Bridle Road** of the breadth the same now is between ditches from and out of the public road herein before described from Moor Mill towards Longcot at or near the guide post through and over the eighth allotment to the said William Lord Craven to a bridle bridge across the brook leading *20* into Fernham Lane (being part of the bridle road from Uffington towards Faringdon.) **One Public Foot Road** or way of the breadth of eight feet nearly in the same tract it now goes from a stile in an old enclosure called Moor Mill Close through and over the fourteenth thirteenth and twelfth allotments to the said William Lord Craven to a stile in an old enclosure belonging to the said William Lord Craven now or late in the occupancy *25* of John Forty (being part of the foot road or way and burying and church way from Moor Mill to Uffington). **One other Public Foot Road** or way of the breadth of four feet from and out of the public road herein before described from Moor Mill towards Longcot through and over the north east side of the eleventh allotment to the said William Lord Craven to a foot plank across the brook between Uffington meadow and Fernham (being *30* other part of the foot road from Uffington and Moor Mill towards Shillingford.) **One other Public Foot Road** or way of the breadth of four feet from and out of the foot road herein before described from Uffington towards Moor Mill through and over the thirteenth fourteenth ninth fifth and eighth allotments to the said William Lord Craven to the said public road herein before described from Moor Mill towards Longcot at or *35* near the guide post (being part of the foot road from the east part of the town of Uffington towards Fernham.) **One other Public Foot Road** or way of the like breadth of four feet branching out of the last described foot way at a place called the Mond plank near the north east corner of the third allotment to the said William Lord Craven though and over the ninth tenth and eleventh allotment to the said William Lord Craven to the aforesaid *40* foot plank across the brook between Uffington meadow and Fernham(being part of another foot road or way from Uffington and Moor Mill towards Shillingford). **One other Public Foot Road** or way of the breadth of four feet from the town of Uffington at or near the pond through and over the twentieth and fourteenth allotments to the said William Lord Craven to a stile in Balking called Balking stile (being part of the footway *45*

bridle roads in Uffington

foot roads in Uffington

46   from Uffington towards Balking.) **One other Public Foot Road** or way of the breadth of four feet from and out of the Town street of Uffington through and over the thirty first allotment to the said William Lord Craven by the south side of an homestead and inclosure belonging to John Lockey into through and over an allotment to the said

50   William Lord Craven and James Mundy his lessee and an allotment to the said James Mundy to a stile called Hook stile between James Mundy's allotment and the twenty second allotment to the said William Lord Craven from thence through and over the said twenty second allotment to the said William Lord Craven by the south east side of an homestead belonging to the said William Lord Craven into through and over the twenty

55   first and first allotments to the said William Lord Craven into the public road herein before described from Uffington to Fawler nearly opposite to the pond on Uffington Green (being a foot road for the easy communication between several parts of the town of Uffington.) **One other Public Foot Road** or way of the like breadth of four feet from and out of the foot road herein before last described through and over the twenty first

60   allotment to the said William Lord Craven by the north side of the twenty second allotment to the said William Lord Craven to the public road hereinbefore described from Uffington to Fawler from thence across the said road into through and over the allotment to the said William Lord Craven and Charles Young and Sarah his wife and Mary Allen his lessees two allotments to the said William Lord Craven and Edmund

65   Cook his lessee the twenty fourth and twenty fifth allotments to the said William Lord Craven and the allotment to the said William Chamberlaine by the side of the said public road from Uffington to Fawler and into the said public road at or near the south west corner of a certain place called the Hitchin (being part of the foot road from Uffington towards Fawler.) **One other Public Foot Road** or way of the like breadth of four feet

70   from and out of the Town street of Uffington at or near the south west corner of the said inclosure belonging to the said John Lockey through and over the thirty first allotment to the said William Lord Craven an allotment to the said William Lord Craven and Edward Warren his lessee exchanged as herein after mentioned by the side of the Town street of Uffington into through and over an allotment to the said John Stallard exchanged with

75   the said William Lord Craven the thirtieth allotment to the said William Lord Craven an allotment to the said William Lord Craven and William Mundy his lessee another allotment to the said William Lord Craven and Edward Warren his lessee an allotment to the Trustees of Uffington School lands and allotments to the Vicar of Uffington by the side of the public road from Uffington to Baydon and Ashdown Park to Ickleton Way and

80   from thence across the said Ickleton Way by the side of the same road into through and over part of the thirty fifth allotment to the said William Lord Craven to a way called Limekiln way in the Several farm belonging to the said William Lord Craven (being part of the foot road from Uffington towards Lambourn.) **One other Public Foot Road** or way of the like breadth of four feet from a stile in an old inclosure in Fawler belonging to

95   Joseph Wirdnam through and over the twenty eighth and thirty fourth allotments to the said William Lord Craven into through and over land allotted to the said Vicar of Uffington in a west direction towards the village of Woolston (being part of the road from Fawler towards Woolston.) **In the Hamlet of Balking** one public road called Portway as now

public roads in Baulking

staked and set out of the breadth of forty feet from a gate at the southwest corner of Old

100   field called Fortisons Gate through and over an allotment to the said Trustees of Robert

Fettiplace and from thence between the north part of allotments to the said Roger *101*
Spanswick Joseph Wirdnam John Hippisley and John Williams respectively and several
old inclosures within the hamlet of Balking and the south part of an allotment to the
Provost and Scholars of Queens College and the said Trustees of Robert Fettiplace their
lessees and allotments to the said Provost and Scholars and the said Philip Brown their *105*
lessee Robert Leaver and Abraham Atkins exchanged with the said William Lord Craven
an allotment to the said William Lord Craven and Robert Quarme his lessee and another
allotment to the said John Hippisley to a gate called Standford gate (being part of the
road from Baulking towards Standford). **One Public Bridle Road** as now staked and set
out of the breadth of thirty feet from and out of the public road called Portway from *110*
Baulking towards Standford in the same tract as a private road is herein before described
for the use of the owners and occupiers of land in Old field through and over the allotment
to the said William Lord Craven and Robert Quarme his lessee an allotment to the said
Abraham Atkins exchanged with the said William Lord Craven on the thirty eighth
allotment to the said William Lord Craven to the north east corner of old inclosures in *115*
Balking and from there by the north side of the said old inclosures through and over
other part of the said thirty eighth allotment to the said William Lord Craven into through
and over the allotment to the said Edward Thornhill and Collier his wife and the first
allotment to the said John Hyde to a gate leading into old inclosures in Balking belonging
to the said John Hyde (being part of the Bridle Road from Standford towards Balking.) *120*
One other Public Bridle Road as now staked and set out of the breadth of fifteen feet
across Bagmoor along the tract of a private carriage road herein before described (being
part of the bridle road from Baulking towards Shillingford.) **One other Public Foot**
Road or way of the breadth of four feet from a stile on the west side of Old field though
and over the said thirty eighth allotment to the said William Lord Craven an allotment to *125*
the said Abraham Atkins exchanged with the said William Lord Craven to a stile in
Standford Grounds (being part of the foot road from Baulking towards Standford.) **One**
other Public Foot Road or way of the breadth of four feet from a stile near the south
west corner of Old field through and over an allotment to the said Trustees of Robert
Fettiplace an allotment to the said Provost and Scholars of Queens College and the said *130*
Abraham Atkins exchanged by him with the said William Lord Craven to the said stile in
Standford Grounds (being part of the foot road from Kingston Lisle towards Standford.)
One other Public Foot Road or way of the breadth of four feet from a stile at

27 **The South** part of the old field called Sparsholt Corner through and over the first allotment to the said John Hippisley to a public road called Portway at or near the north west corner of John William's allotment and from there across the said road into through and over an allotment to the said Abraham Atkins exchanged with the said William Lord Craven an allotment to the said William Lord Craven and Robert Quarme his lessee an allotment to the said John Hippisley and other part of the said allotment to the said Abraham Atkins exchanged as aforesaid to the said stile in Standford Grounds (being part of the footway from Sparsholt to Standford) In the hamlet of Woolston otherwise Woolverston One **Public Road** as now staked and set out of the breadth of forty feet from the public road first herein before awarded through and over the Township of Uffington called Ickleton Way on the north side of the third allotment to the said John Archer the fourth allotment to the said Bartholomew Tipping and the fourth allotment to the said Lovelace Bigg and by the south side of an allotment to the said John Archer the public stone pits in Woolston the third allotment to the said Bartholomew Tipping and the third allotment to the said Lovelace Bigg into Hardwell Farm being other part of the said ancient road or way called Ickleton Way. One other Public Road as now staked and set out of the breadth of forty feet from out of the public road called Ridgeway in the Several Farm in Uffington in the occupation of the said Joseph Lousley through and over the south part of land allotted to the said William Lord Craven in Woolston and across land allotted to the said John Archer and the said Bartholomew Tipping to the north east corner of land allotted to the said William Thatcher and by the north part of the same allotment to the said William Thatcher through and over land allotted to the said Bartholomew Tipping into through and over land allotted to the said Lovelace Bigg to the entrance of the same road upon Hardwell Farm (being part of the said ancient road or way called Ridgeway. One other Public Road as now staked and set out of the breadth of forty feet from a lane on the south part of the village of Woolston through and over land allotted to the said Bartholomew Tipping by the east side of land allotted to the said Lovelace Bigg to the road herein before set out called Ickleton Way across the said road into through and over part of the fourth allotment to the said Bartholomew Tipping a plot of land set out for a public stone pit in Woolston and other part of the said fourth allotment to the said Bartholomew Tipping by the south east and east part of another allotment to the said Lovelace Bigg to Ridgeway across the said Ridgeway by the east side of other part of the said allotment to the said Lovelace Bigg the east part of an inclosure called Botty Barn and the east side of other part of the said allotment to the said Lovelace Bigg through and over an allotment to the said William Thatcher to the south west corner thereof and from thence across other part of the said allotment to the said Lovelace Bigg to Lamborne Downs being part of the road from Woolston towards Lamborne. One other Public Road as now staked and set out of the like breadth of forty feet from and out of the public road last herein before described from Woolston towards Lamborne along a certain path called White Horse Way through and over land allotted to the said Bartholomew Tipping John Archer and William Lord Craven respectively into the road in Uffington Township herein before described from Uffington towards Ashdown park and Baydon being other part of the said road from Ashdown park and Baydon to Uffington. One other Public Road as now staked and set out of the breadth of forty feet from a gate called Claypit gate on the east side of Woolston common through

public roads in Woolstone

and over part of the first allotment to the said Lovelace Bigg to the south east corner of an *46*
allotment to the Vicar of Uffington and through and over the south part of the said
allotment to the south west corner thereof and from thence through and over land allotted
to the said Jeffry Church by a cottage house called Old Gortons into Longcot common
(being part of the road from Uffington towards Shrivenham. One other Public Road as *50*
now staked and set out of the breadth of forty feet from a gate on the west side of Woolston
common called Hardwell Gate through and over land allotted to the said Joseph Mayon
and Jeffry Church respectively by the east side of Hardwell Farm to a place on the west
side of the said common called the Hook and from there through and over other land
allotted to the said Jeffry Church into the road last herein before described from Uffington *55*
towards Shrivenham being part of the road from Hardwell towards Longcot. One other
Public Road as now staked and set out of the like breadth of forty feet from a lane on the
west side of the town of Woolston through and over the first allotment to William Thatcher
by the side of the homesteads of the said Joseph Mayon and Lovelace Bigg and through
and over an allotment to the said Joseph Mayon and the allotments to the said Bartholomew *60*
Tipping Jeffry Church and Lovelace Bigg respectively exchanged with the said Joseph
Mayon by the side of other part of the said allotment to the said William Thatcher and
into through and over other part of the said allotment to the said William Thatcher and
the first allotment to the said Lovelace Bigg to the south west corner of an allotment to
the said provost and scholars of Queens College and the trustees of Robert Fettiplace *65*
their lessees and from thence through and over other part of the said first allotment to the
said Lovelace Bigg by the side of the said allotment to the said provost and scholars and
their lessees aforesaid and by the side of several inclosures called the New Leases into the
public road herein before described from Uffington towards Shrivenham at or near the
said Claypit Gate being part of the road from Woolston towards Longcot. One Public *70*
Bridle Road as now staked and set out of the breadth of fifteen feet from a lane on the

*bridle roads
in Woolstone*

east side of the village of Woolston through and over an allotment to the said John Archer
the second allotment to the said Lovelace Bigg and part of an allotment to the said provost
and scholars and their lessees by the east side of several old inclosures in the town of
Woolston to the north east corner of an old inclosure belonging to the said Lovelace Bigg *75*
called Long Close and from thence in a straight direction through and over other part of
the said allotment to the said provost and scholars and their lessees by the east side of
certain cottage houses called the Lower Town to the inclosed meadow belonging to the
said Bartholomew Tipping called Farm Ham on the same track as a private road is herein
before described to go from Woolston to the said Farm Ham and from the said Ham by *80*
the south side of inclosures belonging to the said Bartholomew Tipping through and over
part of the said allotment to the said provost and scholars and their lessees into a bridle
road in Uffington herein before described from Uffington towards Woolston. One Public
Foot Road or way of the breadth of four feet from the beginning of the last described

*foot roads in
Woolstone*

bridle road through and over land allotted to the said John Archer into a foot road in *95*
Uffington herein before described from Fawler towards Woolston being part of the foot
road from Woolston towards Fawler. One other Public Foot Road or way of the breadth
of four feet from and out of the public road herein before described from Woolston
towards Longcot at or near a farm house called The Upper House belonging to the said
Lovelace Bigg through and over an allotment to the said Joseph Mayon to a stile called *100*

101   Hardwell Stile being part of the foot road from Woolston towards Hardwell. One other Public Foot Road or way of the breadth of four feet from certain houses in Woolston aforesaid called the Lower Town through and over an allotment to the said provost and scholars and their lessees across the public road from Woolston towards Longcot into

105   through and over an allotment to the said Lovelace Bigg and an allotment to the said Joseph Mayon to a stile in the hedge between Woolston fields and Hardwell Farm near to the south west corner of Woolston common being part of the foot road from Uffington and the said Lower Town towards Hardwell and Knighton. One other Public Foot Road or way of the breadth of four feet from and out of the public road herein before described

110   from Uffington towards Shrivenham at or near the said Claypit Gate through and over land allotted to the said Lovelace Bigg in Uffington [Woolstone?] common and [Woolstone?] meadow to a stile entering on Longcot common near the north east [west?] corner of Woolston meadow being part of the foot road from Woolston towards Longcot. One other Public Foot Road or way of the breadth of four feet from out of the same

115   public road from Woolston towards Longcot at the south east corner of Woolston common through and over the first allotment to the said Lovelace Bigg to the north east corner of the allotment to the said Joseph Mayon from thence through and over part of the second allotment to Jeffry Church into the public road in Woolston common at the north west corner of an allotment to the said Vicar of Uffington. And further know ye that

120   the said commissioners in further pursuance of the said Act have directed and do herein **direct** that good and sufficient fences shall be made within eight calendar months from the date of this Award for separating and dividing all such of the aforesaid allotments as are herein before mentioned or allotted on the north or lower side of Ickleton Way aforesaid and that such fences shall be so made by the several proprietors of the allotments

125   on the said north or lower side of Ickleton Way upon their own respective allotments in the several proportions and in the respective parts and places of such allotments herein before mentioned and described (save except that such of the said fences as are herein before ordered and appointed to be made upon the allotments to the said Vicar of Uffington and to the said Trustees of Uffington School Land shall be made at the expence

130   of other proprietors herein after mentioned.) And as to the manner in which the said fences(except upon the allotments to the said Vicar and Trustees) shall be

fences to be made within 8 months

28

Done the said Commissioners do hereby award order and direct that all such fences (except in such parts of the public and private roads where gates or stiles are hereinafter directed to be set up) **shall be** of good quick plants to be planted upon the allotments hereinbefore awarded to the said proprietors respectively at the distance of four feet at the least from the outside of such allotments with a ditch to be made between the said quick plants and the adjoining allotments and for the better enabling of the said proprietors to raise the said quick fences to the best advantage the said Commissioners do hereby order and direct that the said proprietors shall have liberty to set down and place posts and rails or stake hedges on the outside of the respective allotments provided such posts and rails or stake hedges shall not be set down or placed at any greater distance than two feet from the edge of the ditch to be made on their own allotments respectively **and the said** Commissioners do hereby further award order and direct that the said proprietors respectively so place and setting down such posts and rails or stake hedges on the outside of their respective allotments shall and may at any reasonable times during their pleasure take and carry away such posts and rails or stake hedges and remove the same to their own use so as not thereby to injure or damage any standing crops of corn or grass and also that the said several proprietors in moving their boundary fences hereinbefore directed across any public or private road herein awarded and set out (except foot roads) shall make and set **up good and** sufficient swing gates across such roads and also erect and make good and substantial covered drains or stone or brick bridges in such gateways and keep the same gates drains and bridges in good and sufficient repair and that where any such fences shall cross any footway herein awarded and described the respective proprietors making such fence shall in all such places set up and erect **footstiles** with floor planks and handrails across the ditches and keep the same in like good and sufficient repair. And as touching the manner of ascertaining and fixing the boundaries of the respective allotments on the south or upper side of Ickleton Way the said Commissioners have directed and do hereby direct that the owners and proprietors of the said respective allotments shall within three months from the date of this award affix proper and sufficient **moor stones** upon their said allotments respectively in the several parts and places hereinbefore particularly described for their making the boundaries against the adjoining lands and allotments and that all such lines as they are so directed to make the same one such moor stone shall be placed at every corner bend or angle and so many other such moor stones in the straight lines between the said bends or angles respectively as that all such moor stones shall stand within the distance of one hundred yards from each other and that they shall from time to time for ever thereafter renew and keep up such moor stones as often as occasion may require subject nevertheless to the directions of the said Act in case the said proprietors or any of them shall think proper to inclose their said respective allotments on the south or upper side of the said Ickleton Road or Way. **And as** to the **fences** to be made upon the allotments hereinbefore awarded to the said Vicar of Uffington and the Trustees of Uffington School Land which fences are by the said Act directed to be made and for the term of seven years supported by such of the other proprietors in such proportions and in such manner as the said Commissioners should award direct and appoint the said Commissioners have ascertained the expenses thereof and find that the same will amount to the sum of one hundred and sixty two pounds three shillings and four pence which

1

5

10

15

20

25

30

35

40

45

specification of fences

gates drains bridges on roads

stiles plank bridges on foot roads

moor stones

fences for vicar & school land

46 they have caused or directed to be raised amongst the proprietors (except as in the said Act is excepted) in manner hereinafter mentioned and the said George Watts the Vicar of Uffington having proposed to contract for the making of the said fences as are now upon his own allotments as upon the allotment to the said Trustees of Uffington School Land

50 and for maintaining and supporting the same for the term of seven years from the time of making the same and for the said sum of one hundred and sixty two pounds three shillings and four pence and to give security for making maintaining and supporting the same accordingly and for indemnifying the said Commissioners and proprietors of the said fields and commonable lands on account thereof the said Commissioners have complied

55 with such proposal and directed the said sum of one hundred and sixty two shillings and four pence to be paid into the hands of the said George Watts on his giving such security as aforesaid. **And the said Commissioners** in further pursuance of the said act **have** assigned and appointed and by these presents **do** assign and appoint as and for boundary and subdivision fences for the several allotments whereon the same stand the several

60 hedges and fences hereinafter particularly mentioned and described that is to say such and so much of the hedges betwixt Uffington Common and Moor Mill Close betwixt Uffington Common and the Hamlet of Balking and betwixt Uffington Field and Fawler Field as belonged to and were the property of the owners and proprietors of lands in Uffington the hedge between Uffington Fields and West Ham and the hedge betwixt

65 Uffington Common and the Fields such and so much of the hedges betwixt Woolston Fields and Common and Hardwell Farm betwixt Woolston Common and Meadow and the Lordship of Knighton and betwixt Woolston Common and Oxleaze Farm as belonged to and were the property of the owners and proprietors of land in Woolston. The hedge betwixt Woolston Meadow and the parish of Longcot the hedge betwixt Woolston

70 Meadow and Woolston Common and the hedge betwixt Woolston Common and Woolston Field and such and so much of the hedges between Old Field and the Lordship of Standford and betwixt Old Field and Old Inclosures in the hamlet of Balking as belonged to or were the property of the owners and proprietors of lands in Old Field which hedges and fences are in the judgment of the said Commissioners convenient and

75 necessary and are by virtue of the said act to be left uncut for the benefit of the respective persons for whom such new allotments whereon the said hedges and fences are standing do respectively belong to the said several persons having respectively made such allowances or considerations for the same to the former owners thereof as the said commissioners have by a writing under their hands in that behalf order and appointed.

80 **And the said Commissioners** in further pursuance of the said Act have marked out and described and do hereby describe in lieu of the thirty seventh allotment hereinbefore awarded to the said William Lord Craven on which are marked the figure and form or representation of a horse commonly called The White Horse and of a Castle near to the same as hereinbefore mentioned and which allotment is by the said act declared to be

95 forever hereafter deemed and considered as lying within and part of the Manor of

transfer to Manor of Woolstone land to compensate for White Horse 100

Uffington. **One plot** or parcel of land containing twenty acres and twenty three perches lying on the Several Down belonging to the said William Lord Craven and now in the occupation of Joseph Lousley bounded on the east by other part of the said Several Down hereinafter exchanged by the said William Lord Craven with the said John Archer on the south by other part of the said Several Down retained by the said William Lord Craven

on the west by land allotted to the said John Archer in Woolston Down and on the north *101*
by the ancient road called The Ridgeway being so much of the said land belonging to the
said William Lord Craven within the Manor and Township of Uffington now in the
occupation of the said Joseph Lousley and in the judgment of the said Commissioners is
equivalent to the said thirty seventh allotment hereinbefore awarded to the said William *105*
Lord Craven which said plot or parcel of land hereinbefore described part of the said land
in the occupation of the said Joseph Lousley is by the said Act declared to be forever
hereafter deemed and considered as lying within and part of the Manor of Woolston
otherwise Wolverston aforesaid and the said Commissioners do award order and direct
that the said William Lord Craven and the owners thereof for the time being shall make *110*
and forever maintain the boundaries for ascertaining the same against the other part of
the said Several Down retained by the said William Lord Craven in the same manner as
all other boundaries on the south or upper side of Ickleton Way as hereinbefore directed
to be made and ascertained. **And the said Commissioners** in further pursuance of and
in obedience to the directions of the said Act **have** assigned allotted and by these presents *115*
do assign and allot unto and for the said William Lord Craven the said fourth allotment
of land hereinbefore awarded to the said George Watts and his successors Vicars as
aforesaid containing eighteen acres two roods and four perches situate within the said
Township of Uffington and hereinbefore particularly described **in exchange** for a piece
of inclosed land in the Township of Uffington aforesaid now or late in the occupation of *120*
Richard Geering the property of the said William Lord Craven called Farm Piece
containing eight acres or thereabouts lying near to the Vicarage House at Uffington the
site of two cottages lately taken down or intended so be late in the possession of William
Wheeler and Henry Smith and the gardens and orchards thereto belonging and part of
the close containing three roods and twenty perches but which in the said Act is said to *125*
contain one acre one rood and nine perches in the possession of Widow Isles and part of
an orchard called Taylor's orchard containing two roods and four perches but in the said
Act said to contain two roods and twenty perches with a barn and stable thereon erected
also lying near to the said Vicarage House and the property of the said William Lord
Craven which are in and by the said Act declared to be from and after the date and *130*
execution of this award vested in and to be forever enjoyed by the said George Watts and
his successors Vicars of Uffington which said fourth allotment hereinbefore awarded to
the said George Watts and his successors Vicars as aforesaid and now hereby assigned and

exchanges between Lord Craven and Vicar

further exchanges

29 *1* **Allotted** to the said William Lord Craven is in the judgement of the said Commissioners of equal value with the said lands grounds barn and stable as the said Act vested in the said George Watts and his successors Vicars of Uffington **and for the more convenient situation** and disposition of the several

5 farms lands and grounds of the several land owners within the said fields liberties territories and precincts of the Township of Uffington and hamlets of Balking of Woolston otherwise Wolverston upon the said division and inclosure **the several owners** and proprietors of messuages lands and tenements within the parishes of Uffington and Sparsholt to these presents have in pursuance of the power given to or vested in them by

10 the said Act made the several exchanges hereinafter particularly mentioned within the consent and approbation of the said Commissioners ascertained and declared in and by this award. **And first** the said Abraham Atkins with the consent and approbation of the said Commissioners hath exchanged and by these presents doth exchange with the said William Lord Craven **all** that said first allotment of land hereinbefore awarded to the said

15 Abraham Atkins for his manorial rights of soil in the said hamlet of Balking situate in Old Field aforesaid and containing one rood and four perches hereinbefore particularly described **and also all** that the said second allotment of land hereinbefore awarded to the said Abraham Atkins situate in Old Field aforesaid containing ninety three acres two roods and twenty four perches (exclusive of all roads and ways through and over the

20 same) and hereinbefore particularly described **and also all** that coppice called Fawler Coppice situate in the hamlet of Fawler aforesaid containing four acres three roods and twenty six perches bounded on the south east east and south by land in the hamlet of Fawler allotted to the said William Lord Craven on the west and north west by other land allotted to the said William Lord Craven in the same Hamlet of Fawler and on the north

25 by an inclosure belonging to the said Philip Brown Vicar of Sparsholt with all the underwood now growing and being in the said Coppice called Fawler Coppice **for and in lieu of** all these the ninth and tenth allotments of land allotted and awarded or intended to be awarded to the said William Lord Craven by the commissioners named and appointed in and by virtue of the said Act for putting the same into execution touching

30 the hamlets of Kingston Lisle and Fawler in and by their award made or intended to be made touching the same hamlets which said ninth allotment is situate in Kingston Lisle Fields on the south or upper side of Ickleton Way and contains thirty eight acres and twenty perches (exclusive of all roads and ways through and over the same) and is bounded on the east by Westcot Downs on the south west and west by land allotted to the

35 said Edward Thornhill and Collier his wife in the hamlet of Kingston Lisle and on the north by land allotted to the said Abraham Atkins in the same hamlet of Kingston Lisle and by other land allotted to the said Abraham Atkins and William Jordan his copyhold tenant in the same hamlet and the said tenth allotment so awarded or intended to be awarded to the said William Lord Craven is situate in Kingston Lisle Fields north of the

40 village of Kingston Lisle and contains ninety one acres one rood and thirty eight perches (exclusive of all roads and ways through and over the same) bounded on part of the north and other part of the east by the hamlet of Westcot on part of the south and the remaining part of the east by land allotted to the said Abraham Atkins on the remaining part of the south by old inclosures at the village of Kingston Lisle and exchanged with the said

45 William Lord Craven with the said Abraham Atkins on part of the west by the Town

Street of Kingston Lisle and by land allotted to the said Edward Thornhill and Collier his *46*
wife on other part of the north and on the remaining part of the west by an allotment to
the said Edward Thornhill and Collier his wife exchanged with the said Abraham Atkins
and on the remaining part of the north by other land allotted to the said William Lord
Craven and of all that homestead consisting of a tenement farmhouse with the yard *50*
garden orchard buildings and part of the Brickyard thereunto and adjoining and belonging
and two closes of pasture and arable land situate on the east side of the village of Kingston
Lisle containing in the whole seven acres two roods and ten perches bounded on the east
and south by an inclosure belonging to the said Abraham Atkins on part of the west by
the other part of the said Brickyard on other part of the west by the Town Street of *55*
Kingston Lisle on parts of the north and remaining part of the west by cottages and
gardens belonging to the said Abraham Atkins and on the remaining part of the north by
the said tenth allotment to the said William Lord Craven in Kingston Lisle aforesaid. And
also of those two cottages now in the occupation of John Hill and John May or their
undertenants and a barn adjoining or near to the same situate near the chapel on the east *60*
side of the village of Kingston Lisle and all that close of pasture ground late in the
occupation of John May adjoining the same cottage and barn the whole containing one
acre and two roods bounded on the east and south by the gardens of the said Abraham
Atkins and on the west and north by the Town Street of Kingston Lisle and also all those
six pieces or parcels or arable land lying disposed in the open and common fields of *65*
Westcot aforesaid within the said parish of Sparsholt containing three acres one rood and
thirty perches and now in the occupation of the said John Hill. **And the said** William
Lord Craven with the like consent and approbation of the said Commissioners **hath**
exchanged and by these presents **doth** exchange with the said Abraham Atkins **all** those
the said ninth and tenth allotments of land allotted and awarded or intended to be awarded *70*
to the said William Lord Craven by the Commissioners for putting the said Act into
execution touching the said hamlets of Kingston Lisle and Fawler in and by their award
made or intended to be made touching the same hamlets and hereinbefore particularly
described the said ninth allotment being situate in Kingston Lisle Fields on the south or
upper side of Ickleton Way and containing thirty eight acres and twenty perches and the *75*
said tenth allotment being situate in Kingston Lisle Fields north of the village of Kingston
Lisle and containing ninety one acres one rood and thirty eight perches as hereinbefore
mentioned. **And also** the said homestead and two closes of pasture and arable land situate
on the said east side of the village of Kingston Lisle containing seven acres two roods and
ten perches as aforesaid and hereinbefore particularly described **and also** the said cottage *80*
barn and close of pasture ground situate near the chapel on the east side of the said village
of Kingston Lisle containing one acre and two roods and hereinbefore also particularly
described **and also all** those the said six pieces parcels of arable land lying dispersed in
the said open and common fields of Westcot within the said parish of Sparsholt containing
together three acres one rood and thirty perches and now in the occupation of the said *95*
John Hill **for and in lieu of** the said two allotments of land hereinbefore awarded to the
said Abraham Atkins situate in Old Field aforesaid and hereinbefore exchanged or
mentioned to be exchanged by the said Abraham Atkins with the said William Lord
Craven one of them containing one rood and four perches and the other ninety three
acres two roods and twenty one perches as aforesaid and both which allotments are *100*

101   hereinbefore particularly described and of the said coppice called Fawler Coppice situate in the hamlet of Fawler aforesaid containing four acres three roods and twenty six perches and hereinbefore particularly described with the underwood growing thereon. **And the said** William Lord Craven with the consent and approbation of the said Commissioners

105   **hath** exchanged and by these presents **doth** exchange with the said George Watts and his successors Vicars of Uffington aforesaid **all** that close of arable land called Broad Street Close and part of an orchard thereto adjoining as now staked out situate in the town of Uffington containing four acres one rood and twenty four perches bounded on part of the north by another inclosure belonging to the said William Lord Craven on the

110   remaining part of the north and part of the east by a public footway fenced on both sides on part of the south and remaining part of the east by the remaining or other part of the said Orchard on the south east by the Town Street of Uffington called Broad Street on part of the west and remaining part of the south by said Farm Piece vested by the said Act in the said Vicar of Uffington and his successors and on the remaining part of the west by

115   an allotment to the said Vicar in Uffington Meadow. **And also All** that plot or piece of ground whereon a cottage lately stood in the occupation of Caleb Stallard with the garden thereto adjoining and belonging containing together thirteen perches bounded on the north east and south east by land belonging to the said Vicar of Uffington on the south west by the said cottage and garden in the occupation of the said Henry Smith by the said

120   Act vested in the said George Watts Vicar of Uffington and his successors and on the north west by the said street called Broad Street. **And also All** that orchard or inclosed ground in the town of Uffington aforesaid late in the occupation of Henry Cooke containing thirty seven perches bounded on the east by the said street called Broad Street on the south by the house and garden now in the occupation of the said Henry Cooke on

125   the west by Uffington Churchyard and on the north by the said Farm Piece. **And Also** part of a close or meadow or pasture ground situate in the town of Uffington called Pusey's Orchard as now staked out containing three roods and twenty two perches bounded on the east by other part of the said close exchanged by the said William Lord Craven with the said John Stallard on the south by an inclosure belonging to the said William Lord

130   Craven   called   Thrashers   on   the   west   by   an   house   and   garden

30

In the occupation of Thomas James and on the north by a lane in Uffington called Little Lane. **And also all** that messuage or tenement called Taylors situate in Uffington aforesaid with the stable yard garden and remaining part of the said Orchard called Taylor's Orchard thereunto adjoining and belonging containing one rood and eight perches bounded on the east by a close belonging to the said William Lord Craven in the occupation of William Stallard on the south by the said Lane called Little Lane on the west by the aforesaid other part of the said Orchard called Taylors vested by the said Act in the said George Watts and his successors Vicars of Uffington and on the north by other part of the said close in the occupation of the Widow Isles **for and in lieu of** the third allotment of land hereinbefore awarded to the said George Watts and his successors Vicars of Uffington containing twelve acres two roods and four perches **and the said** George Watts Vicar of Uffington aforesaid with the like consent and approbation of the said commissioners **hath** exchanged and by these presents **doth** exchange with the said William Lord Craven **all** that the said third allotment of land hereinbefore awarded to the said George Watts and his successors Vicars of Uffington containing twelve acres two roods and four perches as the same is now staked and set out situate in Uffington Fields on the north or lower side of Ickleton Way and hereinbefore particularly mentioned and described **for and in lieu of** the said several closes gardens orchards yard messuage and stable hereinbefore exchanged by the said William Lord Craven with the said George Watts and his successors Vicars of Uffington aforesaid **and the said** William Lord Craven with the like consent and approbation of the said commissioners **hath** exchanged and by these presents **doth** exchange with the said John Archer (impropriator as aforesaid) **all** that inclosed meadow or pasture ground called West Ham lying contiguous and near to the allotments hereinbefore awarded to the said John Archer containing fifteen acres two roods and eighteen perches bounded on the south east by land allotted to the said John Archer on the west by inclosures in the hamlet of Woolston and on the north west and north east by an allotment to the said John Archer in lieu of land purchased of the said George Watts **and also** part of a small inclosure in the town of Uffington as now staked out containing one rood and twenty four perches bounded on the south by the homestead belonging to the said John Archer and by a garden belonging to Thomas Thatcher on the west by a close now in the possession of the said Charles Young and Sarah his wife and Mary Allen on the north by a close belonging to the said Trustees of Uffington School land and the remaining or other part of the said inclosure retained by the said William Lord Craven and on the east by a cottage and garden belonging to the said William Lord Craven **and also all** that plot or parcel of land being part of the said Several Farm belonging to the said William Lord Craven in the occupation of the said Joseph Lousley as the same is now staked and set out containing seventy two acres two roods and twenty eight perches and which comprehends and includes the same plot or piece of land containing twenty one acres and twenty three perches hereinbefore described as an equivalent for the thirty seventh allotment to the said William Lord Craven bounded on the east and north east by land allotted to the said John Archer in Uffington Fields on the south or upper side of Ickleton Way on the south by other part of the said Several Farm retained by the said William Lord Craven on the west by land allotted to the said John Archer in Woolston Fields and on the north by other part of the said Several Farm likewise retained by the said William Lord Craven **for**

46   **and in lieu of** the first allotment of land hereinbefore awarded to the said John Archer containing fifteen acres of meadow and pasture land in Uffington Meadow and the fifth allotment of land to the said John Archer containing seventy five acres and twenty six perches situate in the said Uffington Fields on the south or upper side of Ickleton Way

50   and also the second allotment to the said John Archer in lieu of tithes of old inclosures at Woolston situate in Uffington Fields on the south or upper side of Ickleton Way containing seventeen acres and twenty nine perches. **And the said** John Archer impropriator as aforesaid with the like consent and approbation of the said commissioners **hath** exchanged and by these presents **doth** exchange with the said William Lord Craven **all** that said first

55   allotment of land hereinbefore awarded to the said John Archer containing fifteen acres of meadow and pasture land in Uffington Meadow **and also all** that the said fifth allotment to the said John Archer containing seventy five acres twenty six perches situate in the said Uffington Fields on the south or upper side of Ickleton way **and also all** that the said second allotment to the said John Archer in lieu of tithes of old inclosures at Woolston

60   situate in Uffington Fields on the south or upper side of Ickleton Way containing seventeen acres and twenty nine perches all which said three allotments of land are hereinbefore particularly mentioned and described **for and in lieu of** the said several closes and parcels of arable meadow and pasture ground hereinbefore exchanged by the said William Lord Craven with the said John Archer as impropriator as aforesaid. **And**

65   **the said** William Lord Craven with the like consent and approbation of the said Commissioners **hath** exchanged and by these presents **doth** exchange with the said John Stallard **all** that the east part of the said close of meadow and pasture ground called Pusey's Orchard containing nine perches as now staked and set out bounded on the east by the garden of the said John Stallard on the south by a lane leading from Friday Street

70   to the said close called Thrashers on the west by other part of the said close called Pusey's Orchard hereinbefore exchanged by the said William Lord Craven with the said George Watts and on the north by the said lane called Little Lane **for and in lieu of** the allotment hereinbefore awarded to the said John Stallard situate in Uffington Fields on the north or lower side of Ickleton Way containing twelve perches and hereinbefore particularly

75   described **and the said** John Stallard with the like consent and approbation of the said Commissioners **hath** exchanged and by these presents **doth** exchange with the said William Lord Craven the said allotment hereinbefore awarded to him the said John Stallard situate in Uffington Fields on the north or lower side of Ickleton Way containing twelve perches **for and in lieu of** the said east part of the said close called Pusey's Orchard

80   hereinbefore exchanged by the said William Lord Craven with the said John Stallard. **And the said** William Lord Craven by and with the like consent and approbation of the said Commissioners **hath** exchanged and by these presents **doth** exchange with the said Edward Warren his lessee **all** that close of pasture ground situate in the Town of Uffington aforesaid called East Coppice Close containing one acres three roods and sixteen perches

95   bounded on the north east and east by that part of the town of Uffington which is called Green Bridge on the south east by land allotted to the said William Lord Craven on the south by land allotted to the said John Archer and on the west by a close now in the possession of the said Edward Warren as lessee of the said William Lord Craven **and also all** that other close of pasture ground likewise situate in the said town of Uffington

100   containing one acre two roods and thirty two perches bounded on the east by some

cottages and gardens belonging to the said William Lord Craven and by the said close in _101_
the possession of the said Edward Warren his lessee on the south by land allotted to the
said John Archer on the north west by an inclosure now in the possession of the said
William Mundy as lessee of the said William Lord Craven and on the north by the Town
Street of Uffington aforesaid **for and in lieu of** a small close of pasture ground held by the _105_
said Edward Warren as lessee of the said William Lord Craven situate in the town of
Uffington aforesaid containing one rood and twenty nine perches bounded on the north
the east and the south by inclosures belonging to the said William Lord Craven and on
the west by the Town Street of Uffington and of the second allotment hereinbefore
awarded to the said William Lord Craven and Edward Warren his lessee situate in _110_
Uffington fields in the north or lower side of Ickleton Way containing four acres one rood
and one perch and hereinbefore more particularly described. **And the said** Edward
Warren the lessee of the said William Lord Craven with the like consent and approbation
of the said Commissioners **hath** exchanged and by these presents **doth** exchange with
the said William Lord Craven the said small close of pasture land held by the said Edward _115_
Warren as lessee of the said William Lord Craven situate in the said town of Uffington
aforesaid containing one rood and twenty nine perches and also the said second allotment
hereinbefore awarded to the said William Lord Craven and Edward Warren his lessee
situate in Uffington Fields on the north or lower side of Ickleton Way containing four
acres one rood and one perch and hereinbefore particularly described **for and in lieu of** _120_
the said two closes of pasture ground hereinbefore exchanged by the said William Lord
Craven with the said Edward Warren his lessee. **And the said** William Lord Craven with
the like consent and approbation of the said Commissioners **hath** exchanged and by
these presents **doth** exchange with the said John Williams Willaume and Abraham
Chambers the Trustees or assignees of the estate of the said Robert Fettiplace **all** that the _125_
said thirty ninth allotment hereinbefore awarded to the said William Lord Craven situate
in Old Field in the hamlet of Balking aforesaid containing one rood and twenty three
perches hereinbefore particularly described **for and in lieu of** a certain plot or parcel of
land in the hamlet of Fawler containing one rood and nineteen perches within the

1   **31** **Parish** of Sparsholt awarded or intended to be awarded to the said Trustees by the commissioners named and appointed in and by virtue of the said Act of Parliament for putting the same into execution touching the hamlets of Kingston Lisle and Fawler and which is in and by the award made or

5   intended to be made touching the said hamlets exchanged or intended to be exchanged by the said John William Willaume and Abraham Chambers with the said William Lord Craven. **And the said** Bartholomew Tipping with the like consent and approbation of the said Commissioners **hath** exchanged and by these presents **doth** exchange with the said Lovelace Bigg **all** that close of arable land called Stamps Close situate in the village

10   of Woolston aforesaid containing one acre two roods and eight perches bounded on the east by land allotted to the said Lovelace Bigg on the south and west by other inclosures in the village of Woolston and on the north east by a lane there **and also all** that close of arable land called Botty Barn situate in the hamlet of Woolston aforesaid on the south or upper side of Ickleton Way containing eight acres three roods and eighteen perches

15   bounded on the east by an allotment to William Thatcher and on every other part thereof by the fourth allotment hereinbefore awarded to the said Lovelace Bigg **and also all** that the north part of a close of meadow ground called The Great Moor as now staked out situate in the hamlet of Woolston aforesaid at a place there called The Moor containing four acres and seventeen perches bounded on the east by a public road called Moor Lane

20   and by a Moor belonging to the said Joseph Mayon on the south by the south or other part of the said Great Moor retained by the said Bartholomew Tipping and on the west and north by other Moors the property of the said William Thatcher Lovelace Bigg and other persons (except and always reserved to the said Bartholomew Tipping and the owners for the time being of the said south or other part of the said close called Great

25   Moor a carriage and drift road from the north east corner of the said south part of the said Great Moor into through and over the said north part of the said great Moor by the side of the said Joseph Mayon's Moor to the said road called Moor Lane and so back again to the said north east corner of the said south part of the said Great Moor) **for and in lieu of** all that close of meadow ground situate at Woolston Moors aforesaid containing five

30   acres and ten perches hereinafter particularly described and the seventh allotment hereinbefore awarded to the said Lovelace Bigg situate in Woolston Meadow containing four acres three roods and twenty seven perches hereinbefore particularly described. **And the said** Lovelace Bigg with the like consent and approbation of the said Commissioners **hath** exchanged and by these presents **doth** exchange with the said

35   Bartholomew Tipping **all** that the said close of meadow situate at Woolston Moors in the hamlet of Woolston aforesaid containing five acres and ten perches bounded on the east and south by other Moors the property of the said Bartholomew Tipping on the west by the said inclosed farm belonging to the said William Lord Craven in the township of Uffington in the occupation of the said Richard Geering and on the north by a Moor

40   belonging to Jeffry Church hereinafter exchanged with the said Bartholomew Tipping **and also all** that the said seventh allotment hereinbefore awarded to the said Lovelace Bigg situate in Woolston Meadow aforesaid containing four acres three roods and twenty seven perches hereinbefore particularly described **for and in lieu of** the said two closes of arable land and the said north part of the said close called Great Moor hereinbefore

45   exchanged by the said Bartholomew Tipping with the said Lovelace Bigg. **And the said**

Bartholomew Tipping with the like consent and approbation of the said Commissioners *46*
hath exchanged and by these presents **doth** exchange with the said Jeffry Church **all** that
the said sixth allotment hereinbefore awarded to the said Bartholomew Tipping situate
in Woolston Fields on the north or lower side of Ickleton Way containing three acres two
roods and thirteen perches hereinbefore particularly described **for and in lieu of** a close *50*
of meadow ground belonging to the said Jeffry Church situate at the said place called The
Moors in the hamlet of Woolston containing four acres one rood and nine perches
hereinafter particularly described. **And the said** Jeffry Church with the like consent and
approbation of the said Commissioners **hath** exchanged and by these presents **doth**
exchange with the said Bartholomew Tipping **all** that the said close of meadow ground *55*
situate at the said place called the Moors in the hamlet of Woolston aforesaid containing
four acres one rood and nine perches bounded on the south by a Moor belonging to the
said Lovelace Bigg hereinbefore exchanged with the said Bartholomew Tipping on the
west by the said inclosed farm belonging to the said William Lord Craven in the occupation
of the said Richard Geering on the north by a Moor belonging to the said William *60*
Thatcher and on the east by the south part of the aforesaid close called Great Moor **for**
and in lieu of the said sixth allotment hereinbefore awarded to the said Bartholomew
Tipping containing three acres two roods and thirteen perches as aforesaid. And the said
Bartholomew Tipping with the like consent and approbation of the said Commissioners
hath exchanged and by these presents **doth** exchange with the said Joseph Mayon **all** that *65*
the seventh allotment hereinbefore awarded to the said Bartholomew Tipping situate in
Woolston Fields on the north or lower side of Ickleton Way containing two roods and six
perches hereinbefore particularly described **for and in lieu of** all that west part of a close
of pasture ground called The Slip adjoining the homestead belonging to the said
Bartholomew Tipping and which is divided from the other part of the said close by a *70*
brook or stream of water there and contains one rood and thirty two perches hereinafter
more particularly described. **And the said** Joseph Mayon with the like consent and
approbation of the said Commissioners **hath** exchanged and by these presents **doth**
exchange with the said Bartholomew Tipping **all** that the said west part of the said close
of pasture ground called The Slip in Woolston aforesaid containing one rood and thirty *75*
two perches bounded on the south east and south west by the homestead and home close
of the said Bartholomew Tipping on the north west by a close called Play Close belonging
to the said Lovelace Bigg hereinafter exchanged with the said Joseph Mayon and on the
north east by other part of the said close called The Slip exchanged by the said Joseph
Mayon with the said Jeffry Church **for and in lieu of** the said seventh allotment *80*
hereinbefore awarded to the said Bartholomew Tipping containing two roods and six
perches. **And the said** Lovelace Bigg with the like consent and approbation of the said
Commissioners **hath** exchanged and by these presents **doth** exchange with the said
Joseph Mayon **all** that close of pasture ground situate in the village of Woolston aforesaid
containing one acre and nineteen perches bounded on the east by that part of the said *95*
close called The Slip which is hereinafter exchanged by the said Joseph Mayon with the
said Jeffry Church on the south by other part of the said close called The Slip hereinbefore
exchanged by the said Joseph Mayon with the said Bartholomew Tipping and by the
home Close of the said Bartholomew Tipping on the west by the town street of Woolston
aforesaid and on the north by the home close of the said Joseph Mayon **and also all** that *100*

101 close of pasture ground as now staked and set out likewise situate in the said village of Woolston containing two roods and thirty one perches bounded on the east and south east by the Town street of Woolston aforesaid on part of the west and on the south by a small inclosure belonging to the said Joseph Mayon on the remaining part of the west by

105 the homestead of the said Lovelace Bigg by him lately purchased of Sir William Guise Baronet and on the north by the homestead of the said Joseph Mayon **and also all** that small part of a close called the Home Close in the occupation of Amariah Church containing eight perches as now staked and set out bounded on the east by the said small inclosure belonging to the said Joseph Mayon on the south by the Town Street of

110 Woolston and on the west by other part of the said close retained by the said Lovelace Bigg **and also all** that small inclosure called The Sheep House Barton in the hamlet of Woolston aforesaid containing twenty perches bounded on the west by another inclosure called by the same name and belonging to the said Joseph Mayon and on every other part thereof by the allotment to the said Joseph Mayon **and also all** that the north part of a

115 close of meadow ground called the Great New Lease situate in the hamlet of Woolston aforesaid containing three acres three roods and thirty eight perches as now staked out bounded on the east by the said Oxleaze Farm on the south by the south part of the said close Great New Lease retained by the said Lovelace Bigg on the west by other closes called The New Lease belonging to the said William Thatcher and Joseph Mayon and the

120 north by a lane called Claypit Lane **and also all** that close of meadow ground situate in the said hamlet of Woolston at the aforesaid place there called The Moors containing three acres one rood and thirty five perches bounded on the east by Uffington Meadow on the south and west by Moors belonging to the said Bartholomew Tipping and on the north by a Moor belonging to the said Joseph Mayon **and also all** that said sixth allotment

125 hereinbefore awarded to the said Lovelace Bigg situate in Woolston Fields on the north or lower side of Ickleton Way containing three roods and twenty eight perches hereinbefore particularly described **for and in lieu of** a close of pasture ground called Lawrences belonging to the said Joseph Mayon in the village of Woolston aforesaid containing thirty one perches a close of pasture called Rout's Close in the said village of Woolston containing

130 two acres two roods and fifteen perches and of two small closes or inclosures called Sheep House Bartons adjoining together in the hamlet of Woolston aforesaid and containing thirty six perches and of two closes of pasture ground called The New Leaze in the said hamlet of Woolston adjoining together and containing three acres two roods and four perches and of a small close or parcel of wood ground in the hamlet of Woolston at the

135 said place there called The Moor containing one acres one rood and fourteen perches and of one other close of meadow ground in the same hamlet of Woolston and at the same place called the Moor containing two acres one rood and nineteen perches all which said several closes and parcels of land last mentioned are hereinafter more particularly described **and the said** Joseph Mayon the said like consent and approbation of the said

32 **Commissioners hath** exchanged and by these presents **doth** exchange with the said Lovelace Bigg **all** that the said close of pasture ground called Lawrences in the village of Woolston aforesaid containing thirty one perches bounded on the east and north east by the homestead belonging to Woolston Mill on the south by cottages and gardens and on the west and north by the town street of Woolston aforesaid **and also all** that the said close of pasture ground called Rout's Close in the said village of Woolston containing two acres two roods and fifteen perches bounded on the east by an inclosure called Pond Close on the south by the Town Street of Woolston aforesaid and on the west and north by several other inclosures in the village of Woolston **and also all** those two small closes or inclosures called Sheep House Bartons adjoining together in the hamlet of Woolston aforesaid and containing thirty six perches bounded on the west by an inclosure called Three Pence a Week hereinafter exchanged by the said Jeffry Church with the said Lovelace Bigg and on every other part thereof by the first allotment hereinbefore awarded to the said Lovelace Bigg **and also all** those two closes of pasture ground called New Leaze in the hamlet of Woolston aforesaid adjoining together and containing three acres two roods and four perches bounded on the east by the south part of the said Great New Leaze hereinbefore mentioned on the south by the first allotment awarded to the said Lovelace Bigg on the west by another inclosure called the New Leaze belonging to the said Lovelace Bigg and on the north by another inclosure called the New Leaze belonging to the said Jeffry Church and by him hereinafter exchanged with the said Lovelace Bigg **and also all** that small close or parcel of wood ground in the hamlet of Woolston aforesaid at the said place called The Moors containing one acre one rood and fourteen perches bounded on the south by several moors belonging to the said Lovelace Bigg on the west by the said Farm belonging to the said William Lord Craven in the occupation of Richard Geering and on the north and east by the said road called Moor Lane **and also all** that close of meadow ground in the same hamlet of Woolston and in the same place called The Moors containing two acres one rood and nineteen perches bounded on the east by Uffington Meadow on the south by a Moor belonging to Thomas Bowles on the west by a Moor belonging to the said Lovelace Bigg and on the north by the said Lordship of Fernham **for and in lieu of** the said several closes and parcels of land hereinbefore mentioned to be exchanged by the said Lovelace Bigg with the said Joseph Mayon. **And the said** Lovelace Bigg with the like consent and approbation of the said Commissioners **hath** exchanged and by these presents **doth** exchange with the said Jeffry Church **all** that close of pasture ground called Upper Close in the village of Woolston aforesaid containing three acres and twenty five perches bounded on part of the east by an allotment to the said Bartholomew Tipping hereinbefore exchanged with the said Jeffry Church on the remaining part of the east and on the south by an allotment to the said Jeffry Church on the west by the homestead of the said Jeffry Church and on the north by a lane or road in the village of Woolston **and also all** that the said fifth allotment hereinbefore awarded to the said Lovelace Bigg situate in Woolston Fields on the north or lower side of Ickleton Way containing two acres and thirty five perches hereinbefore particularly described **for and in lieu of** a small close of pasture ground in the village of Woolston called Councils containing three roods and four perches a close of pasture ground called Three Pence a Week in the hamlet of Woolston aforesaid containing two roods and twenty four perches and a close of pasture

1

5

10

15

20

25

30

35

40

45

46 ground called New Leaze in the said hamlet containing three acres three roods and thirty three perches hereinafter particularly described **and the said** Jeffry Church with the like consent and approbation of the said Commissioners **hath** exchanged and by these presents **doth** exchange with the said Lovelace Bigg **all** that the close of pasture ground

50 in the village of Woolston called Councils containing three roods and four perches bounded on the east by a close called Rents Close on the south by an inclosure belonging to Charles Young the elder on the south west and west by a lane in the village of Woolston and on the north by an inclosure called Coopers belonging to the said Lovelace Bigg **and also all** that the said close of pasture ground called Three Pence a Week in the hamlet of

55 Woolston aforesaid containing three roods and twenty four perches bounded on the east by a small inclosure called Sheep House Barton exchanged by the said Joseph Mayon with the said Lovelace Bigg and on every other part thereof by the first allotment to the said Lovelace Bigg **and also all** that the said close of pasture ground called New Leaze in the same hamlet of Woolston containing three acres three roods and thirty three perches

60 bounded on the north the east and the south by other inclosures called the New Leaze and on the west by the first allotment to the said Lovelace Bigg **for and in lieu of** the said inclosure called Upper Close and the said fifth allotment to the said Lovelace Bigg hereinbefore mentioned to be exchanged by the said Lovelace Bigg with the said Jeffry Church. **And the said** Joseph Mayon with the like consent and approbation of the said

65 Commissioners **hath** exchanged and by these presents **doth** exchange with the said Jeffry Church **all** that east part of the aforesaid close of pasture ground called The Slip situate in the village of Woolston aforesaid and divided from the west part of the said close by the said brook or stream of water hereinbefore mentioned containing two roods and eight perches bounded on the north and part of the east by the homestead of the said Jeffry

70 Church on the remaining part of the east by an allotment to the said Jeffry Church and on every other part thereof by other old inclosures in the village of Woolston **for and in lieu of** the said third allotment hereinbefore awarded to the said Jeffry Church situate in Woolston fields on the north or lower side of Ickleton Way containing two roods and thirty nine perches and hereinbefore particularly described. **And the said** Jeffry Church

75 with the like consent and approbation of the said Commissioners **hath** exchanged and by these presents **doth** exchange with the said Joseph Mayon **all** that the said third allotment hereinbefore awarded to the said Jeffry Church situate in Woolston aforesaid on the north or lower side of Ickleton Way containing two roods and thirty nine perches hereinbefore particularly described **for and in lieu of** the said east part of the said close

80 called The Slip hereinbefore mentioned to be exchanged by the said Joseph Mayon with the said Jeffry Church. **And the said** Robert Leaver with the like consent and approbation of the said Commissioners **hath** exchanged and by these presents **doth** exchange with the said William Lord Craven **all** that allotment hereinbefore awarded to him the said Robert Leaver in Old Field in the hamlet of Balking aforesaid containing four acres one

95 rood and twenty eight perches hereinbefore particularly described **for and in lieu of** a certain plot or parcel of land in Fawler Breach Field within the said parish of Sparsholt containing one acre one rood and ten perches which is awarded or intended to be awarded to the said Robert Leaver by the Commissioners for putting the said Act in execution touching the hamlets of Kingston Lisle and Fawler aforesaid and is in and by

100 the award made or intended to be made touching the same hamlets exchanged or

intended to be exchanged by the said William Lord Craven with the said Robert Leaver *101*
and of two small inclosures or closes or pasture ground containing together two acres
one rood and seven perches situate in Fawler aforesaid within the said Parish of Sparsholt
with the barn now standing in one of the said closes now or late in the occupation of
Baruck West bounded on part of the east and part of the north by land allotted to the said *105*
Robert Leaver in Fawler aforesaid on other part of the east by an old inclosure belonging
to the said William Lord Craven on the south and west by the Lordship of Uffington and
on the remaining parts of the north and west by the home close and homestead belonging
to the said Robert Leaver. **And the said** William Lord Craven with the like consent and
approbation of the said Commissioners **hath** exchanged and by these presents **doth** *110*
exchange with the said Robert Leaver **all** that the said plot or parcel of land in Fawler
aforesaid within the said Parish of Sparsholt containing one acres one rood and ten
perches and which is allotted and awarded or intended to be awarded to the said William
Lord Craven by the commissioners for putting the said Act into execution touching the
said hamlets of Kingston Lisle and Fawler and in the said award described to be the *115*
eleventh allotment to the said William Lord Craven bounded on the east and south by
land allotted to the said Robert Leaver in Fawler aforesaid and on the west by the third
allotment therein awarded to the said William Lord Craven and on the north by Spinney
Farm **and also all** those the said two small inclosures or closes of pasture ground
containing together two acres one rood and seven perches situate in Fawler aforesaid *120*
with the barn standing on one of the said closes and hereinbefore particularly described
for and in lieu of the said allotment of land hereinbefore awarded to the said Robert
Leaver situate in Old Field aforesaid containing four acres one rood and twenty eight
perches hereinbefore particularly described and hereinbefore exchanged by the said
Robert Leaver with the said William Lord Craven **all which** said several exchanges *125*
hereinbefore set forth are hereby ascertaining and declared to be with the consent and
approbation of the said Commissioners as by the said Act is required and are in the
judgment of the said Commissioners fair equitable and just and such of the said exchanges
as extend to lands within the said parish of Sparsholt are made with the like consent and
approbation of the Commissioners for putting the said Act in execution touching the *130*
said hamlets of Kingston Lisle and Fawler and are so declared or intended to be declared
in and by their award made or to be made touching the same hamlets. **And the said**
Commissioners do hereby declare that lands hereditaments and premises in these
presents given by the said Abraham Atkins in exchange with the said William Lord
Craven are so exchanged and subject to all Manorial Rights belonging to the said *135*
Abraham Atkins as Lord of the Manor of Kingston Lisle (except as to the Manorial rights
in the same manner as such rights are reserved or saved to Lords of Manors in and by the
said recited Act of Parliament and as if the said lands hereditaments and premises had
not been exchanged as aforesaid anything in these presents contained to the contrary
thereof   notwithstanding.)   And   the   said   Commissioners   in   further *140*

streams &
water courses

1

33 **Pursuance** of the said Act **do** hereby direct order and award that **all streams** of water and watercourses in the said open and common fields common meadows common pastures downs and commonable lands by the said Act directed to be allotted and divided shall be carried and conveyed in such

5 courses and through such lands and grounds so directed to be divided and allotted as the same have heretofore usually been or of right ought to have been carried and conveyed and not otherwise **and whereas** through the necessity of situation and other circumstances it hath happened that some of the proprietors have not an equal share of boundary mounds or fences allotted to them on the same division and inclosure. **Now further**

10 **know ye** that the said Commissioners have first taking into consideration the interior mounds necessary to be made directed and do hereby direct order and award that the several persons whose names are inserted in the first column of the **First Schedule**

*First
schedule:
payments to
be made to
Townsend*

hereunto annexed and who hath sums placed against their names in the second column of the said First Schedule do pay the several sums so placed against their several and

15 respective names in the said second column of the said First Schedule amounting together to the sum of fifty two pounds nineteen shillings and three pence half penny unto Richard Townsend of Newbury in the County of Berks gentleman whom the commissioners have appointed and do hereby appoint to receive the same and that the said Richard Townsend do immediately on the receipt thereof pay and dispose of the said sum of fifty two pounds

20 nineteen shillings three pence half penny together with the sum of thirty six pounds and six shillings out of the monies hereinafter directed to be raised for their general expenses making together the sum of eighty nine pounds two shillings and three pence halfpenny unto and amongst the several other persons named in the said Schedule who have sums placed against their names in the third column of the said first Schedule such persons

25 having too great a proportion of mounding according to the quantity and value of the lands and grounds allotted to them respectively by virtue of the said Act in such sums shares and proportions as are set against their several and respective names in the said third column of the said First Schedule in order to bring the same boundary mounds and fences as near as may be to a just and equal proportion. **And as to such of the charges**

30 and expenses incident to and attending the obtaining and passing of the said Act as belong to or ought to be paid by the proprietors or owners of lands within the Township of Uffington and the hamlets of Balking and Woolston otherwise Wolverston aforesaid and of the surveying admeasuring dividing and allotting the said common fields common meadows common pastures and downs and other commonable lands in the said

35 Township of Uffington and hamlets of Balking and Woolston by the said Act directed to be allotted and divided as aforesaid and of surveying quantifying exonerating from tithes and exchanging the old inclosures and other hereditaments as aforesaid and of preparing and enrolling this award or instrument of allotments and of making supporting and maintaining the fences **awarded** to be made for the said George Watts Vicar as aforesaid

40 and the Trustees of the said Lands at Uffington given by the said Thomas Saunders and of making maintaining and supporting such fences gates stiles drains and other matters as the said Commissioners have thought reasonable and just to be made supported and maintained by and at the expenses of the proprietors in general or any number of them and which cannot according to the provisions and directions of the said Act contained

45 concerning the fences to be made for the several allotments hereinbefore mentioned or with justice and equity be ordered or directed to be made supported and maintained by *46* and at the separate expense of the said proprietors and all the charges and expenses of the said Commissioners for their own time and trouble in and about the obtaining and executing the said Act so far as relates to the said Township of Uffington and the hamlets of Balking and Woolston otherwise Wolverston and all other necessary expenses of the *50* several persons employed by the said Commissioners before the execution of this award or otherwise in or about the premises and all other necessary expenses in about or concerning the same premises amounts which together with the said sum of thirty six pounds and six shillings decided to be applied towards bringing the said bounds and mounds to an equality in the whole to the sum of two thousand one hundred and ninety *55* eight pounds two shillings and four pence the said Commissioners do in and by this their Award order direct and appoint that the sum shall be paid borne and defrayed by the several proprietors and owners and persons interested in the said open and common fields common meadows common pastures downs and other commonable lands in the said Township of Uffington and in the hamlets of Balking and Woolston otherwise *60* Wolverstone and by the proprietors and owners of such of the said cottages tenements farmhouses and old inclosures as are exchanged or exonerated from tithes by virtue of the said Act in such sums shares and proportions as are set against their respective names in the fourth column of the said First Schedule hereunto annexed under written. **And the said Commissioners** do hereby further order direct and appoint that the same shall *65* within ten days from the date hereof be paid to the said Richard Townsend whom the said Commissioners have appointed and do hereby appoint to receive the same and that the said Richard Townsend do immediately after the same shall come to his hands pay and apply the same for the purpose of repaying and satisfying first all such monies as have been advanced and paid in discharge of the fees and other expenses of obtaining the said *70* Act and for the other purposes aforesaid. **And whereas** the several persons whose names are inserted in the first column of the **Second Schedule** hereunto annexed have under the direction of the said Commissioners sown a wheat crop in certain parts of the fields and lands by the said Act directed to be divided and allotted. **Now further know ye** that the said Commissioners have order and directed and do hereby order and direct that *75* upon payment by the said several persons of the several sums of money set against their said respective names in the second column of the said Second Schedule into the hands of the said Richard Townsend for the use and benefit of the several persons whose names are inserted in the third column of the said Second Schedule in the several shares and proportions set against their names in the fourth column of the said Schedule the said *80* several persons named in the first column of the said Second Schedule shall have and enjoy the crops of wheat so by them sown upon the said fields and lands with free liberty to enter upon the said lands to cut down and carry away such crops when ripe and fit for use leaving the stubble thereof for the benefit of the persons named in the said third column according to their shares and interests in the lands whereon the same grows and *95* the said Commissioners have appointed and do hereby appoint the said Richard Townsend to receive and pay the said several sums of money according to the said Schedule and the direction hereinbefore contained. **And lastly know ye** that the said Commissioners have at the time of signing and executing this award delivered to the said proprietors an account in writing signed by the said Commissioners of all the moneys *100*

Second schedule

101   they have laid out and assessed in about or concerning the said dividing allotting or inclosing **in witness** whereof the said James King William Fillingham John Brothers John Watts and John Mitchell Commissioners as aforesaid have to this their Award fairly engrossed or written on parchment set their hands and seals at a public meeting of the

Award signed at Bear Inn Wantage

105   said Commissioners held by adjournment at the **Bear Inn** in Wantage aforesaid on the twenty ninth day of May in the eighteenth year of our sovereign Lord George the Third by the Grace of God of Great Britain France and Ireland King Defender of the Faith and in the year of our Lord one thousand seven hundred and seventy eight and after the same was so signed and sealed by the said Commissioners the said William Lord Craven

110   Abraham Atkins John Archer Bartholomew Tipping Lovelace Bigg George Watts Jeffry Church Joseph Mayon John Stallard Edward Warren John William Willaume and Abraham Chambers and Robert Leaver have hereunto also set their hands and seals on the same day and year aforesaid

on the side of the document is the following inscription:

Let this Deed be inrolled in His Majesty's Court of Common Pleas at Westminster pursuant to the Act dated the twenty fourth day of November 1778 H. Gould

Appendix 5b

The First Schedule referred to by the Award

1st column	2nd column	3rd column	4th column
	inequality of fencing		general expenses
	to pay	to receive	
	£ s d	£ s d	£ s d
Right Honourable Lord Craven	18-6-3		952-14-4
Right Honourable Earl Spencer	9-18-0		12-9-1
Edward Thornhill Esq			15-19-2
Bartholomew Tipping Esq			124-5-8
John Archer Esq			215-3-2
Lovelace Bigg Esq	16-10-0		317-1-3
Reverend John Hippisley			56-17-4
Reverend Philip Brown as lessee under Queens College in Oxford		4-19-0	1-11-10
Abraham Atkins Esq			96-14-3
John Hyde Esq			39-7-9
Henry Aston Esq	8-5-0		10-19-0
Wm Hazell John Tooley Wm Tripp & Wm Hazell the younger trustees of Presbyterian Society in Wantage			5-12-4
Dean & Chapter of the Collegiate Church of St Peter in Westminster & their lessees			1-15-4
Robert Leaver			4-4-1
John Williams			14-9
Joseph Wirdnam			2-15-1
Roger Spanswick		2-9-6	17-2
John Williams Willaume & Abraham Chambers as trustees or assignees of the Estate & effects of Robert Fettiplace Esq			45-3-5
Jeffry Church			76-18-8
Joseph Mayon		16-10-0	67-18-2
William Thatcher			31-8-6
William Chamberlain			22-19-4
John Stallard		6-12-0	7-15-3
Joseph Cooke			7-8-4
Lawrence Woodroffe		4-19-0	3-17-5
Charles Young & Mary Allen an infant		13-4-0	6-14-6
Joseph Dirkson		7-15-1	2-12-8
Elizabeth Hoare widow		6-12-0	2-5-4
William Mifflin		3-6-0	11-2
James Munday			12-19-2
Robert Quarme Esq		10-14-6	9-0-7
Angel Lockey			8-11-6

1st column	2nd column	3rd column	4th column
	inequality of fencing		
	to pay	to receive	general expenses
	£ s d	£ s d	£ s d
George Read			2-4-1
Richard Hinchman		7-5-2	3-7-4
Edmund Cooke			11-5-6
William Mundy		4-19-0	8-2-6
Edward Warren			18-0-4
Totals	52-19-3	89-2-3	2198-2-4

The Second Schedule referred to by the Award

1st column	2nd column	3rd column	4th column
	£ s d		£ s d
Thomas Thatcher	33-6-8	The Right Honourable Lord Craven	26-11-0
Richard Geering	31-1-5	John Archer Esq	47-8-7
William Munday	9-6-0	The Reverend George Watts	46-3-0
Joseph Lousley	2-12-6	The Trustees for the School land	15-18-10
Joseph Dickson	5-11-5	Edward Warren	14-11-5
Lawrence Woodroffe	2-8-2	William Munday	7-15-1
William Mifflin	7-19-4	Bartholomew Tipping Esq	7-9-4
James Munday	24-1-8		
William Stallard	6-6-7		
Edmund Cooke	14-8		
Mary Stallard	3-6		
Johanna Clarke	8-6		
Richard Hinchman	8-0		
John Lockey	1-14-6		
John Stallard	1-17-7		
Charles Garrot	16-8		
John Qinnall	16-16-1		
Jeffry Church for himself & Amariah Church	11-17-2		
Richard Rye	6-7-10		
John Rhodes	19-8		
Totals	165-17-11		165-17-11

Appendix 5c: Index of names in the Award

S

T

W